"The Life Coach's Tool Kit, Vol. *3 is a masterful compilation that cements the series' reputation as an indispensable resource for both novice and seasoned life coaches.*"

—SARAH BENNETT,
Psychologist and Executive Coach

"*With contributions from experts spanning diverse fields and global locations,* The Life Coach's Tool Kit, Vol. 3 *delivers a wealth of insights and practical strategies tailored for various coaching scenarios. Each chapter stands alone, yet collectively, they form a comprehensive guide to enhancing mindset and peak performance.*"

—JAMES R. CARTER,
Founder of Peak Performance Coaching

"*This book goes beyond mere theory, offering actionable activities that can be seamlessly integrated into any coaching practice. Whether you're looking to refresh your approach or seeking fresh perspectives to elevate your clients' success,* The Life Coach's Tool Kit, Vol. 3 *provides the tools you need to transform lives.*"

—MELISSA RODRIGUEZ,
Certified Life Coach, Podcast Host

"This volume is not just a book; it is a gateway to unlocking your full potential as a life coach and achieving unparalleled growth for your clients. Dive in and discover the transformative power of this essential addition to The Life Coach's Tool Kit *series."*

—Dr. EMILY HUANG,
Positive Psychology Expert

"The Life Coach's Tool Kit, Vol. 3 *is a transformative guide that brings together the wisdom and expertise of leading coaches from around the globe. This book is a comprehensive resource, offering tools for every aspect of coaching, from stress navigation techniques to lessons on enacting positive changes within clients."*

—TARA LAWSON,
Transformational Life Coach,
Host of *The Journey Within* Series.

"The Life Coach's Tool Kit, Vol. 3 *is an essential addition for every life coach's library. This volume gathers wisdom from 27 renowned experts worldwide, offering fresh insights into mindset and peak performance."*

—RAJ PATEL,
Senior VP of Human Resources,
GlobalTech, C-Suite Advisor

THE
LIFE
COACH'S
TOOL KIT
Vol. 3

Ready-to-Use Strategies, Principles, and Activities

THE
LIFE
COACH'S
TOOL KIT
Vol. 3

Authored by:

Erik Seversen, Neil Bailey, Rachelle Buskas, Dana E. Crawford, Skye
Deane, Lara Doherty, Eric Ekle, Jolie Engelbrecht, Adele Frost, Ada Fürst,
Alex Garner, Steve Hammond, June Hans, Chris Ho, Kristelle Kamini,
Elena Kim, René Kok, Irina Kuhlmann, Ashley Kuhnau, Mindy McKibbin,
Tanya Newbould, Joyce de Nooijer, Jennifer Richardson, Nick C.I.
Schaart, Mary Beth Schrudder, Alex Webb, Sabrina Vogler, Po Wu, MD

THIN LEAF PRESS | LOS ANGELES

Library of Congress Cataloging-in-Publication Data
Names: Seversen, Erik, Author, et al.
Title: *The Life Coach's Tool Kit, Vol. 3*
LCCN: 2024914789

ISBN 978-1-953183-54-5 (hardcover) | 978-1-953183-52-1 (paperback)
ISBN 978-1-953183-51-4 (eBook) | 978-1-953183-55-2 (audiobook)
Non-Fiction, Coaching, Self-Help, Personal-Development
Cover Design: 100 Covers
Interior Design: 100 Covers
Editors: Nancy Pile, Kristin Kaye
Thin Leaf Press
Los Angeles

THIN
LEAF

Thank you for reading this book. There are tools found within the following pages that can greatly benefit your life, but don't stop there. Make sure you get the most you can from this book and reach out directly to the expert-authors who want to help you reach your goals by becoming the best life coach you can be and to manifest success in your life. Contact information for each author is found at the end of their respective chapter.

To the pioneer life coaches who have positively transformed lives and to those pursuing to do the same.

CONTENTS

INTRODUCTION

By Erik Seversen
Author of *Ordinary to Extraordinary* and *Explore*
Los Angeles, California

W hen I decided to produce *The Life Coach's Tool Kit*, I knew I wanted to provide value to life coaches, but I had no idea that *The Life Coach's Tool Kit* idea would turn into more than one volume. However, as I gathered the authors and began collecting chapters, I realized that there are so many different types of life coaches and so many different ways to improve the lives of coaching clients, I knew that I couldn't stop with just one book. Now, as the first two volumes of *The Life Coach's Tool Kit* are changing lives, I'm excited about producing volume three, which is filled with another collection of amazing chapters from life coaching experts from around the world.

If you read the introduction to *The Life Coach's Tool Kit, Vol. 1*, you've seen that the concept for this book was me thinking to myself, *I wish I had a book filled with different chapters with different ideas from different experts about life coaching. I wish I had a book with simple coaching activities that would work for various situations.* That book was created, and the effect was extraordinary. I'm now happy to offer another volume of tools that life coaches can use to work with their clients in many different situations.

Like *The Life Coach's Tool Kit, Volumes 1 and 2*, this book is designed for anyone wanting to learn principles, philosophies, ideas, and activities related to life coaching. This book will be a great resource for new life coaches just starting out who want to be the best they can be. This book will also be great for the seasoned life coach who may have been using the same coaching philosophy for years and who wants to inject a few new ideas into their coaching practice, especially with their long-term clients.

I'm excited to share volume three of *The Life Coach's Tool Kit* with the world, and I'm excited about the expert authors who contributed to it. For this book, I solicited the help of 27 experts from various backgrounds and locations. The number one goal in *The Life Coach's Tool Kit, Vol. 3* is to provide more examples and strategies from elite coaches, mentors, psychologists, doctors, therapists, business owners, authors, and lifestyle experts who all have something unique to say about life coaching.

The experts authoring this book are from all over the USA, Canada, the United Kingdom, the Netherlands, Denmark, Switzerland, Romania, and South Africa. They are professionals who are leadership, emotional intelligence, communication, transformation, and self-actualization experts, senior business executives, hypnotists, podcast hosts, TEDx speakers, motivational keynote speakers, military veterans, medical doctors, psychotherapists, C-suite strategists, neuro-linguistic programming masters, retreat facilitators, consultants, neurologists, and more. The one thing the authors of this book have in common is that they all have an idea about life coaching, and these ideas can be applied to multiple life coaching situations. These ideas are available to you now.

Although this book is organized around the united theme of mindset and peak performance for life coaches, each chapter is totally stand-alone. The chapters in the book can be read in any order. I encourage you to look through the table of contents and begin wherever you want. However, I urge you to read all the chapters because, as a whole, they provide a great array of perspectives. The chapters are arranged with a general principle, philosophy, or technique followed by a short activity that coaches should be able to easily review and use with clients. Each chapter is valuable in helping you tap into your full potential by adding unique tools to your life coaching practice and your life.

It is my hope that you discover something in this book that helps take your life coaching performance to the next level, so you can enthusiastically reach new heights as a life coach and rapidly reach your goals—and at the same time assist your clients to do the same.

About the Author

Erik Seversen is on a mission to inspire people. He holds a master's degree in anthropology and is a certified practitioner of neuro-linguistic programming. Erik draws from his years of teaching at the university level and years of real-life experience to motivate people to take action, creating extreme success in business and in life.

Erik is a TEDx and keynote speaker who has reached over one million people through his public speaking and live courses. He has visited 99 countries and all 50 states in the USA and has climbed the highest mountains on four continents, 15 countries, and 18 states. Erik has published 13 bestselling books on topics of mindset, success, and peak performance, and he has helped over 300 people become best-selling authors. He is a full-time writer, book consultant, and speaker, and he lives by the idea that success is available to everyone—that living an extraordinary life is a choice.

Erik lives in Los Angeles with his wife and two teenage boys.

Contact Erik for interviews, speaking, or book publishing consultation.

Email: Erik@ErikSeversen.com
Website: www.ErikSeversen.com
LinkedIn: https://www.linkedin.com/in/erikseversen/

CHAPTER
1

The Power of Humour and Empathy in Coaching

By Neil Bailey
NLP Master Coach, Trainer, & Writer
Chelmsford, England, United Kingdom

Your body cannot heal without play. Your mind cannot heal without laughter. Your soul cannot heal without joy.

—-CATHERINE RIPPENGER FENWICK

In the ever-evolving landscape of coaching, weaving humour and empathy into our sessions is like adding a dash of spice to a recipe—it enhances the flavour and makes the experience richer. So, let's dive into the art of infusing coaching with a generous dose of laughter and understanding.

Humour in coaching isn't about turning the coaching room into a stand-up comedy club. It's more of a subtle art, a tool wielded with precision to create a supportive and dynamic atmosphere. In this context, humour is the unexpected twist, the clever insight, or the well-timed comment that sparks a moment of realisation or a shift in perspective.

Laughter isn't just a pleasant byproduct; in my not-so-humble opinion, it's an active participant in the coaching process. It lightens the mood, reduces tension, and opens the door to vulnerability. A shared laugh creates a bond, turning the coaching space into a haven where clients feel not only supported but also understood.

The Science Behind Laughter

Now then, they often say that laughter is the best medicine. If your leg is torn and hanging off your body or you slipped and your grandma's old silver ladle has embedded in your skull, then I'd suggest getting some proper medical help. Laughing probably won't do the job. But when we are dealing with our emotions and changing things in our lives, then some gentle humorous and metaphorical self-flagellation can make all the difference. Before we delve deeper into how we can use humour in coaching (I was going to stick with "dipping into it," but let's forget ladles for the moment), let's touch on the neuroscience of laughter.

When we laugh, our brain releases "feel-good" chemicals like dopamine and endorphins. These neurotransmitters not only elevate mood but also enhance the learning experience. In the coaching context, this means that incorporating humour can foster a positive emotional state, making it easier for clients to absorb insights and embrace change (and if that's not the purpose of coaching, I don't know what is).

When laughter erupts, it's like a firework display of neurotransmitters. The brain releases endorphins, often referred to as the "feel-good" chemicals. These endorphins act as natural painkillers, creating a sense of euphoria and happiness. For example, oxytocin, sometimes referred to as the "empathy hormone," creates feelings of connection, something of benefit to both coach and client.

Laughter is a potent stress-buster. It prompts the brain to decrease the production of stress hormones, such as cortisol. This hormonal modulation not only reduces feelings of stress but also contributes to a sense of relaxation, yet another tick in the box for the perfect coaching environment. (You might be catching on that humour in coaching is not only positive but necessary. I just thought I'd mention it.)

The Benefits of Balancing Humour and Empathy in Coaching

The observer in you may have noticed I haven't mentioned much about empathy yet. Well, hold your horses, we are getting to it. In fact, let's look at some essential aspects of balancing humour and empathy in our coaching right now:

1. Improving Rapport

Balancing humour and empathy can be a bit of an art. It's important to gauge your client's emotional state and be mindful of when to inject humour to uplift the conversation and when to embrace empathy to navigate deeper emotions. In this delicate artistry, the first step is becoming attuned to your client's emotional frequency. It's like tuning into a radio station to catch the nuances of their feelings. Are they in need of a light-hearted moment, or is it time to delve into the depths of their emotions? It's about reading the emotional room, understanding the rhythm of their mood, and knowing when to sway to the beats of humour or slow dance with empathy. Who knew coaching involved so much dancing!

2. Creating a Comfortable Environment

A supportive and light-hearted coaching environment is the result of intentional effort. Set the tone from the beginning, emphasising that your sessions are a judgement-free zone where laughter is welcome and emotions are validated. In my own experience, if there isn't some laughter during an initial connection/chemistry call, then I'm probably not the coach for the person. Otherwise, rather than a coaching relationship built on connection and rapport, it would feel more transactional and clinical.

Picture this coaching environment as a cosy living room/lounge/comfy cave with beanbags and a drinks cabinet (maybe I've gone too far this time), where clients can kick off their shoes and make themselves at home. Think how much more inviting that picture is than a stuffy "therapy room" with diligently placed certificates, books on the shelves, and a clinically tidy feel. Great coaching is not just about the content of the coaching; it's about the ambiance, where the walls are adorned with the art of trust, and the furniture is arranged for genuine connection. Emphasising the judgement-free zone is like putting up a neon sign that says, "You're welcome here, just as you are." It's an invitation for clients to bring their authentic selves into the coaching space without fear of criticism.

Like a skilled host, you make sure that every guest—every emotion, every vulnerability—is not just acknowledged but embraced. I've mentioned authenticity a few times so far in this chapter, and I'm not just referring to client authenticity. You as the coach need to be authentic too, and for me that includes your own humour. Unless you are a totally humourless individual (and, of course, this is a judgement-free zone), then why would you not show a bit of the real you in your sessions?

3. Using Humour as a Coping Mechanism

When life throws its curveballs, and the weight of circumstances seems overwhelming, humour steps in as the ultimate coping mechanism. Envision yourself as the coach donning the role of a humour mentor, guiding your clients to discover the hidden gems of levity even in the darkest corners.

A memory of a friend from many years ago springs to mind here. I sat in his family home, his parents chatting away to us. I already knew that the mum was terminally ill, and, of course, I was being on my best behaviour. It wasn't long before my friend was arguing, light-heartedly, with his mum because he didn't want to do what she'd suggested. The argument ended with words along the lines of, "Well, you won't be around much longer, so I can do what I like then." This was followed by gales of laughter from all parties, except for me who'd frozen into a very small, frozen me-shaped statue in embarrassed shock. They'd obviously talked openly about death and had reached the stage where banter and humour were welcome even about such a serious issue.

In the coaching arena, helping clients identify moments of humour amidst adversity is akin to handing them a flashlight in the dark labyrinth of challenges. It's not about belittling the seriousness of their struggles; it's about shedding a light-hearted perspective that empowers them to navigate with a lighter heart. The ability to find moments of levity becomes a resilience-building exercise, transforming the daunting into the manageable and infusing a sense of playfulness into the process of overcoming obstacles.

If you or someone you know has ever worked in a hospital, for example, you'll be very aware of hearing what's often very dark humour as a way of coping with the serious and emotionally charged parts of the job. Imagine a coaching session as a joint exploration, where you and your client embark on a quest to uncover the comedic gems scattered amidst the challenges they face. Humour becomes the shield that deflects the blows of adversity, fostering not just resilience but a mindset that says, "I can face this with a smile."

4. Reflecting and Learning

Reflecting and learning are the twin pillars that uphold the structure of your coaching practice. It's not just about the sessions themselves; it's about the continuous refinement of your coaching artistry. Learning from each session is like fine-tuning your coaching instrument. What could be adjusted? When did humour strike the right chord, and when did empathy create a harmonious breakthrough? These reflections, often done with a great coaching supervisor, become the stepping stones to a more refined and seamlessly integrated coaching approach. It's not just about the notes played; it's about the music created together—the dance of laughter and understanding.

Strategies for Introducing Humour

Know Your Audience

Understanding your client's sense of humour is like having a comedy radar finely tuned to their wavelength. Consider it as a personalised humour prescription rather than a one-size-fits-all remedy. I thought it was worth throwing a few thought-nuggets for you to ponder on, so here goes:

Observational Skills

Pay attention to verbal and non-verbal cues during your sessions. Does your client respond positively to light banter or prefer a more serious tone? Adjust your approach based on their reactions, ensuring that your humour aligns with their comfort zone.

Co-Create Humour

As the coaching relationship evolves, collaboratively create humour. Ask for feedback on the type of humour they find most enjoyable. This not only fosters a sense of shared humour but also strengthens the coach-client bond. For example, suppose your client expresses a preference for witty, wordplay-based humour. Tailor your coaching language accordingly, incorporating clever puns or playful linguistic twists to create a coaching environment that resonates with their comedic taste.

Coaching humour isn't a one-size-fits-all deal; it's a versatile tool with various styles, each suited for different coaching scenarios. Here's a peek into the comedic toolbox:

Witty Banter

This is the quick and clever exchange of remarks that keeps the energy flowing. It's like a verbal game of ping-pong, a dance of words that adds a touch of playfulness to the coaching conversation. Use it sparingly to keep the engagement high without overshadowing the coaching focus.

Light-Hearted Observations

Sometimes, a well-placed observation with a sprinkle of humour can be a game-changer. It's about pointing out the elephant in the room with a smile, making the client feel seen and understood. This type of humour builds rapport and creates a comfortable space for exploration. To illustrate, an example from my own coaching happened when I was working with an individual around being vulnerable at work to be a better manager. The comment from the client was along the lines of "I can never articulate what's going on in my head and what I'm feeling. It's just not something I've ever been able to do." To which my response was, "Of course, you can't. I can't imagine you ever being able to open up emotionally to anyone being the emotionless desert that you are!" Just reading that, you may be sweating and shocked at my rudeness. However, we had great rapport and used a smattering of sarcasm at each other. So, imagine me with a mischievous grin on my face and read back my comment with a heavy dose of sarcasm—bearing in mind, the client had just been pouring their heart out to me for the past 40 minutes. I think you get my point!

Reflective Humour

Encourage clients to find humour in their own experiences. Foster a reflective mindset where they can explore challenges from a different perspective, discovering the comedy in life's twists and turns. This not only adds a lightness to the coaching journey but also empowers clients to navigate obstacles with resilience.

Humorous Summaries

Use moments of summary to inject some humour.

Purposeful Vulnerability

Be purposefully vulnerable. Share stories that highlight your own imperfections or humorous mishaps. This authenticity creates an environment where clients feel more comfortable opening up about their own experiences. For example, if discussing adaptability, share a light-hearted story about a time when you had to pivot unexpectedly, injecting humour into the narrative to illustrate the value of flexibility.

Interactive Creation

Co-create humorous metaphors with your client. Ask them to come up with analogies that resonate with them. This not only involves them in the coaching process but also makes the metaphors used meaningful to them and taps into our natural propensity to story tell. Playing along with a client-led metaphor can often tap into creative thinking that steps around the perceived barrier (Fig.1).

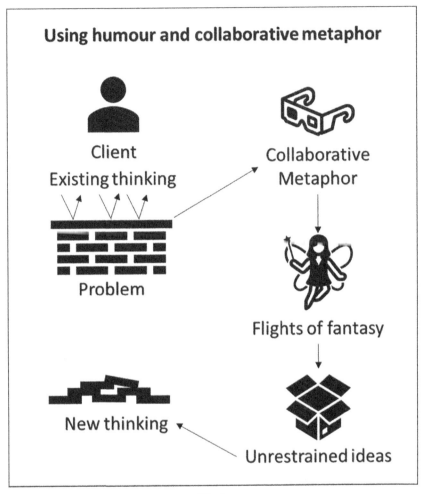

Using humour and collaborative metaphor

Client
Existing thinking

Problem

New thinking

Collaborative
Metaphor

Flights of fantasy

Unrestrained ideas

Fig.1

Let's have a play right now. Maybe the client sees their problem as a solid brick wall. You could suggest they imagine a painted-on tunnel in the style of Wile E. Coyote. Then, let them explore ways they could tunnel through. How would they get through? They could simply bash a hole through, dig under, get an ACME rocket pack and fly over, dig a new tunnel, walk away, and more. Now with all these ideas, how do any of them relate back to ways they could solve their own problem? Of course, humour needs to be used judiciously.

Humour is a powerful tool, but as any skilled craftsman knows, even the finest tools can have unintended consequences. In the realm of coaching, where emotions run deep, the risk of humour being misconstrued is ever-present. How does one navigate this potential comedy minefield?

The first step is awareness. Coaches must be attuned to the individual nuances of each client—knowing when to wield humour and when to tread lightly. Misconstrued humour often stems from a lack of alignment with a client's values, triggers, or current emotional state. To counter this, open communication is key. Establishing a safe space where clients feel comfortable expressing their boundaries and preferences ensures that humour remains a positive force. Regular check-ins and a willingness to adjust the comedic tone based on client feedback can prevent potential misinterpretations.

In those moments where a joke lands flat or takes an unexpected turn, the solution lies in graceful recovery. Acknowledge the misstep, offer a sincere apology if needed, and use the opportunity to deepen the empathetic connection. Humility and authenticity can turn a potentially awkward situation into a moment of shared humanity.

Remember, the goal is not to eliminate humour but to refine it, ensuring that it enhances rather than detracts from the coaching experience.

Tailoring your approach also involves understanding cultural nuances and personal preferences. What may be amusing to one client could be perplexing or offensive to another. Coaches should invest time in getting to know their clients, understanding their unique backgrounds, values, and comfort zones.

Exercises to Develop a Coach's Sense of Humour

Humour isn't a mysterious gift bestowed upon a select few; it's a skill that can be honed and refined. Just like flexing your muscles at the gym, developing your sense of humour requires regular workouts. So, coaches, let's hit the comedy gym with these exercises:

Observational Comedy

Practice finding humour in everyday situations. Observe the quirks, absurdities, and ironies of life. This could be as simple as noticing the funny side of a mundane task or finding amusement in unexpected juxtapositions. The goal is to train your mind to see the lighter side of things.

Stand-Up Reflection

Watch stand-up comedy with a critical eye. Analyse the delivery, timing, and content of jokes. Pay attention to how comedians connect with their audience. This exercise isn't about mimicking but about understanding the art of engaging storytelling and how it can be subtly incorporated into coaching conversations.

Improv Sessions

Improvisation is the ultimate comedy workout. Engage in improv exercises to enhance your spontaneity and creativity. Whether it's a one-word story or role-playing unexpected scenarios, improv strengthens your ability to think on your feet, a valuable skill in navigating coaching conversations with agility.

Humour Journal

Keep a humour journal to jot down funny anecdotes, observations, or thoughts. This serves as your comedic treasure trove, a source of inspiration when you need a dash of wit. Reviewing and reflecting on your entries also allows you to track your evolving comedic style.

Conclusion

In the grand finale of your coaching performance, remember: You are the maestro of your coaching symphony, weaving laughter and empathy into a masterpiece that is uniquely yours. So, coaches, take a bow, continue refining your craft, and let the laughter-infused coaching journey unfold.

ACTIVITY

See *Strategies for Introducing Humour* and *Exercises to Develop a Coach's Sense of Humour* sections within the chapter.

About the Author

In the intricate dance of understanding people, Neil Bailey found his rhythm as an NLP Master Coach, specialising in empowering individuals to be their authentic selves in both work and play. A specific focus for him is supporting those with low support autism to thrive in the professional arena. As an autistic individual, NLP training became his gateway to understanding and building human connection.

Through Neil's journey as a writer on LinkedIn and other websites, he's honed the art of translating intricate ideas into simple, engaging language. This writing voice, sprinkled with humour and authenticity, repeats throughout his coaching practice where humour plays a key role in personal change.

Health isn't just a buzzword for him—it's a lifestyle. Neil blends his NLP coaching and personal training to help clients integrate running fitness into their busy lives to help feel healthier both in body and mind. This extends to working with clients to run the race of their dreams whether that's a 5K or a marathon.

Neil's coaching philosophy is simple: With humour and authenticity, he creates a space where clients can be unapologetically themselves. Through his writing, YouTube videos, and public speaking, Neil hopes to convey the message that positive change is not only possible but achievable in an environment free from judgement.

Email: emailneilbailey@gmail.com
Website: https://www.thenlpmastercoach.co.uk/

CHAPTER
2

Working with Your Client's Subconscious Mind

By Rachelle Buskas
Founder, Limitless You; Rapid Transformational Coach
Calgary, Alberta, Canada

*Until you make the unconscious conscious,
it will direct your life and you will call it fate.*

—CARL JUNG

I've always been fascinated with human behaviour, particularly with how the mind works. We all have a primal brain in which we share common basic traits, yet everyone's mind works differently. Multiple people could be experiencing an event, and they will all interpret this event in different ways, based on their perspectives or "programming" they've acquired over the span of their lives. To put it simply, any event we experience will create thoughts and feelings within us, which then shapes our belief systems about ourselves and the world around us.

Many people don't realize that our beliefs are hardwired into us and set by the time we reach 7 years of age. The mind, from that point on, will then seek validation for those initial beliefs in any given situation. And the mind will always find that validation. "Seek and ye shall find" is the saying, isn't it?

Now it's important to note that everything I have stated above is subconscious. Our subconscious mind is our emotional mind, and many are shocked to find out that we operate from our subconscious minds *95% of the time.* Our subconscious also has saboteurs. These saboteurs are sneaky and powerful. They exist purely to keep us safe from any feelings of discomfort or perceived danger.

In my work as a subconscious coach, I believe there is no greater power and effectiveness than by being able to tap into the subconscious mind by using hypnosis. As coaches, we all have a number of tools at our disposal to assist our clients throughout their coaching journeys. But sometimes we have those clients who just can't seem to get past their limiting beliefs, stalling their progress. Or those clients who keep responding to us with "I don't know" when we confront their thoughts, beliefs, or habits.

Because these blocks and limiting beliefs are so subconsciously embedded in our minds, they truly *don't* know or it's become obvious that the two of you cannot overcome these together through a conscious conversation. This is where hypnosis comes in, allowing your clients to discover things about themselves and how their minds work on a completely different level.

The hypnotic state is often misunderstood. We as humans frequently enter into hypnotic states daily without being aware of it. If you've ever driven your car home on autopilot or gotten lost for a solid hour scrolling on your phone without really being aware of your surroundings, those are both excellent examples of being in hypnosis. In a coaching setting, hypnosis is simply a state of intense focus and relaxation. Through induction methods, I am able to put my clients into an alpha brainwave state, turning down the activity of their conscious minds while allowing the subconscious to take center stage.

Allow me to give you an example of the above. This is a real situation from a client I worked with, she has granted me permission to use her story, and her name has been changed to protect her privacy. Let's look at the development of a woman we will call Serena. The following three scenes were all reviewed while Serena was in hypnosis.

Scene 1

Serena is 2 years old. She is in the living room, looking in at her mother as well as other women in the kitchen. She decides she wants to be with her mother, wants her mother to pick her up and hold her in her arms. But there's a baby gate in the way. She tries to climb over the gate to get to her mother and is instantly told to stop and stay where she is. She tries and tries again, and each attempt is met with her being told to stay away, to stay where she is. Serena doesn't understand why her mother doesn't want her around, and she starts to cry, feeling utterly confused and totally rejected. Her small, undeveloped logical mind cannot make sense of this, but her subconscious *feeling* mind is very present. She adopted this belief right then and there: "If my own mother is rejecting me, then that must mean I'm not lovable. Furthermore, if my own mother doesn't love me, then that means that there is something wrong with me, and no one will ever love me."

Scene 2

Serena at 6 years old. She is beginning to make real friendships at school for the first time. Serena has a best friend. They play together at recess all the time. One day, her best friend has a new friend and invites her to play with them. Over time, the two other girls become closer, and Serena starts to feel left out. Then one day Serena hears that they had a playdate at one of their houses without her. She immediately feels rejected, deceived, and hurt, and that there must be something wrong with her if they didn't invite her to play.

Scene 3

Now Serena is 15. Her first serious boyfriend has just ended their relationship, and she's devastated. He confesses he likes another girl. Serena thinks to herself that she's prettier than this other girl, and she's more outgoing, athletic, etc. So, if her boyfriend is breaking up with her for this other girl who is clearly beneath her from her 15-year-old standards, then there must be something wrong with her, and therefore, no one will ever love her.

Noticing a theme here? Now you might say, "Well, everyone faces rejection growing up, so of course she's going to feel that way. This is a relatively normal human experience, and none of us is spared feelings of rejection!"

However, this is unique for Serena in this way: Serena as an adult struggled with all of her adult relationships, both male and female. She always felt like she was different, like she couldn't really connect with anyone. She put up so many walls, never allowing anyone to see her for who she really was because she convinced herself at 2 years old that there was something wrong with her. Her mind validated that initial belief when she was 6, 15, and at many other moments in her developmental years, hard-wiring that belief further and deeper into her subconscious programming.

The result of this was Serena feeling deeply empty inside, feeling like she was missing out on so much of life because she didn't have any close girl-friends or romantic relationships that lasted longer than a few months. She didn't understand why this was, on a conscious level. She had a basic under-standing of why this might be, but she knew there was something deeper at work here. Serena was tired of feeling lonely and disconnected, wondering why relationships seemed to come so easy for others and not for her.

And so began our work together. Once Serena was under hypnosis, we were able to review the three scenes above from the role of an observer and make sense of them from this heightened and non-judgmental perspective. In the first scene, Serena was able to understand that she was being kept out of the kitchen and away from her mother for her safety. Her mother and aunts were cooking a big family dinner. There was commotion, as well as hot and sharp things in the kitchen, and she would have been at risk of getting injured had she been let in. Serena as an adult was easily and clearly able to see that she was kept away out of love and concern for her safety. Serena has a good relationship with her mother today and has felt loved by her mother her whole life. The fact that Serena at 2 years old adopted a belief that was contrary to this shows you how powerful the subconscious and its saboteurs are!

In the second scene, Serena was easily able to understand that her two friends played without her because they lived on the same street and she lived farther away. It was easy for them to play together, so they did. Serena ended up making more friends at a young age that lived closer to her.

In the third scene, the rejection of her first love still hurt her, but she was able to see the beauty in her boyfriend ending their relationship so that she could find someone better suited for her. She realized that although there was a physical attraction there, they didn't really have a lot in common. She was an athlete; he was into music and video games. There was also an awareness that very rarely does anyone end up marrying the person they started dating at 15! It was bound to end at some point.

Once we were able to review these scenes from her life and find out the root cause of her relationship blocks, we could see the events more clearly for what they actually were. Serena and I were able to heal this part of her that was unconsciously keeping her from experiencing deep and real relationships, and we were able to move forward in her coaching journey regarding relationships effortlessly. It's important to note that for the first two scenes, Serena did not consciously remember the first scene, and the second one she had forgotten about for many years! I find most of my clients are surprised by the memories that their subconscious minds will take them back to. They are seemingly insignificant moments that we all experience, but our subconscious minds and our saboteurs will make quick and easy work out of interpreting those moments as something negative in order to offer us some type of protection. It's simply how our primal minds are wired. Fun, right?

We will remember a lot of things, but usually the root cause, the very first time our minds adopt these harmful and negative beliefs about ourselves, are not situations we remember all that well, if at all. That is why we need to work with the subconscious. *Note: Some of my clients have even regressed back to being in their mother's womb and adopted beliefs even then by picking up on their mother's energy while in utero. Fascinating!

Hypnosis in the coaching journey can be used in more ways than one. While I am not at liberty to share specific tools and techniques, as these are under the copyright of my teacher and mentor Marisa Peer and her RTT School©, I can share with you how you can easily get your client into a relaxed state in order for their subconscious to be more present than their conscious minds. *Note: You do not need to regress your client back to scenes as I did in the example above. I do those longer regressions during their hypnotherapy sessions.

Below is an example of how to use hypnosis quickly and effectively in a coaching session. Have your client roll their eyes up as high as they can while deeply inhaling and exhaling. By having the eyes rolled up in this way, this is signaling to their brain to enter into an alpha brainwave state. Have your client then close their eyes and allow their eyes to relax. Next, use some type of countdown induction. Tell your client to visualize walking down a flight of stairs or traveling down in an elevator as you count down the floors or steps slowly. Guide your client to relax their body and keep their breathing deep and steady. Do this for as long as is necessary until you feel like your client is relatively relaxed and able to visualize without too much effort. Once your client is relaxed, you can then guide them through the following activity.

ACTIVITY

Conversation with Your Future Self Visualization

I love this exercise, as it allows my clients to really feel, see, and hear themselves as they wish to be in the future. They can then have a conversation with their future self and ask any questions they wish in order to help them on their path. The answers will come to them. My script will usually go something like this: *I want you to go now to your favourite spot in the world. Your happy place. Or perhaps this is a place you've always wanted to go. Picture that beautiful place in great detail now. Just be here in this place. See, feel, and hear everything around you. Now look over to your left, and you'll see a figure approaching you. You realize this is you from the future, this is you five years from now. This future you is glowing, happy, and radiant, and they are smiling down at you now. Notice how they look. What are you wearing? What is your posture like? This future version of you sits down next to you now. They are here to show you what's possible for your life. They are here to show you that you ended up creating and getting everything that you desire. And they are here now to offer you advice and wisdom on how to do it. I want you to ask them, "What do you do in your life now? What brings you so much joy? What does a typical day look like for you? What do I need to do now to be where you are in five years? What do I need to know? What do I need to stop doing in order to become you? What is the biggest piece of advice you can give to me right now?"*

Tell your client to answer these questions out loud and naturally. Tell them to answer with the first thing that comes to their minds. Remind them that their conscious, logical thinking mind is not invited to this party. If your client appears to be thinking too much before they answer, remind them to just say whatever comes through and to not think about what they "should" say or try to judge the message that's initially coming through for them. **You can also use this opportunity to ask impactful and powerful** coaching questions, or perhaps questions you asked your client in previous sessions that they frequently responded "I don't know" to. You will be amazed at the wisdom and insights that come through when the conscious mind isn't getting in the way!

This is an incredibly immersive experience for your client. Remind them to really *see* and *feel* and experience themselves five years into the future. Get them to describe to you everything that they are experiencing. You can use one year, three years, five years … it doesn't really matter. Just use a timeline that is most fitting for your client based on their goals. Once you feel like you have asked enough questions and gained enough insight, you can then guide your client to thank their future self for showing them the way and say goodbye.

Bring them back to their full awareness by slowly counting them back in from 5 to 1, such as: *On the count of 5, just slowly coming back to your full awareness. On the count of 4, taking note of the expansion of your understanding of your life's path. On the counts of 3 and 2, begin to start moving your body … wiggling your fingers and your toes … and on the count of 1, feeling **amazing, motivated, energized, and wide awake**, open your eyes and come back to your full awareness right now.* This entire process can be as long as 15 to 25 minutes. It's your call, but that's a great amount of time for your client to be relaxed and having an immersive experience within themselves.

Try this out the next time you feel like you've hit a wall with one of your clients, or just start implementing this into your regular practice! You'll be amazed at how much forward momentum this creates for a client. It's a fascinating thing to experience for you both.

About the Author

Rachelle Buskas is a Rapid Transformational Therapist and Coach, as well as a Beyond Quantum Healing Practitioner. While Rachelle was studying these modalities, she quickly realized how important healing the past was in her coaching work and how important present moment and future planning were in her therapy work. Thus she decided to combine the two together in her work with her clients. Quantum Healing work came into the picture as a way for her clients to also experience healing from past lives, as well as life purpose work and connecting with the spiritual realm.

Rachelle's fascination with the human spirit as well as the human experience is never ending, and it only drives her to continue to find the most efficient and effective ways to heal and empower her clients as we continue to evolve rapidly as a collective.

Rachelle lives in Calgary, Alberta, Canada, and works locally as well as remotely.

Website: www.limitless-you.ca
Instagram: @rachellebuskas

CHAPTER

3

Choosing Thoughts to Manifest Outcome

By Dana E. Crawford
Founder, Evolve Life Coaching; Certified Life Coach
Suwanee, Georgia

Nothing is more easy than to think,
so nothing is more difficult than to think well.

—Thomas Traherne, English Poet and Theologian

The wisdom shared on the importance of thought is not only voluminous but also clear. Many iconic leaders of religion, business, philosophy, and science agree the most critical element determining the outcome of navigating human experience is quite simply, thought. If guiding a bridled horse to a predetermined destination represents intentional thought with a desired outcome, contrastingly jumping on a wild mustang without a map represents the absence of harnessing thought for successful manifestation. Disciplined thinking spotlights the path and directs the mind.

The goal of this chapter is to illuminate the importance of evoking awareness and then choice around thoughts, for the purpose of manifestation. Coaches help elicit permanent mindset changes in clients by introducing this element of control to shape the world around them. The adage of "thoughts become things" was insightfully expressed by Ghandi: "A man is but a product of his thoughts. What he thinks, he becomes."

This is a very personal topic for me. When I first became a coach and began the self-work that accompanies upskilling, I was aghast at the calamity regularly occurring in my head. My inner monologue reflected that I certainly wasn't "my own best friend" as should be the case. My self-talk was brutal, my fears of the future gave way to unproductive worry, overthinking was paralyzing my decision-making, and regrets from the past haunted me. Aristotle knew, "The most important relationship we can all have is the one you have with yourself. The most important journey you can take is one of self-discovery." The prevalence of grace and kindness in self-talk is definitive, and I needed more of both.

Additionally, I began to notice automatic assumptions that stopped me in my tracks, such as distorted black-and-white (perfectionistic) thinking as well as the ever- popular outsourcing of happiness by seeking external validation.

With the help of some wonderful coaches and unwavering determination, my self-talk is now very different. The stoic philosopher, Epictetus, wrote, "Man is not troubled by events, but by the meaning he gives to them." I'm much more careful about interpreting my environment now. There are still challenges, yet I remain armed with mindfulness practices and knowledge of the power to be gained by persevering to create the life I choose. I have experienced how a coach can support the untangling of detrimental thoughts with gentle prompts of "What are you telling yourself?" and how a self-talk journal helps provide an independent excavation of the mind. These lightning-fast messages are subtle, though, and race through the brain in deep, worn grooves, and, unfortunately, if left uninterrupted, this futile torment can be the source of great despair for an entire lifetime. I will articulate the powerful mechanics of how to think in order to support thriving for coaches, who then partner with clients to do the same.

The governance of thought on feelings and actions that culminate in blind spots or pervasive false narratives evidences the need to be vigilant about all thinking. This reinforcing loop is empirically undeniable, and the life that becomes ours is a manifestation of it. Equally significant is how our mind powerfully influences the selection of people in our lives, who enters our lives and who remains, regardless of their capacity to be a resource or liability to our thriving. Understanding the inevitable process of manifestation, either with or without exacting agency, is the cornerstone of accepting responsibility for our own circumstances. Manifestation is the concept of making dreams a reality by first creating a personal vision of who you are through careful and honest introspection. Next, an intentional focus on goals and a belief in the ability to achieve them is essential. Finally, you methodically take actions that move the vision to fruition.

A critical component of stimulating change in thinking is challenging current beliefs, as demonstrated in cognitive behavior therapy (CBT). CBT proposes to recognize specific thoughts, determine their accuracy, and when necessary, replace them with more rational thoughts to promote self-actualization. For example, if a client habitually anticipates the "worst-case scenario" (aka catastrophic thinking), assisting them to consider other more probable outcomes can help them increase optimism. This cognitive shift has many advantageous peripheral consequences, including the reduction of worry.

As penned by Viktor Frankl, Holocaust survivor and psychiatrist, "Between stimulus and response, there is a space. In that space is our power to choose our response. In our response lies our growth and freedom." Successful coaches provide techniques to assist with "growth and freedom." The work of learning how to rule myriad daily thoughts requires focused attention. Supporting a client in the calming of a chaotic mind is singly important to comprehend the significant role thoughts have on an outcome and how they can be conquered to become useful. Once the concept is grasped that not all thoughts are to be trusted for accuracy or edification, "I can't control my thoughts" is replaced with "I choose accurate thoughts and then helpful action."

Problematic thoughts are typically safety mechanisms stemming from past experiences that involve family-of-origin dysfunction or other traumatic life events. Since the human brain is naturally focused on survival, when a stress response is born from a perceived danger, monitoring for similar future threats becomes entrenched. Unfortunately, these negative thought patterns can carry on long after any measure of efficacy or protection. Unpacking the history of these triggers falls outside the coaching lane and is best left to licensed therapists. Thankfully coaches have many tools to assist clients with enhancing awareness around positive thinking habits.

Regardless of the root of maladaptive thinking, the cessation steps remain steadfast. Become aware of thoughts, accept them accordingly as "only" thoughts, and replace them as needed to improve wellness. If thoughts are ties on a railroad track constantly being formed and laid to determine direction, then the client is the train traveling to the destination the ties have assembled. Ensuring ties are laying the track toward the desired destination can prevent a ride of negativity on a runaway train.

Since awareness precedes agency in the work of thought mastery, it is imperative that a person inspect their thought filters, assumptions, self-talk, automatic thoughts, core beliefs, mindsets, interpretations, etc.. As always, sessions are client-directed and oriented around the values and issues presented by the client. Gaining insights about what they are thinking, why they are thinking it, and then how this thinking is affecting behavior can cultivate breakthrough moments that change the trajectory of their journey.

Sometimes sessions involve the exploration of tactical options. Brainstorming about how to schedule an exercise regimen into a packed calendar can be exactly what best serves the client, as indicated by the client's goal. This is in line with behavioral activation theory, which simplified is "Fake it until you make it." Start the desired action so that the motivation and mindset will catch up to eventually be in line with the new habit, which ultimately creates permanent change. The establishment of the new mindset provides the momentum needed for consistency.

Acceptance and commitment therapy (ACT) purports to accept thoughts without emotion, observe a broad array of other contributing realities, including objectivity and centeredness, and finally, commit to valuable action. ACT suggests that accepting emotions without judgment is not the same as approving of them; commitment to actionable progress is foundational here. Each of these applications acknowledge the importance of the fundamental link between measured thinking and directed doing.

A client may be open to immediately exploring thoughts driving an issue. For example, "What makes it challenging to put exercise on the calendar?" This space is where exploration is greater than identifying the solution. After reflection, an underlying issue is discovered: "I am not worthy of self-care; therefore, I do not prioritize it." Kindly challenging this distorted belief can ignite an entirely new perspective as well as permanent thought transformation. Using the affirmation "I am worthy of self-care" can begin "laying the track" in a new direction with far-reaching reverberations in many other aspects of life.

If a client states, "I can't find a good job," a curious coach might uncover a core belief that "I am not as competent as others." A coach can help dispel this negative belief by cultivating self-compassion and inquiring about unique strengths. Reframing past failures as learning opportunities and focusing on successes can be helpful with symptoms of imposter syndrome or low self-esteem. When different thinking becomes possible, navigation of circumstances evolves. In the words of Henry Ford, the famous car maker, "Whether you think you can, or you think you can't, you are right." When the client believes they are competent and displays confidence, they change how they are perceived, which manufactures desired results. It becomes a self-fulfilling prophecy from a germ of thought that is recognized, corrected, and nurtured.

The power of perspective in constructing daily life is revealed in many spiritual tenants, including the Bible, which states in Philippians 4:8, "Whatever is honorable, whatever is right, whatever is pure, whatever is lovely, whatever is of good repute, if there is any excellence and if anything worthy of praise, let your mind dwell on these things." The field of positive psychology also emphasizes the importance of steering the mind toward the good stuff to improve well-being. Marty Seligman, commonly considered the father of positive psychology, once stated, "Let's study why the plane stays in the air instead of why it crashed." After all, don't we want to replicate what works? Research furthering the development of positive psychology practices has solidified the use of mindfulness tools to strengthen the muscles of thinking well.

Practice and patience are necessary to gain skill in reigning thought. Gratitude journals can facilitate self-reflection and optimism. Confidential journaling produces dramatic results in improving overall outlook as it allows for the free flow of thought that is not shared or judged.

Gaining awareness of limiting beliefs is crucial. Once identified, a fixed mindset of "I'm terrible at technology" can transform into a growth mindset of "When I don't give up, I can fix my IT problems." In her book *Grit: The Power of Passion and Perseverance*, Angela Duckworth writes, "'I have a feeling tomorrow will be better' is different from 'I resolve to make tomorrow better.'" Powerful questioning around limiting beliefs can initiate the development of all-important grit that leads to determined manifestation.

The daily regimen of mindfulness habits fosters continued progress far beyond the coaching engagement. These "cognitive bicep curls" of letting thoughts go, discharging emotion from thoughts, staying present-centered, and so much more are rehearsed again and again through mindfulness practices. Thoughts will always need to be monitored, challenged, and evolved to ensure adaptive openness of thinking. Experimenting with mindfulness tools will sharpen the skills needed to observe and choose thoughts that make dreams a reality.

There are a vast number of ways to participate in mindfulness training both formally and informally. Journaling is very popular as it provides an excellent vehicle for surfacing otherwise hidden thinking. Guided meditations and breathing exercises are effective methods of becoming more present; these are now easily accessible through apps that offer a variety of ways to personalize daily "sits" with varying content and duration. Yoga and tai chi are fun ways to dive into exercise and mindfulness with a group. Random acts of kindness are known to promote feelings of well-being and positivity. These acts can be as simple as holding a door for someone or as complex as changing a tire for a stranded motorist. Good deeds foster bodily chemical reactions that can reduce anxiety. The physical discipline of proper sleep and regular exercise both contribute to overall happiness as well as clearer thinking.

Being rooted in the present is a critical component of mindfulness because dwelling on the past can encourage regret and rumination about the future can exacerbate anxiety. Mindfulness means to accept what is now while simultaneously suspending judgment of what has been or what will come. A beneficial re-centering exercise that can be either led or suggested by the coach is the five senses technique. It is a grounding exercise that helps a client focus on the present moment. The client takes a deep breath and slowly releases and then identifies five things they see, four things they can touch, three things they hear, two things they smell, and one thing they taste.

Daily affirmations are short motivational messages that help shift a negative mindset to a positive one, which changes the landscape of a day. Affirmations are client-generated, depending on individualistic goals. Possibilities are: "Control what you can, let the rest go," "I am enough," and "Perfect doesn't exist." A sticky note on a computer screen can make all the difference in tracking thoughts and choosing good ones.

The law of attraction argues that positive thoughts and actions beget positive rewards, and vice versa, for negative ones. Looking on the bright side is linked to better physical health, longer life, and lower risk of heart disease. It's a powerful outlook that helps to manage stress while reducing anxiety and depression; upbeat energy is infectious and gains momentum as it expands.

In her seminal book on the law of attraction called *The Magic*, Rhonda Byrne suggests, "If you want anything to change in your life, change the channel and change the frequency by changing your thoughts." This notion confirms that thoughts construct your day; days create your destiny.

The expectation for doing the hard work of recognizing and then choosing thoughts deliberately is building enough strength to execute discernment consistently in real-time, thereby manifesting a chosen life. Eventually, thought selection is less demanding as good thoughts become automatic and antiquated negative thinking is replaced. Worth noting here is that authentic positivity is balanced and accommodates all human experience. Honed resilience to stay the course in the tough times will pay off in this worthy lifetime investment of learning "to think well."

ACTIVITY

Creating a Vision Board

Every intentional journey requires a North Star. The creation of a vision board assists with focusing on maintaining progress toward the star by providing a constant visual reflection. It clarifies the vision of the future with a collection of images, quotes, affirmations, and inspirations, all aligning with personal values. It displays priorities and passions. This creation should be placed where it is seen frequently. It can be centered around professional goals, personal aspirations, relationships, financial milestones, travel dreams, or self-care. It can portray a one-year plan or a five-year plan. Vision boards are personal and may include elaborate calligraphy or artwork on a cork/white/magnetic board, poster, or framed piece. If you are not artistically inclined, you can also enjoyably create one with printed messages and photos. Nothing is off-limits, and there are no rules about the playful creation of this exciting reminder of what is held by a chosen future.

About the Author

Dana E. Crawford is a Level 2 trained, International Coaching Federation (ICF)-accredited, and nationally certified Life Coach (2014) with a degree in psychology and a post baccalaureate in education. She has deep coach instruction from the BetterUp Coach Foundations Program, Positive Intelligence Training from Sherzad Chamine, ICF Corporate Sponsored Coach Training, and Personal Fitness Training Certification. Dana holds a membership with both the ICF as well as the local ICF Georgia Chapter. She enjoys her conference involvement and membership with the International Positive Psychology Association (IPPA).

In addition to the continued education from ICF and IPPA courses, Dana is grateful for the many other acknowledgements and certificates she earned from Coach Solutions Academy, Rogers Behavioral Health, and PESI Educational Products. These certificates include topics regarding positive psychology, appreciative inquiry, behavioral activation, cultural competency, fierce self-compassion (Kristin Neff), motivational interviewing, and much more.

She passionately partners with clients using strengths-based coaching to support them through the exploration of topics like anxiety, work/life balance, confidence, habit formation/cessation, relationships, and mindfulness, with a focus on the principles of positive psychology. Dana provides a safe and confidential space for clients to direct sessions addressing real-time personal challenges.

Through extensive training and experience as a coach, counselor, teacher, psychometrist, and company director, Dana has witnessed the benefits of increased confidence and awareness following the journey of self-discovery through coaching. Dana finds fulfillment in transformational moments with clients as they own personal agency and ultimately reach their goals.

Dana grew up in Canada and resided in several European and North American countries prior to settling in Atlanta, Georgia. Dana has always enjoyed working with globally diverse populations and myriad cultures.

Email: Canadiandana@comcast.net
LinkedIn: https://www.linkedin.com/in/danacrawford22/

CHAPTER

4

Building Confidence and Self-Worth

By Skye Deane
Co-Founder, Resilient Women Leaders; Consultant, Coach
Surrey, England, United Kingdom

Lack of confidence will always allow doubt,
but strong self-confidence will build courage.

—MARK VILLAREAL

D o you have clients who lack confidence and think they are not good enough? Would you like to explore a framework that helps build confidence and self-worth? Then you are on the right page, and this chapter is for you. Firstly, do not be put off by the term "leader." In this chapter I ask you to think of yourself as a leader. Irrespective of job title, age, sector, background, or experience, whether you lead a team, your family, colleagues, or an organisation, we are all leaders, and we have to lead ourselves well in order to lead others well too.

Within this chapter I introduce you to the Resilient Leaders Elements (RLE™) framework. By building your resilience and leadership muscle and knowing *who you are* and *what you do*, two critical concepts of the framework, you can build confidence and self-worth. Let's start with the definition of a resilient leader:

"A resilient leader knows where they are strong and their areas for development. They know what takes them from pressure to stress and how to rebalance. A resilient leader has confidence in who they are and what they do so they create, build, and take opportunities, bouncing back, knowing they will find a way through uncertainty, change, and even crisis." (RLE™)

With this in mind, take a moment to reflect and answer these questions:

- What are your strengths? What can you rely on in times of challenge?
- What are your areas for development? What do you want to improve?
- What takes you from pressure to stress? Who, what, how, where?
- How do you rebalance? What activity or person helps you return to equilibrium?
- What is it about who you are and what you do that gets people to choose to follow you?

Answering the above questions is a great start. Now, let's add a layer to the definition in order to further understand more of *who you are* and *what you do*. The RLE™ framework consists of four elements, each shown in the diagram below.

The Resilient Leaders Elements

Clarity of Direction

Having a vision and a realistic strategy for the future, communicating effectively to align people to your vision and having the determination to keep going in the face of adversity.

Awareness

Appreciation of your own and others' motivations, cultures, strengths and weaknesses and using this knowledge to adapt to the forces that affect your changing environment.

Resilient Decision Making

Being able to take a valuable idea from concept to reality, challenging your own and others biases and considering the impact, pace and style of your decision making.

Leadership Presence

Being true to yourself, your values and ethical code, being in service to others and bringing a focus and bias for achievement to your organisation and others around you.

Clarity of Direction · What I do · Resilient Decision Making · Awareness · Who I am · Leadership Presence

RLE™ Framework, copyright of RLE Founders
Jeremy Mead and Rachel McGill

This framework:

1. Allows you to reflect on *who you are* and *what you do.*
2. Provides a language to start articulating your strengths and being mindful of them.
3. Allows you to identify your gaps and areas for development.
4. Supports the seven barriers identified for Women in Leadership (Research RLE™ Women as Resilient Leaders (WaRL) March 2020 and 2023).
5. Gives you confidence in *who you are* and *what you do.*

Here are some activities to help you reflect on each of the elements, all with the purpose of building confidence and self-worth:

CLARITY OF DIRECTION

When you have clarity of direction, everyone, including you, knows where they are going and why they are going there. Everyone can work out what they need to do and are determined to succeed.

—RLE™

Activity: How clear are you about your goal, be it personally or professionally? How do you remain focused with all the noise from ever-growing to-do lists, social media, and tensions between personal and professional responsibilities? How do you remove unhelpful distractions?

- Write down the things that are important for you to achieve this week.
- Choose the most important.
- Ask yourself, "Why is this important?" and record your answer.
- Ask the question again for the answer you have written down and keep doing this until you get to the "root" of why this is important.

- Once you know your important task, identify all those things you would describe as "unhelpful distractions" and how they reduce your productivity.
- Before starting work on the task, change something in your environment that reduces the likelihood of the top three distractions being a problem.
- Use this fundamental motivation method to help you stay on track.

> *Your mind is like this water, my friend. When it is agitated, it becomes difficult to see. But if you allow it to settle, the answer becomes clearer.*
>
> —MASTER OOGWAY, *KUNG FU PANDA*

By knowing your why, you can believe in it, and this will increase confidence. Having clarity of direction gives you the strength, courage and confidence to show up.

AWARENESS

> *When you have awareness, everyone, including you, works at their best, resulting in higher productivity and motivation. Diversity is appreciated and used to the benefit of all. Systems and processes serve people in achieving their goals.*
>
> —RLE™

Activity: Where on this RLE™ Uncertainty Spectrum do you do your best work? Mark it.

- Reflect on what happens when you move left or right of this mark.

- Think of examples.
- Does moving left or right of this mark increase pressure/stress on you? Why?
- Investigate the last time you went from pressure (feeling challenged and in control) to stress (unhappy and out of control). When did this happen? What was happening when you first noticed you felt stressed?
- Knowing what triggers your increased pressure/stress helps you prepare for the impact it has on you.

> *The first step toward change is aware-*
> *ness. The second step is acceptance.*
>
> —NATHANIEL BRANDON

Knowing where you are on the Uncertainty Spectrum at any given moment gives you space to rebalance and enables clarity.

LEADERSHIP PRESENCE

> *When you have leadership presence, you have presence*
> *even when you are not in the room because of who you*
> *are when you are in the room. The best person*
> *takes the lead and is fully supported by all around*
> *them leading to greater effectiveness and better results.*
>
> —RLE™

Values are deep within you and define who you are and what you want in your life. It's probably something you fundamentally value if you did it when you were 8 years old, you do it when you are at your most energized and fulfilled, or if it is exciting or even a little frightening.

Activity: How connected and mindful are you of your values? Consider the following list of values and feel free to add your own words if they are not here. Complete this RLE™ Values Exercise.

Acceptance	Freedom of Action	Order
Accuracy	Friendship	Passion
Achievement	Fun	Pleasure
Activity	Generosity	Popularity
Adventure	Genuineness	Power
Attractiveness	Growth	Purpose
Authority	Health (mental)	Quiet
Autonomy	Health (physical)	Rationality
Beauty	Helpfulness	Realism
Caring	Hospitality	Respect
Challenge	Honesty	Responsibility
Change	Hope	Risk
Comfort	Humility	Romance
Commitment	Humour	Safety
Compassion	Included	Self-Acceptance
Contribution	Including	Self-Control
Collaboration	Independence	Self-Determination
Connection	Industrious	Self-Esteem
Courtesy	Inner Peace	Self-Knowledge
Creativity	Intimacy	Service
Dependability	Justice	Sexuality
Dignity	Knowledge	Simplicity
Diversity	Leisure	Solitude
Duty	Loved	Spirituality
Empathy	Loving	Stability
Environment	Mastery	Success
Excitement	Mindfulness	Tolerance
Faithfulness	Moderation	Tradition
Family	Monogamy	Trusting
Fame	Non-conformity	Trusted
Fitness	Nurtured	Virtue
Flexibility	Nurturing	Wealth
Forgiveness	Openness	World Peace

- Highlight the 10 which are most important to you.*
- *Try not to choose any "needs"—if you need it to be happy, it is a need, not a value (make sure you get this need met, as unmet needs slow us down and drain energy).
- *Try not to choose any "should(s)." If you feel you should choose it, then it has probably been defined by someone else, e.g., upbringing, family, friends, etc.
- You can also complete the exercise online at https://tlrdynamics.com/coach/rwl/

Some people get lost for so long they forget what it was like to be themselves. Understanding your core values can help you find yourself again by understanding what matters most to you. Knowing your values and what motivates you helps you be more consistent. It provides clarity, with increased awareness, an ability to show up authentically, and helps inform decisions. How can your three core values help you be more confident in the way you show up?

RESILIENT DECISION-MAKING

When you use resilient decision-making, you can make great decisions at the right time with the right people in the right place. Contingency options are available so that you can manage and deal with the unexpected effectively and confidently.

—RLE™

Activity: Ask yourself "why" for each decision you need to make. Reframe your decisions so that it's not about you or what you'd like, but what's required by the situation.

For each major decision you make this week, ask the following three questions:

1. What's the impact on your goal?
2. How does it respond to the current situation?
3. What purpose does it serve?

Your knowledge and foundations give you the confidence to make a great decision in the right place at the right time.

FINAL ACTIVITY: PULLING ALL THE ELEMENTS TOGETHER

How can you have your most confident self show up? *Who are you* and *what do you do* at your best?

- Prepare a positive statement about yourself that you believe.
- The next time you notice the early signs of lacking confidence, say this statement to yourself.
- Notice what happens. This is your Strength Mantra.

In Summary

Our Belief and Why It Matters

Everyone can be a resilient leader when they are confident in *who they are* and *what they do*. Resilient leaders are able to lead themselves and others through any degree of uncertainty. In a world of increasing uncertainty and volatility, resilient leadership is vital for every one of us.

What We Do

We develop the capability of individuals to lead themselves and others. We help build their resilience and leadership muscle, so they can overcome barriers and perform at their best. We give them the tools to identify the strengths they can rely on in times of change and even crisis. As a result of our work, people feel motivated, empowered, valued, respected, authentic, and trusted. They have confidence and know their self-worth.

How We Do It

We use the four RLE™ Elements that have stood the test of time to form the foundation for a suite of tools and knowledge that help leaders prepare for, cope with, and recover from whatever comes their way. We use the Resilient Leaders Development Programme (RLDP™). This framework is a self-development tool. It can be used in a variety of different sectors, career stages, or for personal or professional development, and it can be applied to all settings.

Next Steps to Being Confident in Who You Are and What You Do

If you want to find out more about how we can help clients optimise their full potential, be their best self, and be confident in *who they are* and *what they do*, so they can lead themselves and others well in their personal and professional lives, then get in touch.

And—start now via the RLE™ Interactive Introduction. Complete the free survey, which provides you with an opportunity to understand more about your strengths and areas of development, indicating where you need the most support.

- Login in here https://rldp.resilientleaderselements.com/register
- Use this code when asked: **RWL02**

ACTIVITY

See *Clarity of Direction, Awareness, Leadership Presence, Resilient Decision-Making,* and *Final Activity* sections within the chapter.

You can find more information and activities using the RLE™ by reading Chapter 25–what takes you from pressure to stress? How do you rebalance? written by Alex Webb, co-founder of RWL.

About the Author

Skye Deane is a former Army Officer and Senior Physiotherapist whose purpose is service to others and making a positive difference to people's lives. Her time in the military was the catalyst for pursuing her interest and lifelong learning of all things resilience, leadership, and well-being. It provided some of the most memorable, challenging, and rewarding work, including Paralympic training camps and deployments to Afghanistan and Iraq, while treating and supporting individuals, some with life-changing injuries, to overcome both their physical and mental barriers. In each of her roles, she was committed to the individuals on her team and the patient population they were responsible for, ensuring the delivery of clinical excellence.

With over 18 years of resilient leadership experience, she specialises in building resilience in leaders to improve both their own and others' performances with the aim to connect, believe, and inspire themselves and others. She supports leaders to really understand their values and strengths in order to build confidence, take opportunity, improve well-being, and prevent overwhelm, so they can be the best version of themselves.

Skye set up her own business to work flexibly as a military wife and as a mum of two young children. Alongside her clinical role, she pursued her passion to develop people and became accredited as a Resilient Leaders

Consultant (RLC). Using the Resilient Leaders Elements (RLE™), plus her skills and experience as a coach, Skye works with individuals and groups to develop their leadership and support their personal and professional growth and development. She also helps teams to work more collaboratively and communicate more effectively, resulting in higher productivity and motivation.

Skye is co-founder of Resilient Women Leaders with her RLC colleague, Alex Webb. The RLE™ framework and RLDP™ is at the heart of all their programmes and workshops which are specifically designed to develop the capability of women, irrespective of age, stage of career, or sector, to lead themselves and others, supporting and helping build strength in their resilience and leadership muscle. She is no stranger to functioning in high-pressured environments and is known for her ability to perform under pressure both professionally and personally, be that as a sportswoman or on the stage. Skye also facilitates the RLE™ accreditation programme, training future RLCs.

Emails:
hello@skyedeaneconsulting.com
hello@resilientwomenleaders.com

Websites:
www.skyedeaneconsulting.com
www.resilientwomenleaders.com
www.resilientleaderselements.com

Facebook:
https://www.facebook.com/groups/skyedeaneconsulting
https://www.facebook.com/groups/643060069718939
Instagram: @skyedeaneconsulting
LinkedIn: https://www.linkedin.com/in/skyedeaneleadershipconsultant/

CHAPTER
5

Building Resilience and Empowerment in Leadership

By Lara Doherty
Founder, The Motivation Clinic; Bullying Expert
Guildford, England, United Kingdom

Becoming "The Bully Coach" in February 2024 marked the culmination of a long and transformative journey in my professional life. My varied experiences in the corporate world have profoundly shaped my understanding of leadership and management. As life coaches, it is essential to help clients navigate their paths to becoming effective managers while avoiding the pitfalls of bullying behaviors, both as perpetrators and as victims. This chapter aims to provide insights and practical strategies to achieve this goal, emphasizing the importance of understanding the root causes of workplace issues, including personal and corporate bullying.

My corporate journey began in 1990 at a large travel company in Sydney, Australia. Here, I had the pleasure of being managed by a woman for the first time—a positive and unforgettable experience that set a high standard for my expectations of leadership. This initial encounter with effective management shaped my belief in the importance of supportive and empowering leadership.

However, subsequent roles presented significant challenges. I worked for a Japanese company where cultural norms dictated that women were seen as unequal, expected to perform menial tasks and manage the financial aspects often without recognition or respect. This experience was a stark contrast to my previous role and highlighted the impact of corporate cultural attitudes on workplace dynamics.

Later, I joined a private bank in Mayfair, where I worked for eight years, climbing the corporate ladder through hard work and dedication. Unfortunately, this period was marred by instances of sexual harassment and an incident that left lasting scars. Despite the toxic environment, I persevered and eventually found a supportive company where I spent five fulfilling years and built lasting friendships.

Reflecting on my corporate journey, it is clear that mismanagement and challenging experiences equipped me to become the leader I always aspired to be. When I joined TenUK as a manager, I faced immense pressure to perform and initially struggled with my new responsibilities. In my quest to improve, I purchased the book, *Leadership for Dummies*, but soon realized that practical experience and feedback from my team were far more valuable.

A pivotal moment came when I sought feedback from my team, only to discover that my management style was perceived as bossy and overbearing. This revelation was a turning point that compelled me to rethink my approach to leadership.

The Role of Feedback in Transformation

Understanding the importance of feedback is crucial for any leader. Conducting a 360-degree feedback exercise with my team was one of the most transformative steps I took. This process involved soliciting honest feedback about my leadership style from my team members and providing them with the same opportunity. The insights gained from this exercise were invaluable and fundamentally changed the way I managed my team. Here is what I did and this might also be useful for any coaching clients you have who aim to become good leaders themselves.

Seven Steps of Positive Leadership

1. **Conduct a 360-degree Feedback Exercise**: Engaging in honest feedback fosters transparency and trust. It allows leaders to understand how their actions impact their team and identify areas for improvement.
2. **Embrace Feedback**: Taking criticism seriously and using it for growth is essential for effective leadership. Listening to your team not only helps you improve but also shows that you value their opinions.
3. **Implement Team Ideas**: Encouraging your team to share their ideas and implementing them when feasible empowers your team and validates their contributions. This approach fosters a sense of ownership and motivation among team members.
4. **Foster a Positive Environment**: Celebrating successes, providing regular feedback, and ensuring your team feels valued and appreciated boosts morale and productivity. A positive work environment is crucial for employee well-being and retention.
5. **Monday Morning Meetings**: Starting the week with a meeting where team members share something positive from their weekend builds camaraderie and sets a positive tone for the week. This practice helps create a supportive and cohesive team culture.
6. **Reward and Recognize**: Acknowledging exceptional work with rewards, whether through bonuses, lunches, or personalized notes, fosters loyalty and motivation. Recognition is a powerful tool for reinforcing positive behaviors and performance.
7. **Personal Touch**: Showing genuine care for your team members strengthens bonds and makes them feel valued. Personalized gestures, like birthday cards, demonstrate that you see them as individuals, not just employees.

Addressing Personal and Corporate Bullying

As life coaches, it is vital to understand whether your clients' issues might stem from personal or corporate bullying. Bullying, in any form, can have devastating effects on an individual's mental health, performance, and overall well-being. Identifying the root cause of their challenges is the first step in helping them overcome these obstacles and build resilience.

Bullying can take many forms, including verbal abuse, exclusion, manipulation, and even physical intimidation. In a corporate setting, bullying can be systemic, perpetuated by organizational culture, policies, or specific individuals in positions of power. Personal bullying, on the other hand, may arise from interpersonal conflicts and power dynamics within smaller groups or teams.

The consequences of bullying are far-reaching. Victims often experience anxiety, depression, low self-esteem, and decreased job satisfaction. In severe cases, bullying can lead to absenteeism, high turnover rates, and even physical health issues. For organizations, the cost of bullying includes reduced productivity, damaged reputation, and potential legal liabilities.

Identifying Bullying in Clients

As a life coach, it is crucial to recognize the signs of bullying in your clients. These may include:

- **Behavioral Changes**: Withdrawal, increased irritability, or noticeable changes in mood or demeanor.
- **Performance Issues**: Declining performance, missed deadlines, or a sudden lack of motivation.
- **Physical Symptoms**: Unexplained illnesses, frequent headaches, or other stress-related symptoms.
- **Reluctance to Discuss Work**: Hesitation or discomfort when talking about their job or colleagues.

When these signs are present, it is essential to explore the underlying causes through open and empathetic dialogue. Encourage your clients to share their experiences and feelings about their work environment and relationships.

Strategies for Addressing Bullying

- **Create a Safe Space**: Ensure your clients feel safe and supported when discussing their experiences. Building trust is fundamental to helping them open up about sensitive issues.

- **Empower Clients**: Help your clients recognize their worth and build confidence. Empowering them to stand up for themselves and set boundaries is critical in addressing bullying.
- **Develop Coping Strategies**: Teach clients effective coping mechanisms to manage stress and anxiety. Mindfulness, relaxation techniques, and positive self-talk can help them navigate challenging situations.
- **Encourage Reporting**: If bullying is systemic, encourage clients to report the behavior to HR or higher management. Guide them on how to document incidents and present their case effectively.
- **Support Network**: Encourage clients to build a support network within and outside the workplace. Trusted colleagues, friends, and family can provide emotional support and practical advice.
- **Professional Help**: In cases of severe bullying, recommend seeking professional help, such as counseling or therapy. Mental health professionals can provide specialized support and interventions.

Implementing these strategies can transform a disempowered and demotivated team into an inspired and productive one. As life coaches, guiding your clients to adopt these practices can help them become effective, compassionate leaders. Encouraging a supportive and inclusive environment will not only enhance team performance but also create a workplace where everyone feels respected and empowered.

Empower your clients to build resilient, motivated teams by fostering open communication, valuing feedback, and showing genuine care for their team members. The impact of these changes can be profound, leading to lasting positive outcomes for individuals and the organization as a whole.

By understanding the importance of addressing bullying and its impact on individuals and teams, you can provide your clients with the tools and strategies they need to overcome these challenges. Help them recognize the signs of bullying, develop resilience, and create a positive and empowering work environment. In doing so, you will enable them to become the kind of leaders who inspire and uplift their teams, driving success and well-being for all.

ACTIVITY

See Seven Steps to Positive Leadership within chapter

About the Author

Lara Doherty has been a life coach for six years working with midlife women who are miserable about life and she helps them get excited about life again. When she drills down into the reasons why these women are so miserable she saw a theme—bullying. The women had all been bullied (as had Lara) in childhood and then through into adulthood.

Lara became "The Bully Coach™" in February 2024, and she is now on a mission to eradicate bullying in workplaces and schools with education, coaching and healing.

Nobody deserves to be bullied and over the last six years Lara has developed a method to heal the lives of people affected by bullying.

Email: lara@themotivationclinic.co.uk
Website: https://www.themotivationclinic.co.uk/

CHAPTER
6

Living Your Highest Purpose

By Eric Ekle
Transformational Coach
Glenwood Springs, Colorado

*Your gift is the thing you do the
absolute best with the least amount of effort.*

—STEVE HARVEY

Everyone is a genius. Not just Einstein, or Isaac Newton, or any well-known philosopher or mathematician throughout history. Every human being has their own "genius," meaning their own purpose in life. It's their unique way to contribute to other people. It's like a fingerprint in that each genius is different from any other.

This chapter is a guide for coaches to support clients in truly knowing their highest purpose—and then, showing them how to put it into action. This chapter can also be used as a guide for coaches to find their niche of the type of people they coach and what area of life to coach them on. When a coach's niche is based around their purpose, it allows them to have maximum impact in the world.

On that note, I believe the reason there is continued suffering and conflict on our planet is that only a small portion of people are living their purpose. I believe someday everyone on the planet will be living their highest purpose. When everyone does that, humanity will thrive, and we'll figure out how to solve problems without going to war or having major economic instability, as a few examples.

The tricky thing about this is our society as a whole doesn't guide people to live their calling. So, you have to find methods that allow you to find what you really love to do and that you also can do for others. This is your purpose. To find your highest calling, there are three main components. First, find your passions. These are the things that really light you up. Then, discover your purpose. That means turning your passions around into some way that you use them to serve others. The last component is the courageous step of living your purpose.

Part One: Finding Your Passions

Finding out what you're passionate about means getting away from living the way most of us are taught in school, which is to take information in and spit it back out on a test. This mentality can work in a lot of careers, yet doesn't teach us who we really are. So, a person has to reconnect with themselves to find their passions. And they may already know their passions, but not consciously.

Reconnecting to Playing

To help someone be aware of their passions, the best thing to ask is "When you were a child, how did you play?" It may have been board games, action figures, dolls, or made-up games they played outside. A key to their answers is what brought them the most joy.

There will be a theme or multiple themes that come up when they tell you how they played. For example, one client shared that they played with Batman, Terminator, and Robocop action figures. The theme there is those were individuals that independently created justice in the world. So, one of this person's passions is about correcting injustice and corruption, even on topics that no one else is speaking up about because they're uncomfortable to deal with.

Following Signs

The next thing for people to do in finding their passions is to refine the childhood play themes to specific hobbies or actions they can take on nowadays. An easy way to do this is to follow signs and symbols that show up in their life. For example, someone might see certain numbers showing up over and over again over the course of a month—such as repeating digits 111, 333, or 999, or the symbol of an animal showing up repeatedly. These tell us that the actions we're taking in life, or about to take, are the right path for us. Other examples of this would be that if you imagined public speaking, and then you see a flier for a public speaking class or a social media ad about how to create a great speech, then it's possible those are signs for you to do public speaking and share your message with the world. The key with this is to check in with your gut intuition. When you see a symbol and also feel a sense of knowing in your gut about what you're meant to do, then you're heading in the right direction.

Once you've figured out the things you loved to do in your youth and let the universe guide you towards new activities, you're now living a more passionate life. The universe tends to guide people not only to what they're meant to do, but also to meeting certain people that end up becoming an important part of their life. This leads into the next phase of the journey.

Part Two: Discovering Your Purpose

Discovering your purpose means turning your passions into something that you give to others. And following signs towards hobbies you're passionate about will naturally allow you to meet two types of people—a mentor and a community. These both provide a support system to become great at something.

Mentoring

When you look at the mentors you've had in life, what they do is to help you become proficient at something more quickly than you would on your own. Mentors can train you in methods they've refined through experience. They help you find blind spots—those things you do unconsciously that hold you back. Mentors also encourage you to keep going when you feel like giving up.

In those moments that you feel you're never going to be good at the thing you're training in, they might see that you're only a few steps away from success because they were once in your position.

Embrace Community

The mentor that shows up in your life likely has a community of students around them that are training in the same thing you are. If you're training to be a chef, your mentor is probably going to have classes of people all doing that as well, who you may form new friendships with. And the great thing about these new friendships is that you all can support one another through the ups and downs of life that come with mastering something. This is because you're going to fail a lot when you do a new activity, and it can be emotionally draining. So, you can lean on one another as a community, so the stress and frustration of making mistakes are easier to take.

The bottom line is being in community makes things easier because your old friends who aren't joining you on this new journey won't be able to relate to what you're going through, and people on the same path as you will. Also, another perk of community is collaboration with some of your team members. Maybe a handful of chefs that graduate together decides to open a restaurant together where each one brings their different culinary interests to the menu.

Inner Knowing

After honing new skills with a mentor and community, it's time to tap into your "inner knowing." I believe we all have a sense deep inside of what we're really meant to do in life. We typically hear famous actors and singers talk about how they knew when they were young that they'd be in show business. Everyone may have this gut intuition as well, but if someone's life purpose isn't something that's been done before—say, they're supposed to create a cure for cancer—then they may not see it as easily as someone who's following a well-known career path like acting in movies. Because of that, they may have a lot more doubts to overcome to fully see what their purpose is.

Another aspect of listening to your inner knowing is to look at what limiting beliefs you've had to overcome because those can tell you what you're meant to do for others. For example, with the limiting belief that "my voice doesn't matter," a person may have not spoken up throughout their life, and their purpose comes from flipping that limiting belief upside down and using it in public speaking. This may encourage others in their audiences to speak up when there's something important to be said.

A great way to find out what you're supposed to do in life is to look at your top five limiting beliefs and look at the opposites of them. This can show you specific things you're supposed to do and possibly the type of people you're meant to serve. For example, say you've gone to culinary school and have a fear of being seen, a fear of connecting with people, and a belief of "I don't have anything to offer." Then you can find something involving cooking where you're visible, connecting with people, and giving value in some way. That may be to teach group cooking classes, so people learn to make great Italian dishes at home.

Acknowledge Your Gifts

Next, you get to acknowledge your innate gifts. We're all born with unique gifts, and these allow each person to carry out that specific purpose that their internal sense tells them about. Some are gifted with humor; some are great at creating a plan and leading a team to execute it. Some have great hand-eye coordination and become athletes. Whatever your gifts might be, they allow you to bring what you're meant to do out into the world. The activity at the end of this chapter is a guide for tying your gifts to your purpose.

Part Three: Living Your Purpose

Now that you've looked at the things that bring you joy, enhanced your skills with a mentor, and figured out your gifts, you have clarity about ways you can serve other people. At this point, the thing that typically comes up is overcoming fear and being courageous, so you put your purpose into action.

Courage is the thing that's needed because it's the way to get through that wall of impostor syndrome that typically shows up before someone does something they've never done before. Each one of us sees something that needs to be done in the world—something where we sense that we could contribute. And then doubt comes in: "Will I do a good job? Am I actually qualified? Someone else is meant to take the lead here, not me." These types of thoughts come up because of the mind trying to keep us safe. If you're not the one to do it, then that means you don't have to do anything that scares you, and you get to stay in the safety of the life you're used to.

Courage is the key to life itself.

—Morgan Freeman

Fill the Void

When you see a problem in a specific situation and you have an idea to solve that problem, but no one else is talking about the idea that could be the solution, then you are internally sensing a void of action in that situation. You may feel that void because you're the only person who can see the solution, and it seems obvious to you. It's likely that when something is obvious to you and not to others, it's because your natural gifts allow you to see it clearly. Another way of saying this is that you sense a void in the world that needs to be filled with a solution. And there's a three-step process to use any time this comes up. I call it "Void-Vow-Validate."

With this three-step memory tool, once you see something that needs to be done (a "void"), it's up to you to make a "vow" to do something about it. You get to use your gifts, your skills, and perhaps team up with other people in your life to make it happen. It may feel tough to do, and you may feel uncomfortable and continue having doubts, but in the end, the struggle is worth it because you now have the result of accomplishing a dream from your highest nature. That's where the third step comes in—you get to "validate" your efforts—meaning celebrate that you stretched out of your comfort zone and made a change in the world. This builds confidence to go after the next purposeful goal in your life.

An example in this situation is that for me, I saw a void in the world that many people don't seem to be living their purpose and don't feel fulfilled. So, I decided (made a "vow") to put on my first workshop for people to connect with their highest purpose. I aimed for having ten people in the room, and two showed up. It was nerve racking to put something out there that I created, yet I delivered it anyway. I used the communication skills I learned from mentors who are public speakers and had people start digging into what they really want to do in their life. I received positive feedback and celebrated that ("validate"), which boosted my confidence for the next big step into my purpose.

Embracing Your Vision

As you begin to take action from your purpose, there's a catch to keep yourself going. I say this because sometimes people get a high at first when doing something new, and then their enthusiasm may fade after a while. You need a way to inspire yourself whenever this happens. And that's where creating a vision statement comes into play. A vision can also get you through tough days when impostor syndrome kicks in again. Here are some tips on making a vision:

- It's the big *why* statement about what you do for others.
- It creates a *feeling* for you and the people you serve.
- It inspires you to keep taking action.
- It can help to make it short and sweet, so you can memorize it easily, although this is not necessary.

Here's my vision as an example: *A world where every person passionately lives their highest purpose, so we all experience freedom and fulfillment.* Here's another example:

> *To bring inspiration and innovation*
> *to every athlete in the world.*
>
> —NIKE

Whatever your vision is, it's important to remember and state your vision to yourself every day, so you re-energize yourself and stay committed to your goals.

Closing

We all have a unique calling, which is like a fingerprint—no two are alike. The tips and tools given here accelerate the growth for a coach in finding their specific calling of who they're meant to work with and what they'll help them with. These tools can also be used to accelerate a client's growth into their full potential.

Another thing to keep in mind is that people don't just have one purpose. We all may have one overall theme with our purpose, but it can play out in different ways. For example, Benjamin Franklin helped write the United States Constitution, was a newspaper editor, was an ambassador to France, invented bifocals, and was Postmaster General of America where he introduced some innovative changes. Maybe the underlying theme of all these was to make improvements in society that benefit everyone.

Whatever someone finds their purpose to be, they can look to the next level of what they're capable of—to keep expanding so they bring all aspects of their purpose into the world. I believe that when a person does this, they feel the most fulfillment in life.

The Golden Shadow Exercise

This activity helps people figure out their gifts that support their highest purpose. Here's how to do this:

1. Have your client pick three people they really admire. They can be people from history, famous people living right now, or people from their own life such as teachers or family members.

2. Tell them to write down one or two positive qualities they observe in each of those people. For example: "Do they live with integrity? Are they naturally confident? Great at leading others?" These can be one-word values that they live by or states of being they naturally live with, such as kindness, confidence, generosity, or wit.

3. Now, let your client know that these qualities are the qualities in them too! The values and states of being they see in their heroes are their own "gold" that they can't see because they're unconsciously putting them in the shadow in their mind.

When people know their gold, they gain confidence about what they have to provide others from their highest purpose. Also, an extra bit about this exercise is that when someone looks at the people they admire, there are certain things their heroes did in their life that they may be meant to do also. For example, if one of the people they picked is Dr. Martin Luther King Jr., then they might one day lead a non-profit that peacefully acts against some injustice in the world.

About the Author

Eric Ekle grew up in central Illinois. He worked for years in the aircraft industry as a structural engineer, yet it wasn't his ultimate calling. When he began seeking other things he truly cared about, he ended up being guided to the mountains of Colorado to study the Baha'i spiritual teachings. He later became a transformational coach and is on a mission to help people become the highest version of themselves by stepping into their purpose. He also became a Baha'i Teacher and has written about spirituality in his local newspaper. When not coaching or teaching, he enjoys hiking and playing disc golf.

Email: ericekle@capstonecoaching.co
Website: https://capstonecoaching.co
LinkedIn: https://www.linkedin.com/in/ericekle/

CHAPTER
7

Empowering Change: Strategies for Creating Breakthroughs

By Jolie Engelbrecht
People Change Specialist, NLP, Life Coach, Hypnotist
Regina, Saskatchewan, Canada

*As we look ahead into the next century,
leaders will be those who empower others.*

—BILL GATES

Change can be scary.

Some may find it exhilarating, but the vast majority of us find it unnerving, in some cases terrifying and, at best, uncomfortable. We all seem to agree change is necessary to drive a person or a business forward, but that doesn't make it fun for most people.

In my work as a people change manager at a large corporation and in my personal business as a master life coach and hypnotist, I have seen many parallels regarding change that I will share today. The thing is, in an organization and with coaching clients, change only really happens one person at a time. Empowering people can become easy if you follow a strategy.

Let's break it down.

Acknowledging the Need for Change

In business, making a change can come out of necessity, like software becoming obsolete, because of an opportunity that has been observed, a desire for the business to run more efficiently, or perhaps the business landscape has changed. Sometimes it can occur due to outside influences that you are obligated to deal with. With this tool set as a coach you can assess what is creating the need for change with your client and help them understand and acknowledge why it is happening. Creating awareness is key in understanding and acknowledging the need to change.

Often clients show up frustrated and wanting to move forward and really don't understand what the problem actually is. As a coach, you have the ability to ask questions to get to the core of the problem and often have the distance and perspective to identify patterns in the client that give you clues about what the true problem is. Let's look at an example.

A client came to my office complaining that no matter how hard she worked at her business, she could never break a certain ceiling of income. She had created a number of innovations but felt like whatever she did she couldn't be successful. She came to me exasperated and exhausted. I noticed that whenever we talked about people with money, she became sarcastic and tended to roll her eyes a lot. I started questioning her in various ways, testing her reaction to abundance and wealth, and almost every reaction was negative. When I brought it up to her, her first reaction was disbelief, then denial, then, as we talked about her "evil" rich relatives and dug into her feelings about them, she slowly acknowledged that she unconsciously despised people who she perceived as wealthy.

At one point I asked her why she was working hard to be wealthy if all wealthy people were evil. We discussed this at length and I challenged her to make a change with this belief. The biggest jump for her was figuring out her unconscious bias and admitting it may be hindering her success. We used a number of methodologies to deal with this block, and the cool thing is that soon after this work together, she increased her business by 80% with no effort. By the next year her business had bloomed, increasing a full 500% using some of her former innovations. It all started with acknowledging the need for a change in her subconscious beliefs.

Trust Is Vital

How can you create trust? The first way you can create trust is to ask the affected teams questions, often this is done with a subject matter expert from the affected team. When a team feels heard they become part of the solution instead of part of the problem. Often you get one or two people who complain loudly. All too often they get labeled as resistors. Remember to listen especially well to these people. It is human nature to want to avoid them, but not only do they often have good information, but they can also become your loudest ally when they understand and feel heard as part of the change. This works in coaching and everyday life as well. Ask your client questions and really listen to both what they are saying and what they are not saying. Work with them where they are. When you create a vision for them in the next step, it becomes much more effective if you can use their own words and phrases. People believe their own facts.

Recently I went for a consultation at a medical aesthetics business. I had talked to the owner on the telephone and agreed to come in to use their magical machine that would tell me more about my skin. Although I personally choose to wear makeup daily, I decided to go in with a fresh face. When I arrived, I was greeted by a woman who promptly put me in a small room with a clipboard and left me alone for a long time to fill out five lines of information. When I say the room was small, I mean my knees were touching the desk when I sat in the chair. I am 5' 2".

Later, the woman entered the tiny room, stationed herself on the other side of the desk, looked at the form, and frowned at a line I had left blank. She had not yet introduced herself. She opened with, "You don't know what this means?" immediately making me feel judged and found inadequate. I replied I had questions about the line and felt that we could fill it in together. She went through the rest of the short survey, lecturing me on this and that. She didn't know anything about me except that I was in my 50s. She hadn't bothered to create any trust and didn't work with me where I was. In addition, she was telling my horrible future from a skin perspective as if it was fact. I am a hypnotist and take those kinds of subconscious suggestions seriously. It wasn't information I wanted floating around in my brain.

As I sat there, all I could think was (1) "Why am I letting this woman dictate my future reality?", (2) "Why should I trust her opinion?", and (3) "She does not care about me as a person at all". I knew in her mind she was setting me up to buy more things in the future, but I don't believe scare tactics are the best policy. She thought she was coaching, but not coaching in a way that was at all effective. After 25 minutes of lecture and no use of the magical machine in sight, I walked out. This was a good reminder for me of what it feels like to be on the bad side of a one-way coaching relationship.

Create trust. It's worth it.

Use What You Can When You Can to Support the Change

Using what you can when you can to help a client support a change will help them immensely. Another way you can create trust is to leverage existing relationships. In a corporation, this may be their manager or their senior leadership. In a coaching relationship, it may be that you have built up a relationship over time, or you have them leverage an accountability partner. From there, they use that shared trust as a motivation tool. You can also utilize a thought leader that you both resonate with as well.

Creating the Vision

Depending on the change management methodology you adhere to, when you create the vision for change, it could be called creating desire, sharing the strategy, or even something else. This works from a coaching perspective as well. People need to want to change in order to make it happen. In order for this to be a smooth process we figure out what success looks like from the client's perspective. We often hear that WIFM or "What's in it for me?" is important. In business we are really mindful of thinking of all of the possible reasons why a change can be an advantage to a person or a group of people. Your client is the same. Essentially in both cases we are "selling the future state". Our person needs to have a clear vision, so when and if making the change gets difficult, they can keep moving through. The stronger the vision, the easier it is to pull it up and refer to it. In this case you may want to help your client envision their future state. Think of a memorable television commercial. Maybe it is a powerful car roaring down a beautiful road with horses galloping in the distance. You can almost smell the pine trees and the ocean on the coastal road. The more senses you can include in the vision, the better. For my corporate clients, sometimes I create a video that embodies the future state. For your clients, a vision board can do the same thing.

If you are creating a vision board with your clients, remember to encourage them to include images and words that take them towards what they want.

I recently attended a retreat where we were given the means to make vision boards but no instructions, and I observed things like the word "debt" with an X through it being used. Your subconscious mind will just read "debt" and will work towards giving you that. Vision boards are wonderful tools if used correctly. Encourage your clients to capture not only the material representation of what they want, but images that convey the feelings they want as well.

Provide the Tools or the Means to Learn the Tools

Clients in corporations or in a one-on-one setting need to learn or understand the tools to work well in their new reality. In a corporation this can include training, communication, goals, and resources. Coaching clients are similar. For a person who needs to take a step into a new way of being, maybe it is creating a list of skills that they possess that they can refer to, a great meditation, or a book that is relevant. Perhaps it is custom homework that will drive them forward. Maybe it is providing the name of an expert in the needed field from your network, like an accountant or organizer, to help them get what they need done. Looking at new contacts, books, and even videos you come across as potential tools for your business can help you be ready to meet your clients where they are and help them increase their knowledge dramatically. Something I often do is, I buy extra copies of some of my favorite books, so I can hand them to clients on the spot without losing my personal copies.

Reinforcement Is Key

No matter what industry a change occurs in, it is important to remind your client why they put effort into a change. It allows that change to become a permanent habit. It gives you a forum to refine any bits that need refining and creates confidence and momentum for more change. It lets the client see the results of their change. Quite often although someone has created a change, it takes a while for their self-image to catch up.

I had a client who told me that they could no longer listen to music after some trauma. Music can be one of the great joys in life, so we made it a priority to find a way to allow her to enjoy it again. After a few hypnosis sessions she casually mentioned a song she had heard on the drive to my office, and we happily discussed it. A little later she referred to herself as broken because she didn't listen to music anymore. When I gently reminded her of our earlier conversation, she stopped and realized that this thing she was so used to saying about herself was no longer true. It was a breakthrough moment for her. Reminding clients of success is one of the best parts of being a coach. Allow yourself that joy often.

Remember to Have Fun

You are walking your clients down an empowering road. Find some ways to keep things fun for both of you. The energy you create when change is happening stays with people and becomes part of the upgraded version of them. Smiles can make great stories and stories make things sticky in our brains. Ask yourself (and them) for ways to make this process fun and you may be surprised by the answers.

It is such a gift to be able to empower and witness people changing for the better. Remember, coaching is not just a process or a strategy, it is a calling. Take the time often to celebrate your clients and your successes, and it will remind you why you do this special work. The true power of coaching comes from your genuine desire to be of service in the world. Keep learning. Keep growing. Keep shining.

ACTIVITY

Empowering Your Vision: Create a Vision Board

Welcome to the journey of manifesting your dreams and goals through the power of vision boards. Below are some simple yet effective guidelines to help you craft a vision board that resonates with your desires and empowers you to manifest them into reality.

1. **Set clear intentions.** Before you start, take a moment to clarify your intentions. What specific goals or dreams do you want to manifest? Visualize them clearly in your mind and infuse them with positive energy. Really feel it.

2. **Choose positive affirmations.** Select affirmations that reflect your desired outcomes. Use positive wording to frame your affirmations. For example, instead of saying, "I don't want to be stressed," say, "I am calm and at peace." Remember, the subconscious mind responds best to positive language.

3. **Create a visual representation.** Find images and words that resonate with your intentions. Choose visuals that evoke positive emotions and inspire you to take action towards your goals. Whether it's pictures from magazines, printed quotes, or your own drawings, make sure they align with your vision.

4. **Keep it simple and specific.** Focus on your top priorities and avoid cluttering your vision board with too many goals. Be specific about what you want to manifest, and keep each element on your board meaningful and relevant to your vision.

5. **Create a balanced board.** Incorporate various aspects of your life into your vision board, including career, relationships, health, and

personal growth. This will ensure that your vision is holistic and aligned with your overall well-being.

6. **Visualize daily**. Place your vision board in a prominent location where you'll see it every day. Take a few moments each day to visualize yourself living your desired reality. Feel the emotions associated with achieving your goals as if they have already manifested.

7. **Stay open and flexible**. While it's essential to have a clear vision, remain open to unexpected opportunities and outcomes. Trust that the universe has a plan for you, and be willing to adapt as you progress towards your goals.

8. **Believe in yourself**. Cultivate a deep sense of belief in your ability to manifest your dreams. Trust in the power of your subconscious mind and the universe to bring your vision to fruition. Let go of doubt and embrace unwavering faith in your journey.

9. **Celebrate your successes**. As you start to see manifestations of your vision, celebrate each success along the way. Acknowledge the progress you've made and express gratitude for the abundance flowing into your life.

10. **Review and update regularly**. Periodically review your vision board to ensure it still reflects your aspirations and desires. As you achieve goals or your priorities shift, update your vision board accordingly to keep it aligned with your evolving vision for the future.

By following these best practices, you'll not only create a powerful vision board but also set yourself on a path towards realizing your dreams and living the life you truly desire. Embrace the journey, trust the process, and watch as your vision unfolds before your eyes!

About the Author

Jolie Engelbrecht is an enthusiastic Master Life and Executive Coach, Hypnotist, Reiki, and NLP Practitioner. She is an experienced facilitator and loves to teach workshops. She brings her sunny disposition and positive attitude to everything she does, including her work with a large communication company, managing the people side of change. She often calls herself people's "personal cheerleader" and is delighted when those around her succeed. She is passionate about books, furry creatures, and musical theater, and loves to travel. She created Simply Inspired Coaching and Facilitation because she believes some of the most effective change is created in simple steps that are easy to implement.

Email: angelfish@sasktel.net
Website: https://www.jolieengelbrecht.com/
Facebook https://www.facebook.com/SimplyInspiredCoach
LinkedIn https://www.linkedin.com/in/jolie-engelbrecht-5969a8b
Instagram @joliessmiling
Twitter/X @joliessmiling

CHAPTER
8

Holistic Life Transformation Through the AFISA Elements© Identity Card Game

By Adele Frost, M.Ed.
Founder, Adele Frost Institute of Self Actualization Elements©
Middletown, Connecticut

Let me call your attention to a great power which is under your control, a power which is greater than poverty, greater than the lack of education, greater than all your fears and superstitions combined. It is the power to take possession of your own mind and direct it to whatever ends that you may desire ... The Gift of The Creator ... attracting circumstances to you. Whatever your mind feeds upon, your mind attracts to you.

—NAPOLEON HILL

The New You—Creating your AFISA Elements© Identity Card Game

N avigating life during compromised health, life-and-death situations, grad-uations from one level to another, scaling businesses, becoming a parent, aging, changes in career, etc.—these are all examples of when a person may require support such as life coaching. The AFISA Elements© Identity Card Game is a fun way to open up dialog between the life coach and their client. It allows room for expansion of ideas, provoking thought, respecting responsibili-ties, unfurling the client's deepest desires, and discerning priorities of self.

The process of this game teaches the client that they can learn, they can build skills, and they can make positive and progressive choices toward what they desire. It reminds them that they are in control of their thoughts, their mind. This process will help the client to focus on what is important, thereby creating their own environment by recreating their identity to com-pliment the desired lifestyle. This exercise, and tool, helps the client and life coach to gain clarity in the new identity of the person's character, mission, purpose, and passions for living. It allows space for new personal develop-ment concepts of foundational goals, over-riding goals, means goals, or end goals for the person who is learning the concepts of self-actualizing.

Life coaches can use this tool to assist clients in recreating a positive story of success, a new identity. The answers to the questions in the game support the new identity for who and what the client is striving for, especially during periods of transition. The AFISA Elements© Identity Card can feed a person's mind with direction, confidence, and a path to success by aiding them to understand their future identity in manifesting what they desire.

The AFISA Elements© Identity Card Game sets the path in motion for the life coach to guide their client in setting clear daily routines and practices to achieve five-year goals. With you as their life coach, this is an effective and necessary tool that your client will revisit often, re-aligning their identity toward their ultimate goals, their North Star. The AFISA Elements© Identity Card is a quick reference for life coaches to remember their client's history, present focus, and discernment of next steps for success on their path of personal development.

The AFISA Elements© Identity Card Game is a "complete the sentence" game that respects the 12 categories of a person's life as demonstrated in Jon & Missy Butcher's Lifebook® personal development program. Aligning prompt questions with Lifebook's© 12 categories creates a holistic, personalized approach when navigating transitional timeframes. The 12 life categories in Lifebook© and the respective questions on the "AFISA Elements© Identity Card Questions Page" are Health & Fitness (8), Intellect (3 &10), Emotional (6), Character (2), Spirituality (11), Love Relationships (1 & 7), Parenting (1), Social Life (1 & 3), Financial (12, 14 & 15), Career (1, 13 & 14), Quality of Life (4 & 17) and Life Vision (4, 5, 9 & 16). Some questions have the influence of combined categories and weigh more heavily within a person's life based on their answers.

Methodology

The AFISA Elements© Identity Card Game is easy and should take less than a half hour to answer. The life coach should instruct the client to answer the prompt questions with the first thought(s) that come to mind, reminding them that there are no wrong answers. (The client has the power to change their mind and their answers at the end of the game.) The life coach reads the prompt questions and writes the answers on the AFISA Elements© Identity Card Page of the game, respective to the associating letter/combination. Once the client completes the game, the life coach reads the identity card out loud with their reported answers.

Feedback is encouraged after reading the identity card to the individual. The following conversations can bring even more clarity to the person's new identity, their priorities under the 12 categories of life, their dreams, and their goals. These questions will reinforce what ultimate pursuits they have in life and serve as on-going topics for discussions throughout the individual's growth and progress with the life coach.

Discuss answers on the AFISA Elements© Identity Card and any desire the person may have to change those answers. Discuss the need for change. What barriers or blocks to progress can they immediately identify?

Discuss non-negotiable routines and systems that may impact the preferred priority goals. Provoke thought on which category may be the over-riding goal category.

Discuss categories which are the person's foundational goals to build their dreams on. Discuss the skill development that is necessary for next steps.

Discuss the person's missions, passions, and purpose. Discuss timelines for the mission, methods to fulfill passions, and ways to implement purpose through methods of learning: degrees, licenses, self-development learning, responsibilities, and contributions.

- Discuss the character that is necessary to obtain these goals. Reinforce the AFISA Elements© Identity Card for on-going focus and re-centering of self.
- Discuss the means to obtain the ultimate end goals. Develop means goals to get to the end goals, recognizing current responsibilities, daily priorities, delegation of tasks, and necessary finances to go to the next level.
- Discuss behavior that the client controls and how the client can support others in their life that they cannot control, learn to role model, and teach through dignity to risk and incidental learning opportunity/technique; support responsibility and contribution.
- Discuss scheduling daily/weekly/monthly/yearly goals for implementation.
- Discuss methods for documenting progress and follow-up discussions.
- Prompt the client to revise, delete, or continue the AFISA Elements© Identity Card with self-awareness, growth, and achievements.

Intentions of the AFISA Elements© Identity Card

In the spirit of the great self-help author Napoleon Hill, the client is to read the card daily to remind themselves of the character they will take on to achieve their *Life Vision.* It reminds them what they are working on daily and what they are working towards. It clarifies their journey towards self-actualizing as their best-self here on Earth. This card helps the person to realize their true potential in life and how they can affect others. It motivates them to keep going. They can change any aspect of the identity card as they grow, progress, change, or reprioritize what they want in life.

The life coach can teach the client to use the identity card during various meditations. One suggested meditation is MindValley® founder, Vishen Lakhiani's Six Phase Meditation Method®. This method has six phases: Connection, Gratitude, Forgiveness, Visualization, Intention, and The Blessing. The AFISA Elements© Identity Card can be used for the

Visualization and Intention phases. Through guidance from the life coach, the individual reads the identity card out loud. The individual will close their eyes, actively visualizing the metamorphosis of their identity as portrayed on the card one to five years from now.

The intention of this exercise is for the individual to be prompted by the life coach to picture, hear, feel, smell, and taste different experiences on their identity card. The life coach emphasizes the client's emotional aspect once they've assumed this new identity. The experienced or licensed life coach can implement neurolinguistic programming techniques of interpreting any feelings and experiences that the client has questions or concerns with. The life coach can help the client identify where alignment in the person's visualization needs to be rewritten or is compromised, developing/implementing strategies to move through the discomfort. Gently advocating, supporting, and encouraging the client to push through discomfort, and reminding them that they can try new things, react differently, and learn new behaviors is imperative for the life coach to teach. The client may have a-ha moments of discovery on how to implement their daily/weekly/monthly/quarterly/annual goals.

Past practice of successful *identity shifts* has included:

- The client rewriting the card until the preferred identity is clear and desirable.
- The client reading the AFISA Elements© Identity Card in the morning prior to starting the day serves as a reminder of the character traits, behaviors, and goals of focus the person will work on throughout the day and evening.
- The client takes any action(s) toward what is identified on the card.
- The client makes slow to fast progress by changing their current behavior to the behavior/aspects as written on the card.
- Carrying the AFISA Elements© Identity Card on the person and rereading the card during times of doubt, hardship, anxiety, procrastination, or illness can reprioritize, realign, and refocus the client toward taking action on their current needs, wants, or desires, now or through steps towards the future—the end goal.
- A life coach is present in the client's life.
- The client is held accountable for their actions and progress toward goals.
- The client is in a formal *accountability group*.

ACTIVITY

Identity Card Game Prompt Questions

Adele Frost, LLC AFISA Elements©   Level 1: Life Vision Clarity

Adele Frost, LLC AFISA Elements© Identity Card Game Questions Level 1: Clarity

Answer these questions with the first thing that comes to mind. Don't overthink this! There is no wrong answer. You can always change your answers later.

1. List five roles that you play in life. (i.e., mother, co-worker, friend)
   Fill in areas A, B, C, D, E
2. What are three things that your role model does on a daily basis?
   Fill in areas F, G, H
3. Where is one place you'd like to meet "like-minded" people?
   Fill in area I
4. What is your most important role from Question 1 to achieve your dream goal this year?
   Fill in area J
5. What are three things that you really want to accomplish this year?
   Fill in areas K, L, M
6. What are three feelings that you yearn for in life? (i.e., to be safe, to be loved, to be happy)
   Fill in areas N, O, P
7. List three ways you can show someone that you love them.
   Fill in areas Q, R, S

8. List three activities you enjoy that move your body.
    Fill in areas T, U, V

9. If your future self were to talk to you about discipline and pro-
    ductivity, what three secrets would they tell you?
    Fill in areas W, X, Y

10. List four ways to stimulate your mind.
    Fill in areas Z, Aa, Bb, Cc

11. What are two things you can do to connect to your God and
    higher self on a spiritual level?
    Fill in areas Dd and Ee

12. State here the exact amount of gross income you'd like to have by
    the end of the year.
    Fill in area Ff

13. What are you willing to do or trade to obtain that money?
    Fill in area Gg

14. What are three steps you can identify in the process of doing or
    trading to get that money?
    Fill in areas Hh, Ii, Jj

15. If you were to receive $100,000 in free money, list five ways you
    would spend it to take care of yourself and/or your family?
    Fill in areas Kk, Ll, Mm, Nn, Oo

16. What are three major accomplishments you'd like to achieve
    before age 75?
    Fill in areas Pp, Qq, Rr

17. What are five things on your bucket list that you would like to do
    before you die?
    Fill in areas Ss, Tt, Uu, Vv, Ww

Adele Frost, LLC AFISA Elements© Identity Card Page Level 1: Clarity

I, (your name)_____, am a (A)_____,
(B)_____, (C)_____, (D)_____,
and (E)_____, who (F)_____, (G)_____,
(H)_____, just like people from (I)_____.
I am a successful (J)_____ who is actively work-
ing on (K)_____, (L)_____ and
(M)_____. I am (past tense) (N)_____,
(O)_____, and (P)_____ unconditionally,
and I give thanks and gratitude by giving (Q)_____,
(R)_____ and (S)_____ to others. I am healthy,
taking care of myself by (T)_____, (U)_____,
(V)_____. I am successful because I (W)_____,
(X)_____, (Y)_____. To build my
skills I (Z)_____, (Aa)_____,
(Bb)_____, (Cc)_____. The two
most important things I can do daily are (Dd)_____ and
(Ee)_____ as I bring forth (Ff)_____ toward
me by (Gg)_____. As I (Hh)_____,
(Ii)_____, and (Jj)_____, I develop
my skills towards self-actualizing. I take care of myself and my loved ones
by (Kk)_____, (Ll)_____,
(Mm)_____, (Nn)_____, and
(Oo)_____. Every day, I take small action steps or
big leaps toward (Pp)_____, (Qq)_____
_____, and (Rr)_____. I make sure to schedule time to (Ss)_____, (Tt)_____,
(Uu)_____, (Vv) _____, and
(Ww)_____. I ask Divine Providence for the riches
to help fund me and my family to become our best selves through our current means to reach our end goals. I ask Divine Providence for the moral
wisdom with which I accept and use these riches wisely, the riches I received
at birth, and the form of power to control and direct my mind to whatever
ends I desire.

About the Author

Adele Frost has a master's degree in education from the University of Connecticut, specializing in rehabilitation psychology. She has been in the health, human, and social services field, for both the private and public sectors, over the past 30-plus years. Her experience includes positive behavioral clinical support and services and case management, coordinating supports and services in the areas of residential, day program, employment, community access and healthcare for individuals with intellectual disabilities, mental health, dual diagnoses, autism, forensics, and drug addiction. Her current superpower during the day is providing case management services for individuals with autism and various developmental abilities.

At night and on the weekends, Adele prioritizes her family and friends, but somehow, you will find her crafting and fulfilling orders for The Paper Fascinator, a paper party product store on Etsy. You will also see her on the Lifebook© Platform, delivering international workshops, providing life coaching sessions through her second business, Adele Frost, LLC, and/or on Zoom, delivering seminars for her Facebook followers. As a perpetual student and personal development junky, she "Quests" on MindValley®, attends various guru seminars, views workshops on Brendon Burchard's Growth Day®, listens to self-help audio books while exercising, and researches personal development and healthcare material to develop more content for her followers. Every night, she reads for leisure in various genres on paper and Kindle books. And to answer—no, she hardly watches TV, and, yes, she takes time to eat, relax, and sleep (so long as it's scheduled in her weekly day/night planner, and her dolphin brain allows her to sleep).

You can access the AFISA Elements© Personal Development Programs under her Life Coaching business, Adele Frost, LLC.

Email: AdeleFrost.LifeCoach@gmail.com
Website: https://www.AdeleFrost.com; https://adele-frost.mykajabi.com
Facebook: https://www.facebook.com/AdeleFrostLifeCoach/

You can access her paper party product store at:

Website: https://paperfascinator.com
Etsy: https://www.etsy.com/shop/ThePaperFascinator/
Facebook: https://www.facebook.com/PaperFascinator/

CHAPTER

9

Leadership Coaching Mastery: Integrating HR Strategies for Personal and Professional Growth

By Ada Fürst

HR Business Leader, HR Consultant, Executive Coach

Switzerland | Hungary

Flexibility is strength ... And it's true for the psyche as well as for the body ... So get up each morning and STRETCH. Develop the mental range of motion that keeps you free.

—EDITH EVA EGER

As a practicing HR professional who has been working across multiple countries and industries, I have experienced and shaped various HR strategies, which helped me to develop my **S T R E T C H** mindset and coaching method for continuous personal growth and advancement. I call it "mindset" as it can be used alone to strategically plan your professional growth and the project plan connected to your goals. However, in our careers, as in sports, we all sometimes need the support of a coach to make the process more efficient and bring out the best in us. Therefore, it is also a coaching method. While the clients are the experts of their own domain, a coach helps them to explore new directions, giving undivided attention and allowing a safe space and time for reflection. This ultimately helps clients in their own personal growth by getting a better line of sight of their next step in building their own strategic plan and to follow up on it. Therefore, the different elements of **S T R E T C H** are perfectly usable in any coaching process and also connected to the different HR strategy pillars, which you can learn about more in detail below.

S T R E T C H is good for anyone. It can be good for those who miss a bit of self-motivation and, therefore, need an external partner, a coach, to help them to keep on moving. At the same time, it is intended to help those who continuously have the inner thrive and, rather, need help to pace their own ambition in order to keep their balance (both mental and physical).

Professional development requires personal investment, willingness to grow, and change. It takes time and effort; hence, why working together with a coach is often useful to keep you going on the defined road restlessly despite any obstacles. In the core of any company's success there are people— people who develop new technologies and ways of doing things through collaboratively challenging one another, their customers, and competitors. People strategies, therefore, became a key strategic pillar in companies. HR leaders nowadays rightfully have a seat in management boards. The name of the function also recently changed, commonly including "people" (People Department, Chief People Officer, etc). The goal of an HR strategy is to enable the business vision via aligning, translating it to the people strategies. Depending on the life cycle of a company, it requires emphasis on different pillars, similar to a professional career. In the corporate world, as in executive coaching, this requires business savviness. As ultimately, any people strategy is there to serve the overall profitability of the company. The financial success of an organization defines the capability level of investment toward the different strategic pillars as well.

The following pillars of an HR strategy are an extract of those elements, which are the most relevant for personal career planning and enablers for professional success regardless of field or career maturity. Coaching is one of the most effective ways to support professional development during any pillar of the career cycle to overcome obstacles and boost and elevate the efficiency of the learning curve. The following are HR strategic pillars translated to the career life cycle:

Talent Assessment and Identification

This is one of the key pillars of any HR strategy, even more so in the era of rapid technological advancement. It is important to define interest, motivation, the level of knowledge already gained, and the desired level to achieve. However, talent in itself is not enough if not paired with a good level of each of the following quotients and some winning personality traits as well. Some of the most recently used quotients to be explored in a coaching process are:

- EQ (Emotional Quotient) plays a big role in leadership skills and includes being able to listen and interpret people via self-awareness.
- AQ (Adversity or Adaptability Quotient)—Adversity in psychology, and recently also used as adaptability quotient in leadership materials, this became even more important in our ever-changing environment.
- CQ (Cultural Quotient) is key in our globalized workplaces.
- VQ (Virtual Quotient)—Most recently the VQ refers to the ability to build rapport, effectively communicate, and collaborate with others virtually.

Personality traits, which foster successful career advancement, include, but are not limited to, a person's level of adaptability, resilience, and growth mindset. People who look at setbacks as learning and as opportunities to develop and try something new are generally more successful and more likable—which also correlates to the likelihood of a promotion (until a certain level). Popularity enables collaboration, thus the correlation. However, it is a fine line and dependent on level and field. In leadership roles, especially on executive levels, respect comes before popularity. Natural leaders are followed by people not because of the reporting line but because of their authenticity, knowledge, leadership style, inclusivity, humbleness, etc. Most of these can be learned and developed with the right motivation level.

I believe in magic happening out of our comfort zone, but I am equally a believer of balanced, achievable, smart goals. As it's in human nature, we need feedback and positive reinforcement for the success that fuels constant re-birthing of motivation from within. **S T R E T C H** fosters personal growth, which supports professional advancement by encouraging a person to maintain inner curiosity and constantly develop new personal strategies to support transformation in changing environments. In coaching—especially in solution-oriented coaching—a baseline is important to find and call out the resources of the coachee, on which further success can be built.

Talent Development

Defining a coachee's area(s) of development and its return on investment for them is key in such mid- to long-term strategies. The *"What's in it for me?"* and *"How does this support my future personal and professional plans?"* is extremely important for self-motivation and engagement. It takes courage, knowledge, practice, and resilience to change and constantly move forward. Learning new skills and growth takes time and can only happen if you constantly but gradually push yourself to move forward to your next level.

As an HR professional experienced in corporate cultures, I have often witnessed firsthand how high-performance orientation can sometimes lead to burnout, demotivation, lower performance, or other unwanted outcomes. For example, promoting a talent just too early, expecting "above and beyond" performance even from "good performers," and the constant overuse of the word "challenge" to rationalize such situations. Furthermore, "challenge" is often used as the synonym for impossible targets to reach, impossible deadlines to be kept, and extra responsibilities for someone without them really being ready and trained for it just to suddenly fill a gap in the organization.

Another typical trap in talent development is the "gap culture." Instead of defining what is missing, I believe in defining the resources on which further successful learnings can be gained. Good leaders identify the different strengths needed in a team and aim for diverse teams, not only as defined by diversity targets, but equally, as per subject matter experts in different fields. In personal coaching as well, quick positive outcomes mainly come from building on the resources someone already has within and further stretching those. Often the "gap culture" leads to trying to develop over short time periods personality traits that would require a longer time investment. Due to the short time period available for change (for example, in a company development or coaching program), failure is almost always guaranteed, which could be avoided by looking at it from the other direction—the "right person in the right position" approach. A person may be perfect in one role and not in another in the same company, or someone may be a perfect fit in one organization while a total mismatch in another. Therefore, another example during career coaching sessions, when this pillar gets addressed, is career re-orientation.

Talent Acquisition (Recruitment)

Interviewing requires good pitching and sales skills. Self-awareness, personal branding, a good elevator speech, and expanding your network, paired with good communication skills, are complementary key elements in career planning as well. In career planning or redirection, the first key step is to do your own market research and channel plan. Define which are the target companies and what is the name of the role in these segments, which includes the key tasks and responsibilities of the desired position. During an interview, it is key to keep the answers short and sharp to ensure there is sufficient time for both sides to learn enough about each other to be able to decide on next steps. A few questions to support defining the desired role during the preparation may include: "What are the most important factors, my non-negotiables, upon defining my role and company I would like to work for?" (This may also require a bit of deeper self-reflection on the stage you are at in your life-journey.) "How marketable am I?" "How can I ensure my employability?" "What do I bring to the table?" "What makes me good in my profession?" Besides these questions in a coaching process, you can also focus on the way the coachee communicates to ensure that their message is getting through and aligning to the audience as much as possible.

Compensation and Benefits (C&B)

Part of interviewing—be it internal in a company or external—compensation negotiation is also an important element, as it is of any HR strategy. Self-awareness also includes the translation of a person's skills and experience to a monetary value. This also partially drives someone's level of satisfaction at the workplace. However, the main dissatisfaction, or primary reason, why people quit is still due to cultural or leadership reasons. Recently, the purpose of an organization and its support of employees' personal lives (hybrid or remote work, travel time—distance from the office, sabbatical and extra holiday opportunities, four-day work weeks, paid learning time, etc.) have also become key differentiator factors. Such non-direct monetary benefits are now more important to people when evaluating a potential future employer. In coaching, depending on the needs of the client, you may need to explore what is utmost important and where there is still room for negotiation for the coachee. Purpose, content, or benefits may or may not be the most important factors. The coachee can also draw up a matrix to visualize the importance of the different criteria to support and define the right focus for the coaching sessions.

Employee Well-Being, Company and Leadership Culture

This element has never been so important and recently gained a more significant part of HR strategic pillars. For companies, it is paired with their C&B strategies (as it has a cost but equally it is an investment in talent retention and attraction), and for individuals as well, as written above, it is a highly important element of the non-monetary employment conditions. This also requires self-awareness to define what a person's values are. Dissatisfaction, demotivation, and disengagement often derive from a mismatch between personal and company values (not only a mismatch on a skill and experience level when it comes to the "right person in the right role" approach). Major disconnects between company values and leadership styles, both of which are key factors of the company culture in practice, leads to regretted losses (talents moving to other companies).

During coaching sessions, you can further explore this field with a coachee to help them to understand not only their situation but also other factors that are influencing their situation. If you do this further exploration with them, using the question "Is it something I can influence or directly change?" can further help the coachee to define their personal strategies and non-negotiables (often it is easier to start from "what I don't want" in order to derive from that a broader spectrum of acceptable options to keep the adversity quotient high enough to ensure employability).

S T R E T C H and each of its elements are here to address this current people-centric paradigm shift where business results are fostered by prioritizing culture, employee well-being, and learning ability while also being conscious about the performance-oriented culture of workplaces. S T R E T C H is linking the important pillars of this shift with the human element, when "people are our biggest asset" is truly embraced. **S T R E T C H** can be used on individual, team, and organization levels, as well as for personal and professional growth—as these often go hand in hand.

What Is S T R E T C H?

Sport

Find your sport, whatever makes you happy and relaxed. Other—nonphysical—hobbies are also important in burnout prevention, but sport is ideally something that can be practiced in nature, has a great positive effect on personal growth, and supports not only physical but mental well-being as well. Active relaxation leads to shorter and better learning cycles upon learning new skills.

Technology

Learning new skills, especially in the field of technology, is a key factor in up- and re-skilling and also in ensuring a person's long-term employability. As the speed of technological innovation is very high, constant learning is inevitable. Trying out a new application at work usually is the most effective way to do daily micro learning, which supports life-long learning without significant extra effort or overwhelming non-technically savvy people, or anyone for that matter, in the busy lives we live.

Resilience

As in sports, so it is in our professional lives, endurance is key. Resilience can also be trained through several ways, for example: practicing sports in nature, other active relaxation techniques, developing new hobbies, practicing self-compassion, etc.

Emotions

Know your emotions. The better you know yourself, the better you can get to know others, which helps in building and maintaining efficient professional relationships and collaborating with others.

Transformation

Adaptability and agility are key. Change is constant, both personally and professionally. Learning your own change strategies can support your professional goals as well.

Communication

Excellence in communication is key both in face-to-face and in virtual co-working situations regardless of your field. Communication skills can be co-trained with the emotional awareness skills.

Humbleness

We are all humans. We are all fallible, and we all have a unique style and strengths. In well-functioning teams, successful individuals are aware of their shortcomings and are not afraid to show vulnerability by revealing the areas in which they need support from others.

ACTIVITY

STRETCH Exercise

S T R E T C H is best used in coaching processes; however, it may also be used alone. I suggest breaking down the different elements and the goals connected to each one. Once you define the goal, progress towards it can happen in shorter time periods. As is commonly known, taking on new habits takes approximately 21 days, but making them stick is closer to 90 days—it's called the "21/90 rule." Therefore, I suggest spending at least one month when working on a pillar(s) that requires developing something completely new, or the least known domain, to avoid overwhelming situations, quitting, etc. Furthermore, the elements of S T R E T C H build on one another. R for Resilience can easily be combined with S for Sport or T for Technology to make sure you continue to build a new habit with the 21/90 rule effortlessly, making it imprinted in your life going forward. It is important, however, to ensure all elements of S T R E T C H are present during the coaching process.

Sport

- What's your sport that you can practice in nature?
- How are you going to **STRETCH** it during the next two weeks? Define your goal. Example: I will run one kilometer more at least once (it can be as small as this).
- What extra effort will you start/continue?

Technology

- What is one skill that you would like to know by tomorrow morning if you could wish one as a new "superpower"?

- Why this one?
- How will you start learning this one skill during the next [timeframe]?

Resilience

- What helps you to keep on learning/doing sports?
- Name two things that you can do for yourself to re-energize. It is important to note that it has to be dependent only on you and practicable in any environment (during travels, etc.).

Emotions

- How did you feel this week at work?
- How did you react?
- If you reacted poorly to something, what could you do differently next time when a similar feeling arises to have a different outcome?

Transformation

Pick a topic which keeps your mind overly busy, and play with it from the following angle:

- Why is this topic difficult for me now?
- What exactly makes this difficult for me? Summarize it in three lines.
- What can I learn from this current event/scenario? Name two things.

Communication

- During self-reflection, before or after a professional situation, name what/how you feel yourself (silently or you can share that with your coach, etc.). Examine the words you have been using and the way you have formulated your sentences.

Humbleness

Remain humble throughout the entire process. You are learning something new—stretching yourself. Self-compassion exercises can compliment this step if needed.

About the Author

Ada Fürst is a practicing HR Business Leader in the world of multinational organizations. She has been successfully supporting business leaders across various industries in multiple countries with growing responsibilities to drive their departments' HR strategies. In her roles, she coaches employees, leaders, and executives. She became a trained coach by attending several coaching trainings designed and delivered by her employers, which she complemented with studying Solution-Oriented Brief coaching as well.

Ada also devotes time to helping organizations and individuals through career and leadership coaching and personalized consultancy across multiple countries and industries. She has delivered tailored workshops and been a mentor in non-profit corporations.

She is an ex-karate competitor, a sport enthusiast, and now an avid runner. She is the founder of **S T R E T C H**, which she has been successfully using in coaching processes with her clients and for her own personal benefit. Originally born and raised in Hungary, now she lives in Switzerland.

Website: https://www.adafurst.com/

CHAPTER

10

The Significance of Life Coach Certification

By Alex Garner, CLC
Enrollment Advisor for Jay Shetty Certification School
Los Angeles, California, USA

*When you change the way you look at
things, the things you look at change.*

—MAX PLANCK

n today's fast-paced world, the demand for personal development and
self-improvement has never been higher. The waiting list at your average
therapist's office is six months. People constantly seek guidance and support
to navigate life's challenges, achieve their goals, and find fulfillment. This is
where life coaches play a crucial role: offering clients the tools and insights to
unlock their full potential. However, in an industry that lacks strict regulations, the question arises: Why is getting certified as a life coach important?

The Evolution of Life Coaching

Life coaching has evolved over the years from various influences, including psychology, counseling, and business consulting. It encompasses a wide range of techniques and approaches aimed at helping clients clarify their goals, overcome obstacles, and develop a plan for personal and professional growth. With its diverse toolkit, life coaching can address a multitude of issues, such as career transitions, relationship challenges, health and wellness goals, and more.

The nature of life coaching allows individuals to choose their niches and adapt their methods to suit their clients' unique needs. It's a profession that calls for excellent communication skills, empathy, and a deep understanding of human behavior. However, being a good listener and having a genuine desire to help others are just the starting points.

The Role of Certification

Certification in the field of life coaching serves several critical purposes. It's a means to distinguish competent and ethical practitioners from those who may lack the necessary skills, knowledge, or professionalism. Here are some compelling reasons why life coach certification is of paramount importance:

1. Credibility and Trust

When certified as a life coach, you demonstrate your commitment to your profession and clients. We're dealing with people's lives here, and it's important that the tools and techniques we give them are from a credible source. In turn, clients will feel more confident in your abilities. It's a signal that you've undergone training, have met certain standards, and adhere to a code of ethics. It shows that you've invested your time and effort into your profession, which builds trust with your clients and demonstrates that you will invest your time and effort into them.

2. Ethical Standards

Ethical considerations are central to the practice of life coaching. Clients entrust their personal and professional aspirations to their coaches, making ethical behavior and confidentiality essential. Certification programs typically include training on ethical guidelines, ensuring coaches understand the importance of maintaining confidentiality, respecting client autonomy, and avoiding conflicts of interest.

3. Mastery of Skills

Now that we got the two big ones out of the way, we come to building the foundation needed as a life coach. Programs are designed to ensure that life coaches acquire a solid foundation of skills and knowledge. It requires a deep understanding of certain concepts and how to apply them in real-world coaching scenarios. It's not just about acquiring knowledge; it's about honing your skills and putting them into practice. Certification involves practical training and assessments, which help you become a more effective and confident coach.

Just like a foundation is needed for any building structure, it's needed for life coaching too. The ABC Framework that I learned at Jay Shetty's Certification School (JSCS) gave me the framework I needed to feel confident in the services I provide to my clients. Not only did I learn the framework, but I learned how to apply it to my life coaching sessions. We can have all the knowledge in the world, but if we don't know how to apply it, it's not worth much.

4. Marketability

Certification can give you a significant advantage in the competitive market. Many organizations and employers require certified coaches when seeking external support for their employees. Being certified can open doors to a wider range of opportunities, whether it's working independently, within an organization, or with specific niches like executive coaching or wellness coaching.

My experience with JSCS changed my whole view of owning a life coaching business. They helped me with how to get clients, how to manage clients, how to manage my brand, and pricing structures. They also helped me select a niche and create a marketing message that hit my niche. This helped me find my market within the sober coaching space.

5. Continuous Learning

Since it's an ever-evolving field, new research, techniques, and approaches are constantly emerging. Certification recommends coaches to engage in ongoing professional development, which keeps them up to date with the latest trends and best practices. When you invest in a certification, you're investing in yourself. Not only will that attract clients who will do the same, but you have an example to show that you were one time in their space, making the decision to invest in yourself. Be who you want to attract.

6. Networking and Support

Certification programs often provide access to a supportive community of coaches. This network can be invaluable for sharing experiences, learning from others, and collaborating on projects. It's a source of encouragement and mentorship that can be essential for personal and professional growth.

Moreover, certification organizations may offer resources, such as templates, tools, and marketing support, that can help you establish and grow your coaching practice. My experience at Jay Shetty's school resulted in me changing my whole contact list on my phone. I essentially leveled up because of the people I surrounded myself with at the school. Imagine a school full of like-minded individuals, all with the same goals and values as you have. It's extremely powerful when you get a group like that together.

Choosing the Right Certification Program

While the importance of certification is evident, not all certification programs are created equal. It's essential to select a program that aligns with your goals and values as a coach. Here are some key considerations:

Accreditation

Look for programs that are accredited by recognized coaching associations or governing bodies. The big three are AC (Association for Coaching), ICF (International Coaching Federation), and EMCC. They have joined together to make the Global Coaching Alliance (GCMA). These programs are more likely to have rigorous standards and quality education.

Curriculum

Review the program's curriculum to ensure it covers the essential skills and knowledge areas you want to master. Some programs may also offer specialization in areas like career coaching, wellness coaching, or leadership coaching.

Practical Experience

Seek programs that include practical training and opportunities for coaching real clients, not just mock or role play. The best way to learn coaching is by doing it. You may be uncomfortable here, but that's okay because we grow in discomfort. We don't grow when we're comfortable.

Code of Ethics

Ensure the program emphasizes ethical standards and guidelines. All of the programs under GCMA will have these. It's crucial to understand the ethical considerations in coaching to build trust with your clients.

Support and Community

Consider the level of support and community provided by the certification program. Having access to mentors, resources, and a network of fellow coaches can be incredibly valuable.

In conclusion, becoming a certified life coach is not only important but also a professional imperative in today's coaching landscape. Certification provides you with the credibility, skills, and ethical foundation needed to thrive in a competitive industry. It ensures you are well prepared to help your clients navigate their life challenges, reach their goals, and experience personal transformation. So, if you're aspiring to become a life coach, don't hesitate to invest in the certification that can set you on the path to success and make a real difference in the lives of your clients.

What I Got Out of My Certification

I realize that this might not be the same for everyone, but I believe I have a very special story when it comes to my journey of getting certified as a life coach. I don't know where I would be if I didn't get certified. It will help if we start at the beginning where everything started to fall apart for me.

I'm a sober life coach. I help people get and stay sober. I struggled with substances for 17 years—to the point where I was homeless for a year and a half in Chicago. I use the term "homeless" lightly because I always had a home I could go to, but I had to get clean and sober in order to be there. So, I chose the alternative of being homeless to pursue what I thought I wanted.

When I finally had enough, I got help. It was in rehab that my sister gifted me the book *Think Like a Monk* by Jay Shetty that changed my life. For the first time in my life, I saw something that I wanted more than substances, and that was a "monk mindset." In the book, Jay describes two different mindsets: the monk mindset and the monkey mindset. A monkey mindset is exactly what you picture when you think about it—ideas bouncing off of ideas, never finishing a complete thought or plan of action to acquire a goal. The monk mindset is one of peace, able to get through anything that life throws at it with ease. A mindset that is peaceful and clear. It was evident that I had the monkey mindset, but for the first time I had a goal. I had something to acquire.

I finished the book in three weeks. The first book I had ever read cover to cover in my life. I had a clear picture of what I wanted and the steps to get there. I was experiencing exactly what a life coach does for their clients, but by myself (with Jay's help). I started implementing the tools and techniques in the book, and I was amazed because they worked. I had been to rehab four times before this, and nothing ever worked like this. Nothing even came close. As I started to research, I found that Jay was a life coach, and he had his own certification school. From that point on, I had a new goal.

I entered the school at six months sober. To say that I was open-minded and willing to do the work ahead of me would be an understatement. I took every lesson, every technique, every tool that I had at my disposal and started to implement them into my own life. They kept working, and I kept growing. All of a sudden, I was launching my own life coaching business with a new-found confidence in not only myself but the services that I could provide, and I was ecstatic! I had made new friends from all around the world who thought like I did and had service-oriented goals like I had. That meant the world to me because, during all of those years of addiction, I'd felt alone. This was more than a certification for me. This was my new home.

After gaining the knowledge that I needed through the Business Launchpad at JSCS, things took off. I had set a one-year goal of where I wanted my income to be, and I hit it by month two. Fast forward, I saw a posting that the school was looking for an enrollment advisor. With my work history, it made sense to apply. Now, I work for the school that helped save my life, and I help empower others to join in on the journey.

You see, this certification school is and was everything to me. I don't know where I'd be without it. You, too, can have this profound of an experience if you take a chance on yourself and your growth. You are powerful, and your decisions carry more power than you could ever imagine.

ACTIVITY

Cancel Your Limiting Beliefs

Begin by setting an intention that you are going to be focused during this exercise. Take deep breaths—in through your nose, out through your mouth. Pick a limiting belief that is holding you back from living up to your potential—something that makes you feel bad about yourself lately. Some examples may include: "I'm not performing well at work right now," "I'm not good at my job," "I did something out of character and feel bad for it," and "I am not worthy." Hold this belief in your mind. Now answer these questions:

1. Is the belief actually true?
    *   Don't close this off with an answer right away. Think about it—focus on it. Is the belief true? Sit with it for a bit.
2. Can you know for certain that this belief is true?
    *   Don't close this off with an answer right away. Think about it—focus on it. Do you know *for certain* that it is true?
3. What happens when you believe this thought or story? How do you react to it?
    *   How does it make you feel? What happens when you think about it? Dig deep.
    *   How does your body react to it physically? Tension in a certain area? Where? Is it a tired feeling all over? Exhausted from thinking about it?
4. Who would you be without this belief?
    *   What do you see? What do you feel?

5. Imagine how it would feel to not believe that anymore—canceling this limiting belief.
   - How does it feel? Describe it to yourself.
6. Who do you become when you stop believing that?
   - Go through your five senses here—immerse yourself as much as you can in feeling that you don't believe this anymore.
7. What's the opposite of your limiting belief?
   - See what it's like to believe the opposite. How does it feel?
8. Is this belief useful or worth getting rid of? Can you let it go?
9. Can you let it go right now?
   - Pay attention and focus on the physical release of the limiting belief on your body.
   - Go through your five senses again—immerse yourself in this new and improved you.

Now that we've demolished this limiting belief, let's replace it with a new, positive, and empowering "I am …" belief. For example, "I am good at my job," "I am a good person," and "I am worthy." Repeat this ten times out loud and ten times internally. Continue stating affirmations every day, multiple times a day if needed. The more you do it, the better the outcome and results.

About the Author

Once grappling with homelessness and the weight of burnout, Alex Garner emerged from the depths of personal struggles to redefine his life's trajectory. Drawing from his own experiences, he transitioned into a sober life coach, leveraging his journey as a source of strength and inspiration. Having navigated the challenges, he discovered a profound sense of purpose in guiding others toward their goals.

This transformative journey not only allowed him to break free from the shackles of his past but also empowered him to facilitate positive change in the lives of those facing similar struggles. Through his work as a life coach, he imparts valuable insights, strategies, and unwavering support to individuals seeking sobriety, transforming adversity into a catalyst for personal growth. Alex's narrative serves as a testament to the transformative power of resilience, self-discovery, and the unwavering commitment to helping others navigate the path to a fulfilling life.

Email: Alexander.Stanley.Garner@gmail.com
Website: https://www.alexsgarner.com
Website: https://heal.me/practitioner/alex-garner-sober-life-coach
LinkedIn: Alex Garner—https://www.linkedin.com/in/alexgarner6/
Instagram: @AlexGarnerLifeCoach
TikTok: @Alex.Garner.Life.Coach

CHAPTER
11

Connecting with Our Inner Self: A practical Guide to Elevating Client Transformation

By Steve Hammond
Business Trainer and Life Coach
Nyborg, Denmark

Don't let the fear of the time it will take to accomplish something stand in the way of you doing it. The time will pass anyway; we might just as well put that passing time to the best possible use.

—Earl Nightingale

I stopped being a Global IT Director in London to become a coach, mentor, and trainer in 2002. After leaving my job, I embarked on a two-year journey up some of the world's highest mountains and diving in some of the most beautiful oceans. It was a journey full of physical and mental adventure. On returning, I wrote this:

My world tour took two years of planning and a lifetime of dreaming. It all finally led to the most extraordinary two years of my life to date. A world tour across seven continents, 35+ countries, and 110,000 Km by plane, train, boat, automobile, and foot ... Now I have had time to think. I am still amazed that I had the means to do it and feel very lucky. I would like to say thank you to all the people that helped me during my journey with a kind word, a helping hand, and good company over a meal in some remote place or bar. The experience has changed me, but what shall I say about it? I have had so many traveling experiences, each building on the last. Traveling has been everything I expected it to be and more: Blazingly awesome, mundane, lonely, overcrowded, beautifully solitary, mind bending, happy, sad, humbling, arrogant, painful to the mind and body, culturally rich, blindingly drunk, reflective, adrenaline rich, educational, confusing, frustrating, and lifelong friendships made. Sharing brief rich encounters with people, places, animals and the stars at night, music, laughter and tears, hellos, and goodbyes. It has been the most profound thing I have done to date.

I met my beautiful wife in Nepal, and we now live in Denmark with three kids and a dog, on another incredible adventure.

The Journey's First Step

During my journey to the top table as a Global IT Director, I realized that it was my connection with my people—leaders and team members—that gave me the greatest reward, not the IT technology, big car, salary, or bonus. I can remember after getting my promotion I sat in my new office talking with a friend, reflecting on my journey to this point. I looked at the person and said, "You know what it feels like? I've been climbing a mountain, and I am finally at the top, but guess what? As I pulled myself up and onto the summit, I immediately saw 2,000 new mountains to climb, people to meet, places to explore." In that moment, I wanted to find a way that I could explore those new experiences and blend them into a new focus and direction. On reflection, these are my takeaways having gone through that whole experience:

- Our **dreams** are out there waiting. Just pick one and make it your goal.
- It is down to us to take the first step toward our **goal**.
- **Plan** as much as possible, **nurture** your **will**, and be **persistent**.
- Do not take that step lightly. It **requires consideration**.
- Knowing when to **rest** and where to rest is vital. You need your energy.
- Make the step knowing there will be **pain** and **uncertainty** on the way.
- Take the step knowing you will **have to let certain things go**.
- But know that beyond that pain and loss lies your **reward** and **lesson**.
- You are **never alone**. Keep your eyes open and suck in the experience.

The Territory of Self-Development

Navigating the territory of self-development needs planning, training, preparation, a place to rest, energy both physically and mentally, and tools that help navigation. You would not step onto a mountain without this, and yet, we can find ourselves in the middle of challenges (metaphorical mountains) in our professional and personal life, with nothing more than metaphorical flip-flops, shorts, and a t-shirt. As a life coach, we need to help our clients plan, execute their new path/direction, and provide awareness of tools and techniques that will help them to navigate and prosper.

How often have you found yourself in a position where things have been going well, but you are now feeling low on energy and struggling to recharge, stress levels are high, and you are feeling overloaded? You are still performing externally, but inside you are just managing to keep it all together. Even when in the middle of this internal chaos, we have choices, enabled by having awareness and a well-planned support structure. For example, when climbing a mountain, in the beginning we have a steady approach with access to a base camp full of all the things we need to recharge, such as food, water, companionship, resources, time for reflection, and preparation. In this moment, things are relatively easy, and energy is high. As we start to climb, things are initially going well, but as we get higher, the altitude takes its toll on all of us, no matter how well prepared. Preparation helps us to manage the increasing challenges, but at some point, we will need access to a base camp. The problem is it can be a long way below us. We need to have planned for this moment, stocked high-altitude camps with the essentials we need to survive, and go on—finish the climb and return safely.

The above can be an analogy for how things can be in our professional and personal lives. You would never climb a mountain without a plan, training, key resources, and the aid of both a basecamp and a series of high-altitude camps. Yet, we sometimes embark on new projects, leadership challenges, and life projects without much thought on how we will stay energized. We can even ignore or stop engaging with sources of energy that are still available as we become obsessed with achieving the goal.

Tips for Managing the Territory of Self-Development

- Plan your sources of energy, support, and rest in advance—stock your camps.
- Know the situation will always have a beginning, middle, and end.
- If not, find a way to break it down so that it does.
- Use all your resources both in and outside of work—you are not alone.
- Do not forget to reflect and evaluate throughout your journey.
- Consider all outcomes, good and bad—great lessons lie in both.
- Take time to see things from different angles—this helps in finding the way.
- Ensure you celebrate your achievements—large and small.
- Things that weigh heavily on your shoulders can always be put down.

Remembering to unburden is a key step. It allows us to breathe from the metaphorical oxygen mask and take care of ourselves and others around us. It enables a break amongst the chaos, a chance to recharge, before picking up the burden again. Ensure that before moving on, you ask yourself the question: "Am I carrying unnecessary baggage?" If you are, then leave it behind. You can pick it up again on the way down, if it is still of value.

We sometimes cannot let go—we must hold on—so be aware and seek out help that will enable you to share the burden while finding a place to rest. If you don't, you will collapse, and then you have no choice but to let it go. So, ensure you find a way to energize that enables you to manage your choices.

Staying recharged is a vital step, and if it's not built into any development program, it can stop development dead in its tracks.

Stocking the Base Camp

What should your clients place in their base camp? The answer is very personal. It depends on what gives them energy. Get them to think about energizers for the mind, body, soul, and timeouts. You should help them to explore the times when they have found themselves high with energy. Ask them where, what, why, and when. You must also challenge them to think about how they will energize when their base camp is not accessible due to work pressure, deadlines, or personal challenges. Also, ensure you help your clients to find a way back to their base camp because energy will be draining even with altitude support.

Having a stocked base camp and altitude support enables people to start the journey towards their chosen goal. Your aim should be to help them manage the ups and downs and build in enough awareness and tools for it to be self-manageable. You want your clients to be their own Sardar (Sherpa) lead guide after you are gone. Figure 1 is to help you start a conversation with your clients regarding what they can have in their base camp and what they require for high-altitude support.

Figure 1. Energizer Checklist

Activity	Base	High	Activity	Base	High
Time with family			Be creative		
Time with friends			Watch sport		
Go to the gym			Play sport		
Walk the dog			Travel		
Paint			Take a holiday		
Do nothing			Take a short break		
Gardening			Talk with friends		
Read a book			Mindfulness		
Yoga			Talk with a coach		
Stretch			Talk with mum / dad		
Take walk			Talk with siblings		
Time for lunch			Feed the ducks		
Ride a bike / horse			Sit on a swing		
Swim			Play a game		
Sleep			Do a puzzle		
Drink water			Do the crossword		
Breathe, relax, meditate			Do Sudoku		
Watch a film			Listen to / Play music		
Go to the theatre			Dance / Sing		
Write a diary			Power nap		
Cook			Say no...		

Tools for Navigation

Once sustainable energy is available and people start moving towards their chosen goal, having navigation tools becomes a priority. I have found that navigation tools used in the corporate world can be utilized during life coaching. Having worked with many companies delivering leadership development programs, I have found one skill that is often requested is the skill of influencing others that we have no direct authority over. I have found a model created by Cohen and Bradford from their book *Influence Without Authority* to be particularly useful. Figure 2, which is inspired by this model, shows how it can be used to help clients influence themselves during life coaching. You would think that we have authority over our own actions, but due to a lack of awareness or overbearing negative self-beliefs, we can find ourselves lacking that authority. This is why it is critical that we can successfully influence not just others but our own selves.

Figure 2. Self-Enabling Model

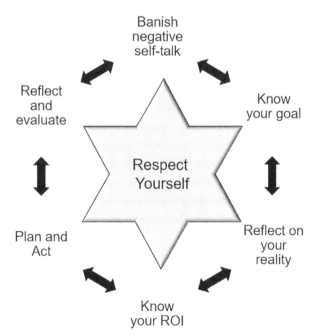

Figure 2. Inspired by Cohen-Bradfords Model of
Influence Without Authority.

Influencing Without Authority *Model* / Self-Enabling Model

1. View people as allies. / **See yourself as an enabler—banish negative self-talk.**
2. Be clear about what you need and want. / **Know your goal and direction.**
3. Analyze the world of others. / **Reflect and learn from your experiences to date.**
4. Identify value for exchange. / **Know your personal return on investment.**
5. Plan and make the exchange. / **Commit to a plan and act on it.**
6. **Reflect and evaluate.**
7. Relationships matter. / **Be good to yourself—respect your needs.**

Step 1: Banish Negative Self-Talk

As a life coach, it is important to help your clients know they have the power to take the first step and that it can be our negative self-beliefs that are holding us back. You should take time to explore the source of any negative beliefs with your client. Negative beliefs are like weeds strangling the shoots of self-development. You want to help your client be a self-enabler.

Step 2: Know the Goal

Knowing the goal is vital. Your clients will sometimes need your help to clearly know what it is they are aiming for. It is important to use active listening. Focus on using open questions and clarify your understanding. Your aim is to help them uncover the path for themselves. Having a well-thought-out goal is an amazing catalyst.

Step 3: Reflect on the Reality

Enable the client to discover what has led them to this point. Explore if they have tried to grasp the goal before and what was the outcome. It gives them the chance to learn from past experiences. It's a balancing game, so ensure they reflect, assess, respond, and move on.

Step 4: Identify the Return on Investment (ROI)

They must confirm "Why" they want it in their lives, thier return on invest-ment (ROI). In business, the ROI is the reason for spending the time and effort. Take time getting your client to think about how it will feel and what it would be like to have achieved the goal. You must ensure they are aware of all outcomes triggered by attaining the goal, both gains and losses, and the effect on others and themselves.

Step 5: Plan and Act

Getting commitment from your client from themselves to themselves is vital *(see Planning Tool at the end of this chapter).* Help your client to create a plan and identify the how. At this point, the task might feel too big. So, help them to break the task down into smaller steps, just like stepping stones leading across a river. Get them to think about tactics that will help them to achieve their goal:

- Commit to a start date and share it on a dream chart with a friend.
- Identify ways to keep inspired and motivated—celebration helps.
- Identify possible contributors and collaborators.
- Keep an eye on creeping negative self-belief.
- Creating a plan offers you and your client two things:
- A checklist to use during reflection and follow-up.
- The opportunity to celebrate when ticking off achievements.

Step 6: Reflection and Follow-Up

When you see your client again, it is important to reflect on progress using the plan and ensure negative self-beliefs have not crept back. Enabling self-reflec-tion in the current moment is like giving self-feedback, and our future actions and results are shaped by it. Ensure you use it with your clients and help them to make it a habit in their lives.

Reflection and follow-up are valuable resources that we often forget to use. We must choose to look at these resources with an open mind and seek actions that will enable positive self-growth. Avoid over analysis. Reflection and follow-up are key in helping us to find our next choice and step. In summary, reflection and follow-up:

- Help keep the path clear and enable new ideas to grow.
- Create space for celebration and for discarding what is not working.
- Help clients stay focused, motivated, and engaged.
- Help clients to shape their future development themes and goals.

Step 7: Respect Yourself

By placing a client at the center of the "Self-Enabling Model," you show them that they control the process and pace. Ensure they know their current limits and how far they should currently stretch (see figure 3).

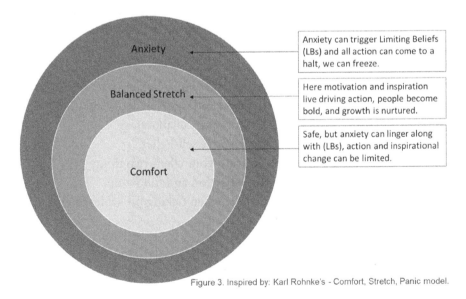

Figure 3. Inspired by: Karl Rohnke's - Comfort, Stretch, Panic model.

We are all artists, and we are all creating our own masterpiece, our legacy. Don't let negative self-belief erase it from existence. Helping people believe in their own creativity is a vital part of life coaching!

—STEVE HAMMOND

Conclusion

The "Self-Enabling Model" is a navigation aid, and as a life coach, we need to help our clients traverse each step. It is OK to find yourself moving freely between steps, going backwards and forward, as you progress with your client. When such navigation tools are used often, they can become a part of our clients' DNA and help them to navigate when we are long gone. If we can do this, then our job is done.

Key Takeaways in This Chapter:

- Help your clients to know "The first step belongs to them."
- Look out for creeping negative self-belief.
- Help them to identify the end goal and the steps that will get them there.
- Consider both gains and losses and the impact on self and others.
- Enable them to stay focused and energized.
- Ensure they know they are not alone.
- Help your client to identify tactics to help them stay on track.
- Urge them to commit to their plan and make it visible.
- Ensure they embrace reflection and follow up.
- Celebrate. It is a key motivator and energizer.
- Ensure your client has respect for their needs and current limits. Help them to know how far to stretch and find the right pace.

ACTIVITY

Planning Tool

Reference and use the numerous check list within this chapter.

As you work through the "Self-Enabling Model," you will start to be able to complete the initial plan. Begin with the discovery steps 1, 2, 3, and 4 (*What* and *Why?*), move on to define step 5 (*How?*), and finally, deliver the commitment (*When?*). (You may find that negative self-beliefs dominate the action plan these must be delt with before any associated goals can be achieved effectively.)

Personal Development Plan for:

Discover (What and Why?)
- What is most important in your personal development?
- Identify why it is important to you your return on investment.

Define (How?)
- How will you develop what is important to you?

Deliver (When?)
- When will you start and what are you committing to do?

Measuring Success

When considering your actions, it is worth thinking about how you are going to measure your achievements. Here are some ideas to help you kickstart the measuring process:
- Set a measurement period—for example, three months.
- Self-evaluation once a month. Make space for celebration.
- Write an email to yourself once a month explaining your progress and challenges faced, with next steps to be taken. Collect feedback and act on it.

Discover	*What is important to you?*		
	Why is it important? (ROI)		
Define	**How** will you develop what is important to you? **Tasks and Resources.**	**Deliver** the **When?**	
		Start	Finished

About the Author

Steve Hammond is an inspirational trainer and coach who has built his business on extensive experience gained at all levels as a team member, leader, and global board director. It has proved to be a dynamic combination when mixed with his personal drive and hunger for self-development, fueled by his extensive global travel and desire for adventure. He has also played a key role in setting up a global company as a board member with a turnover of more than £400 million per year, along with helping companies and teams develop core skills training programs—designing and implementing workshops in human behavior, project management, influencing skills, holistic leadership, change management, conflict handling, and high-performance team principles, to name a few. He has also helped people close the gap between thinking about and attaining their dreams and goals in life and work.

Email: sh@vitalsteps.org
LinkedIn: linkedin.com/in/steve-hammond-21439112

CHAPTER
12

Connecting with Your Coaching Client's to Cultivate a Wealth Builder Mindset

By June Hans
Wealth Coach and Educator
Talent, Oregon

If you want to be financially free, you need to become a different person than you are today and let go of whatever has held you back in the past.

—ROBERT KIYOSAKI

In the realm of personal development and coaching, cultivating a wealth builder mindset is paramount for long-term financial success and fulfillment. Eighty-five percent of Gen Y would like some form of behavioral coaching to keep them from making mistakes, procrastinating, or making rash decisions (versus just 25% of Baby Boomers). This generation does not want a financial advisor. They want a life coach with a side of financial planning and investment advice. The financial services industry caters to the wealthy, but everyone needs education and awareness when it comes to financial skills, and the schools are failing our students when it comes to teaching these important life skills. In this chapter we will delve into various strategies and techniques to help coaching clients adopt and nurture a healthy mindset, enabling them to build wealth sustainably and achieve their financial goals.

Understanding the core strategies for wealth accumulation is crucial for assisting your clients in achieving financial stability. Key principles to master include diversification of investments, long-term financial planning, creating passive income sources, maintaining consistent saving practices, and effectively managing risks. By incorporating these principles into your client's financial approach, you lay the foundation for a secure and prosperous future. Long-term planning ensures sustainable growth and wealth preservation over time. Passive income streams offer financial security and independence, reducing reliance on a single income source. Consistent saving habits build a strong financial base, enabling you to weather unforeseen challenges. Effective risk management safeguards your investments and ensures financial stability in volatile markets. By embracing these strategies, it sets your client on a path to financial success and resilience. Having a positive attitude about money can help to break out of the cycle of financial stress and open up a world of wealth and abundance.

Understanding the Wealth Builder Mindset

At its core, a wealth builder mindset is a combination of attitudes, beliefs, and behaviors that foster financial growth and prosperity. It goes beyond mere accumulation of wealth to encompass a holistic approach to money management, investment, and mindset cultivation.

Shifting Perspectives on Wealth

Encourage clients to redefine their relationship with money, moving away from a scarcity mindset toward an abundance mindset. Explore underlying beliefs and attitudes toward wealth and success, addressing any limiting beliefs that may hinder progress. Emphasize the importance of viewing wealth as a tool for personal enrichment and generosity rather than a source of greed or materialism.

Reprogram Beliefs About Money

Many of us have money beliefs that were formed in childhood, and they can hold us back from creating the wealthy life we desire. To create a positive money mindset and attract wealth and abundance, we must reprogram our beliefs about money. One way to reprogram our beliefs about money is to become aware of the stories we tell ourselves about money and then reframe them into positive, empowering statements. We can start by replacing negative messages like "I can't afford it" with more positive ones like "I choose to save for something I really want." This shift in thinking can open up possibilities we never realized were available to us.

Another way to reprogram our beliefs about money is to find role models who demonstrate a positive money mindset. When we surround ourselves with people who are successful financially, we learn from their successes and can adopt those same positive attitudes toward money. Finally, we can reprogram our beliefs about money by choosing to take responsibility for our finances. When we accept responsibility for our current financial situation, we become empowered to make better decisions that will improve our future financial prospects. We can start by tracking our spending, creating a budget, and setting financial goals. By becoming aware of our beliefs about money and taking steps to reframe them in a positive light, we can create a healthy money mindset that will lead us toward greater wealth and abundance.

Past-Present-Future

> *Money is a life skill—and as parents, grandparents,*
> *adults—it's up to us to make sure our children are*
> *prepared for the financial world they are going to face.*
>
> —Sharon Lechter

Past

To help your client begin this process, have them go back to their childhood and remember their first memories about money, for example, their parents talking about finances, fighting about money, etc. What are the words they remember their parents saying about money, for example, "We can't afford it," "Do you think money grows on trees?", "It's rude to talk about money."

Present

What are their beliefs about money now that they are adults? Identify what is working and what is holding them back.

Future

Dreaming bigger dreams. What are some of their dreams that have fallen out of view because of money? Take them on a dream journey and help them realize that perhaps their dream machine has been on the fritz and that it's time to dust it off and start dreaming again.

What Is the Money Imprint You Want to Leave on Your Children?

If your client has kids (their own children, nieces or nephews, grandchildren, or children in their community), they probably get how important it is to raise them with a solid financial foundation. So how do we talk to this next generation about money and success in a way that they can have a good money mindset? This is a really important topic for everyone to talk about (whether you have kids or not) because we are all influencing this next generation, and this next generation is going to have a huge impact on the planet.

Setting Clear Financial Goals

Guide clients in setting specific, measurable, achievable, relevant, and time-bound (SMART) financial goals. Help clients identify their values and priorities, aligning their financial goals with their overarching life goals. Break down long-term goals into smaller, actionable steps, fostering a sense of progress and accomplishment.

Assisting clients in setting clear financial goals is crucial for their long-term success. By providing coaching and guidance, you can help a client establish a solid foundation for their financial future. Together, you can create a plan that aligns with their aspirations and ensures they stay on track to achieve their goals. Setting precise financial objectives is essential for attaining lasting financial success. By defining clear targets, your client can craft a well-organized roadmap for their financial journey. Whether it entails saving for a future home, securing a comfortable retirement, or starting a new venture, establishing specific goals will guide and drive them forward. Regularly reassessing and adjusting objectives is key to realizing goals.

Embracing a Growth Mindset

Introduce the concept of a growth mindset, emphasizing the belief that abilities and intelligence can be developed through dedication and effort. Encourage clients to embrace challenges, view setbacks as learning opportunities, and persist in the face of obstacles. Foster a culture of continuous learning and self-improvement, empowering clients to expand their financial knowledge and skills.

Practicing Financial Discipline

Educate clients on the importance of spending, saving, and living within their means. Advocate for the establishment of emergency funds and long-term savings goals, instilling a sense of financial security and stability. Maintaining financial discipline remains a cornerstone for achieving stability and long-term financial success. It is imperative to diligently track expenses and prioritize savings to secure a strong financial future. By establishing a comprehensive budget and sticking to it, individuals can efficiently work towards their financial goals. Remember, even small financial sacrifices made now can yield substantial rewards in the future, ensuring a more secure and prosperous tomorrow. Embracing prudent financial habits today paves the way for a financially resilient future.

Cultivating an Entrepreneurial Mindset

Many times, our clients really need to make more money. Working with them to identify ways they can increase their cash flow and income is a perfect place to start. Inspire clients to think entrepreneurially, seeking out opportunities for innovation, creativity, and value creation. Encourage risk-taking and resilience in pursuit of entrepreneurial ventures, recognizing that failure is often a stepping stone to success. Support clients in developing skills such as networking, negotiation, and problem-solving, essential for entrepreneurial success. Discuss the possibility of multiple streams of income. Diversifying your income through multiple streams is a smart financial move by exploring various avenues such as investments, side hustles, or passive income sources that can secure their financial future.

Investing for Long-Term Wealth

Encourage your clients to educate themselves on the principles of investing, including asset allocation, diversification, and risk management. Help clients explore their risk tolerance and investment objectives, tailoring investment strategies to their individual needs and preferences. One size does not fit all. Emphasize the importance of long-term thinking and patience in investment decisions, avoiding impulsive actions driven by short-term rewards and market fluctuations.

Cultivating Gratitude and Generosity

Encourage clients to cultivate gratitude for their current financial situation, regardless of its magnitude. Promote the practice of generosity and giving back to others, recognizing that true wealth extends beyond financial abundance to include relationships, experiences, and contributions to society. Help clients develop a mindset of abundance, where generosity and goodwill are seen as integral components of a fulfilling and meaningful life.

 Assisting individuals in nurturing gratitude and empathy is a fundamental aspect of coaching. Guiding clients to recognize and be thankful for their present blessings while also encouraging them to give back to others can result in substantial personal development and satisfaction. By cultivating these virtues, individuals can fortify their relationships, enhance their mental health, and make meaningful contributions to society. Embracing a mindset centered on appreciation and benevolence has the power to truly revolutionize lives, fostering a ripple effect of positivity and growth.

Conclusion

Cultivating a wealth builder mindset is a journey that requires dedication, discipline, and continuous growth. As coaches, our role is to empower and support our clients along this journey, providing them with the tools, knowledge, and guidance they need to achieve their financial goals and unlock their full potential. By fostering a mindset of abundance, resilience, and gratitude, we can help our clients build wealth not only for themselves but also for future generations to come.

ACTIVITY

See *Past-Present-Future* section within the chapter.

About the Author

June Hans, a retired Wall Street executive turned financial educator, author, licensed financial professional, and agency owner, has dedicated her retirement years to promoting financial literacy. Through her expertise, she guides her clients in determining their Financial Independence Number and devising a strategy for long-term financial success. Her focus areas include personal finance understanding, debt solutions, wealth preservation, tax reduction, insurance protection, retirement planning, legacy and estate planning, multiple income streams, and business services. With a passion for helping individuals reach their full potential in health, wealth, and personal growth, June's commitment to continuous learning and empowerment shines through. She is a mother, grandmother, sister, aunt, and devoted friend. Outside of her work her passions are travel, photography, and cooking.

Email: jhansrevolution@gmail.com
LinkedIn: https://www.linkedin.com/in/june-hans-60374a5

CHAPTER
13

From Cancer to Coaching: Powerful Lessons on What Is Important

By Chris Ho
Senior Coach & Consultant, Cancer Survivor
Vancouver, British Columbia, Canada

Things turn out best for those that make the best out of the way things turn out.

—JOHN WOODEN

"You have cancer."

I remember those words echoing from my doctor as if it were yesterday. Three words that most people dread hearing from their doctor. And there I was in the fall of 2013 where my life would never be the same afterwards. The next thing I knew, I found myself sitting beside the scheduling clerk, booking an emergency surgery to remove the cancer on one of my testicles in two weeks' time.

After a successful surgery in October that year, a follow-up CT scan revealed another large tumor on my right adrenal gland. "It's probably a spread of the original cancer, you'll probably lose your right kidney, parts of your liver along with your right adrenal gland. If we don't get this out soon, you'll probably die". That was Christmas of 2013.

On Valentine's Day 2014, I had a successful surgery to remove my right adrenal gland and was able to save my right kidney and liver.

Cancer unfortunately came back to my life, but this time it was my dad. In 2016 my dad asked me to come over one night, and he wanted to share some tough news. I watched as he stared into the living room wall and told me he had stage 4 lung cancer and was already undergoing treatment. At 63 years of age, this was the first time I ever saw my dad cry. Later that night, I went home to tell my wife the news. After we embraced and shared some deep emotions, she turned to me and said, "I'm pregnant." It would be our first child.

My dad passed after a two-year courageous battle of cancer, yet he lived long enough to meet his first grandson, Caden Ho.

Cancer came back yet again, this time in 2020 on my remaining testicle after a routine follow up. After another successful surgery to remove my remaining testicle, I am and continue to be in great health since.

What does this challenging health story about my life have anything to do with coaching? For me, this was the turning point in my life that changed everything. Sure, I was always a leader professionally in my life, leading high-performing teams in finance, technology, and professional services over the span of 15-plus years. Coaching, leadership, and development were always a deep passion of mine, something that came naturally to me. And yet it wasn't until I faced these personal challenges in my life that I learned my biggest lesson: the importance of being present and understanding what's truly most important in our lives.

In the world of leadership coaching, the ability to stay present is not just a skill—it's a necessity. As a coach, I witnessed firsthand the transformative power of presence in coaching sessions. It is through being fully engaged and attentive that coaches can truly connect with clients, understand their needs, and guide them toward meaningful growth. Staying present requires more than just active listening though; it involves cultivating a deep awareness of the moment and fully embracing the here and now. Facing testicular cancer in my life and losing my dad were pivotal moments that reshaped my perspective on being present. These experiences taught me the value of truly living in the moment, not just in my personal life but also in my professional life as a coach.

When I faced my first diagnosis, the uncertainty and fear were overwhelming. It was during this time that I learned to focus on the present, appreciating each day as it came. This shift in mindset not only helped me through my treatment but also deepened my understanding of what it means to be in the moment at all times, especially during coaching calls with clients.

Similarly, losing my dad was a profound loss that reinforced the importance of cherishing the time we have. It was a reminder that life is fleeting, tomorrow is never guaranteed, and every moment counts. These personal challenges have made me a more empathetic and grounded coach, enabling me to connect with my clients on a deeper level.

Now you may be thinking, "Does facing tough challenges in life as deep as loss and sickness act as a precursor to becoming a great coach?" Of course not. However, without deep inner work, reflection, and a coach's own personal development to identify what's most important in their life, you leave a lot of your coaching impact off the table.

Being Present While Striving for Performance

Being present with your clients, so you can listen deeply, ask, coach around what's really being said, and identify what's most important is one of the hardest skills for a coach. Going through my health experience provided me with a different lens, perspective, and paradigm to appreciate the present moment and all it has to offer. Through this experience of gratitude, appreciation, and presence, I was then able to have a different perspective when helping senior leaders in my coaching practice. I leverage my experience with cancer, not so much in coaching conversations (because it's more about them than me) but as a way to remind me as a coach to think about the underlying importance of what's being said and what's most important. Gaining perspective is key to the success of a coachee, and our role is to pivot, adjust, and zoom in and out so that the client can see their situation, story, values, and wants in a whole new way.

Putting in Our Own Work

As a coach, how are we preparing and doing our own inner work to decide and determine what's most important for us before we can show up in a way that helps serve our clients? This is not to say we should share our story in our coaching (it should be all about the client), but it's more about how much of the work we are doing personally to be able to show up and support our clients who are exploring the work they need to do to become better themselves. Ever heard the phrase, "Eating your own dog food"? While I hate the phrase (I have two dogs myself and think their food smells great, FYI), it begs the question: are we, as executive leadership coaches, spending and investing in our own development, or are we just pretending to "eat our own dog food"?

The strategy includes making sure you, as a coach, have gone through these deep perspective-shifting exercises yourself, so you can show up as present as you can be in your conversations with clients. There is an energy that is aligned when a coach has "done the work" themselves before coaching clients towards their outcomes. The perspective I'm talking about here is not about remembering all the great questions you can ask in the moment or thinking about that catchy phrase or word to say but more about aligning your energy, your own development, and your own intuition in a way that best serves the client when they need it.

Identifying What's Most Important (For Coaches and Clients)

As coaches, one of our key responsibilities is to help our clients identify what truly matters in their lives. My own journey through cancer was a catalyst for discovering my core values and priorities. Facing such a significant challenge forced me to confront what was genuinely important to me—family, health, and meaningful work. This clarity has not only enriched my personal life but has also become a cornerstone of my coaching practice.

One of the most effective tools I use with my clients to help them determine their priorities is the Eisenhower Box, also known as the Urgent-Important Matrix. This simple yet powerful tool helps individuals categorize tasks based on their urgency and importance, allowing them to focus on what truly matters.

The Eisenhower Box is divided into four quadrants:

- **Urgent and Important**: Tasks that require immediate attention and are critical to achieving your goals, personally and professionally.

- **Not Urgent but Important**: Tasks that are crucial for long-term success but do not need immediate action. These are often neglected but should be prioritized and acted on.
- **Urgent but Not Important**: Tasks that require quick action but do not significantly contribute to your long-term goals. These can often be delegated or politely dismissed. This area is all about boundaries.
- **Not Urgent and Not Important**: Tasks that are neither time-sensitive nor crucial to your goals. These can be eliminated to free up time for more important activities.

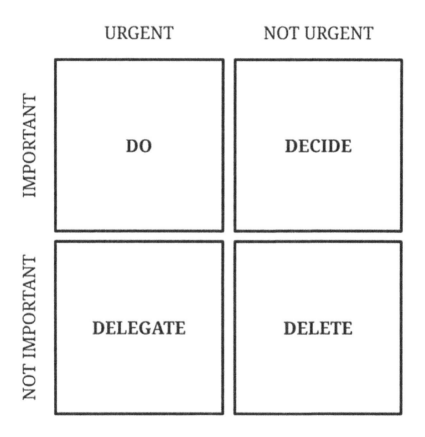

By guiding clients through this matrix, I help them gain clarity on their priorities and make more intentional choices about how they spend their time. This process not only enhances their productivity but also aligns their actions with their values and long-term goals.

Balancing Presence and Future Performance

As coaches, one of the most significant challenges we help our clients navigate is balancing the act of being present and grateful for today while still striving for high performance in the future. This delicate balance requires a mindset that embraces both mindfulness and ambition, allowing individuals to appreciate the journey without losing sight of their long-term goals.

To achieve this balance, I often guide my clients through several key strategies:

1. **Mindful Goal Setting**: Encourage clients to set goals that align with their core values and passions. When goals are deeply meaningful, they naturally foster a sense of gratitude and fulfillment in the present moment, even as clients work toward future achievements.

2. **Regular Reflection**: Incorporate regular reflection practices, such as journaling or mindfulness meditation, to help clients stay connected to their current experiences. Reflecting on daily progress and small wins fosters a sense of appreciation and keeps the focus on the present.

3. **Gratitude Practices**: Encourage daily gratitude practices, such as writing down three things they are grateful for each day and sharing it with a friend, partner, or family members. This simple habit shifts the focus to the positive aspects of their current life, fostering a mindset of appreciation.

4. **Flexible Planning**: Help clients develop flexible plans that allow for adjustments as needed. This approach reduces the pressure of rigid timelines and creates space for them to adapt to new opportunities and challenges, maintaining a sense of presence while working toward future goals.

5. **Celebrating Milestones**: Emphasize the importance of celebrating milestones and achievements along the way. Recognizing progress keeps a client motivated and grounded in their journey, reinforcing the connection between present actions and future success. Celebrate, celebrate, celebrate!

By integrating these strategies into their life, a client can cultivate a mindset that honors both the present moment and their aspirations for the future. This balanced approach not only enhances their well-being but also leads to more sustainable and meaningful success.

In the end, I would use, practice, and implement these to help your client gain a better and different perspective, so they can make the best decision and choice for themselves. With that said, the most important work a coach can do is to lead in that work for themselves, to determine what's most important for the coach, so they can show up as the best versions of themselves to then support the coachee the best way they need the support.

ACTIVITY

See the Eisenhower Box within the chapter.

About the Author

Chris Ho is on a passionate, purpose-driven journey to make a meaningful impact to as many lives as possible. Professionally he holds a business degree in finance and marketing and is a Certified Organizational and Executive Leadership coach with over 15 years' experience of leadership, coaching, and sales development. Personally, he is a two-time testicular cancer survivor, past cancer caregiver to his late father, and uses this life experience to live each day in the present, on purpose, full of passion.

Chris has held several leadership roles in finance, media, technology, and leadership and development industries. He has hundreds of hours of coaching experience and draws from his personal and professional experience to help his clients live the life that they want to. His goal is to help create the best leaders in the world, at work and at home. Chris is passionate about his contributions to his community including BC Cancer Agency, Movember, and other organizations that promote men's mental and physical health and positive masculinity.

Chris lives in Vancouver with his amazing wife, Maggie, two boys, Caden and Liam, and fur babies, Sam and Zoe.

Contact Chris for coaching, speaking, or leadership and team development workshops.

Email: chris@consciousstudio.ca
Website: www.consciousstudio.ca

CHAPTER
14

The Executive Compass: Guiding Teams in a Global Landscape

By Kristelle Kamini
Strategic Business Partner
London, England, United Kingdom

*The best time to plant a tree was 20 years
ago. The second best time is now.*

—CHINESE PROVERB

In the intricate tapestry of today's global business landscape, senior executives and their teams shoulder immense responsibilities. They must navigate constant change, spearhead innovation, and make high-consequence decisions—all while ensuring profitability and sustainability. In this high-stakes environment, executive coaching has emerged as a powerful tool for unlocking leadership potential, enhancing team dynamics, and driving transformative growth.

Throughout my career, I've had the privilege of working alongside brilliant senior executives and global teams. This collaborative experience has provided invaluable insights into the unique challenges and opportunities faced by those leading in dynamic, high-pressure environments. Witnessing firsthand the complexities of global operations, the need for rapid decision-making, and the relentless focus on results has shaped my understanding of the support life coaches can offer. My success in this diverse landscape stems from a few core values I've always embraced: a deep-rooted belief in human potential, an unwavering commitment to adaptability, and a passion for igniting authentic empowerment in others. This potent combination allows me to connect with leaders on a human level, navigate the complexities of global dynamics, and cultivate lasting transformative experiences for my clients. In addition to this, it is important to recognise that a wide range of tools and strategies exist for guiding global teams effectively. There is no one-size-fits-all solution. In this chapter, my hope is to enlighten you on the unique challenges faced by those in leadership positions and provide you with strategies and insights needed to successfully navigate these complexities.

Harnessing the Power of the Brain

Coaching stands on the fascinating principle of neuroplasticity—the brain's remarkable capacity to change, adapt, and form new connections throughout life. By employing carefully designed conversations, exercises, and reflective practices, coaching leverages this inherent ability to reshape neural pathways. Let's delve into the ways this transformation occurs.

Rewiring Thought Patterns

Our brains are remarkable pattern-forming machines, constantly creating neural pathways that shape our thoughts, emotions, and behaviours. Some of these pathways serve us well, while others can become deeply ingrained obstacles to growth and effectiveness. Coaching offers a powerful tool for leaders and team members to identify these limiting patterns and beliefs— including unconscious biases that might be influencing their perceptions and decisions. Unconscious biases are those automatic, often hidden, preferences or prejudices that can unintentionally impact how we interact with and judge others. Through focused coaching techniques, new pathways are formed, supporting the development of more empowering approaches to challenges, decision-making, and overall leadership style. This could involve exercises that challenge assumptions, perspective-taking activities to encourage empathy, and techniques for becoming more mindful of unconscious biases when managing teams or addressing complex situations.

Fostering Innovation

When leaders and teams learn to break out of established thought patterns, they open space for creativity and innovation. Coaching facilitates this by encouraging individuals to challenge assumptions, explore new perspectives, and experiment with different approaches. This brain rewiring promotes a more agile and innovative mindset.

Enhanced Problem-Solving Skills

Neuroplasticity allows the brain to develop enhanced problem-solving capabilities. Coaching creates a safe space to analyse challenges from multiple angles. New neural pathways are developed, expanding the leader's ability to think strategically, consider various solutions, and arrive at well-informed decisions.

Emotional Intelligence Growth

Emotional intelligence (EQ) is a core skill for effective leadership and teamwork. The science behind coaching reveals that EQ can be cultivated through targeted techniques. Coaching delves into behavioural patterns and emotional responses, fostering self-awareness. Leaders and team members learn to recognise their own emotional states and those of others. They develop strategies to regulate emotions, enhancing empathy, communication, and overall relationship management. In essence, coaching is fundamentally aligned with how our brains learn and adapt. It's not merely about providing advice but about empowering individuals to transform their own thinking and responses for lasting, positive change.

Understanding the Executive Mindset

Successful executive coaching starts with an in-depth understanding of the executive mindset. What is the underlying reason for an executive's persistent pattern of misprioritisation? Coaching probes deeper: Are there fears about missing out? Is there difficulty saying no? These underlying drivers must be addressed for sustainable change. Key factors include:

The High-Pressure Environment

Executives face a relentless torrent of demands. Balancing strategic vision with day-to-day operations, managing complex stakeholder relationships, and driving results within ever-shrinking timelines creates a pressure-cooker environment. The executive mindset is often characterised by a need for rapid analysis, decisive action, and continuous recalibration of priorities as circumstances change.

Prioritisation and Focus

Amidst competing demands, executives must maintain laser-focus on critical business objectives. This requires relentless prioritisation. They must distinguish between the urgent and the truly important, ensuring that time-sensitive tasks don't overshadow longer-term strategic goals. Effective executives develop systems to filter information, delegate effectively, and protect time for high-level strategic thinking amidst the chaos.

The coach's role is to provide executives with focused support. Rather than dictating solutions, they assist executives in developing individualised systems that cater to their needs. These systems could include decision-making frameworks like the Eisenhower Matrix, time management techniques like time-blocking, or training on effective methods for prioritising and managing communications.

Calculated Risk-Taking

Time pressures often force executives to make decisions with incomplete information. Success hinges on the ability to assess risks intelligently, weigh the pros and cons decisively, and pivot quickly if results diverge from expectations. The executive mindset is marked by a willingness to act based on the best available data, even when there's an element of uncertainty.

Resilience and Mental Agility

Today's fast-paced business world places immense pressure on executives, demanding exceptional resilience to manage stress, bounce back from setbacks, and maintain optimism. Mental agility is equally crucial, allowing executives to adapt quickly, think creatively, and make sound decisions under pressure. Clarity of thought is also vital for focus and effective decision-making in high-stakes situations.

Practices like mindfulness, healthy habits, and strong support systems help executives develop these qualities. Smart delegation and team empowerment are also key—skilled teams led by trusting executives share the burden and drive greater success. This mental resilience and agility benefit not only the executive but cascade down to their team. Leaders who model these qualities foster a more positive, adaptable, and focused work environment where everyone can thrive, even under tight deadlines.

Leveraging a Team

The most effective executives understand they cannot operate in a silo. Surrounding themselves with skilled teams and delegating strategically are critical to achieving goals within time constraints. The executive mindset values building trust, aligning teams around critical objectives, and empowering their people to take calculated risks within their spheres of authority. In the face of time constraints, executives must navigate a complex landscape that demands a blend of strategic thinking, decisive action, risk tolerance, resilience, and skillful resource utilisation. This delicate balance between immediate priorities and long-term vision calls for both adaptability and unwavering focus on critical business goals.

Building a Strong Coaching Alliance

A strong coaching alliance between the coach, executive, and sponsoring organisation is vital for success. To optimise the coaching relationship, coaches should begin by clarifying expectations and roles. This includes initiating conversations that establish the scope of the coaching engagement and clearly define the responsibilities of the coach, the executive, and organisational stakeholders.

Alongside this, coaches should collaborate with the executive to set realistic and measurable goals that align with both personal and organisational objectives. Maintaining confidentiality is crucial for building trust, especially within high-pressure environments where executives may feel hesitant to be vulnerable. Finally, coaches who demonstrate empathy, genuine interest, and a non-judgmental approach will develop stronger rapport with their executive clients.

Tailoring Coaching Approaches to the Executive

In executive coaching, a one-size-fits-all approach simply won't yield optimal results. Effective coaches understand the importance of tailoring their methodologies and techniques to the specific needs and preferences of the individual executive. This customization might involve considering the executive's personality traits and preferred learning styles. For example, some executives might thrive with direct feedback while others respond more favourably to a Socratic questioning approach.

Additionally, a coach should take into account the executive's prior coaching experience. Seasoned executives might feel comfortable bypassing foundational steps and diving straight into more advanced concepts, whereas those new to coaching could benefit from a more structured process. Finally, the nature of the challenge the executive is facing is a significant factor in tailoring the coaching approach. Whether the focus is on technical skill development, behavioural change, or strategic decision-making will guide the selection of the most appropriate coaching models and interventions.

Navigating the Complexities of Global Leadership

Global leadership presents a unique set of challenges that require leaders to be adaptable, aware, and resilient. Leaders must navigate diverse cultural norms, bridge communication gaps across time zones, manage remote teams effectively, and remain informed about geo-political landscapes. Coaching addresses these complexities by focusing on the leader's internal development. Coaches help global leaders build cross-cultural competence by identifying biases and tailoring communication styles to resonate with various cultures.

They foster a global mindset, enabling leaders to break free from regional perspectives and embrace the interconnected nature of global business along with its geopolitical influences.

Coaching plays a vital role in developing the skills essential for effectively managing virtual teams. Leaders learn to build trust in a remote environment, communicate expectations with exceptional clarity, and manage conflict constructively despite the lack of in-person interaction. Because the global environment is often unpredictable, coaches help leaders become more comfortable with ambiguity and enhance their decision-making under pressure. Moreover, as the stresses of global leadership can be significant, coaching offers tools for building resilience, helping leaders develop coping mechanisms and preserve their mental well-being. Overall, coaching augments theoretical leadership training with a personalised approach. It's a crucial support system for global leaders, enabling them to navigate the complex world of international business with greater adaptability, cultural sensitivity, and inner strength.

The Subtle Strength of Small Changes

It's easy to get caught up in the desire for radical life transformations. Yet, true and lasting change often happens incrementally. Here's how coaches can empower clients by focusing on the potential of micro-shifts:

Celebrate the Tiny Victories

Emphasise that small actions matter a lot. Instead of fixating on distant milestones, help clients identify and celebrate the daily micro-shifts they make. Whether it's drinking an extra glass of water or taking five minutes to meditate, reinforce how these add up to significant progress.

The Actionable Goal

Break ambitions into bite-sized tasks. Want to write a novel? Start with committing to ten minutes of writing a day. Aiming to be more organised? Focus on decluttering one drawer a week. Small, achievable goals prevent overwhelm and build confidence.

Gratitude as a Game-Changer

The gratitude journal, often regarded as a potent practice, thrives on the provision of context. It serves to retrain the brain's focus, shifting it from negativity towards an abundance mindset. This transformation, from mere activity to a holistic mindset, nurtures resilience and fosters a more optimistic outlook.

Essentially, your responsibility as a coach goes beyond presenting grand concepts. It lies in helping your clients experience breakthrough moments of realisation. Your role is to guide them in recognising how even seemingly insignificant choices and actions can bring about tangible transformation.

The Impact of COVID-19: Reshaping the Landscape

I witnessed firsthand how the pandemic dramatically transformed the landscape of executive and global team coaching, leading to several fundamental shifts. The rise of virtual coaching made coaching sessions more accessible by eliminating geographic barriers and reducing travel costs, with video conferencing becoming the primary delivery method. Coaches increasingly focused on helping leaders build resilience, navigate uncertainty, and manage stress—skills that were crucial for navigating the pandemic's challenges. With remote and hybrid work models becoming prevalent, cross-cultural sensitivity in coaching became even more important for bridging communication gaps created by distance. Finally, the challenges of isolation and disconnection faced by global teams led to a surge in team building, where coaches played a vital role in fostering trust, cohesion, and effective collaboration within dispersed teams.

The Value of Coaching: Essential for Personal and Professional Growth

Coaches act as strategic partners, empowering executives to develop personalised systems for effective prioritisation. This goes beyond surface-level tactics—it might involve employing decision matrices like the Eisenhower Matrix, practising time-blocking for greater focus, or training on how to filter communications for clarity.

To create lasting change, coaching delves deeper, addressing the root causes of misprioritisation. By exploring an executive's fears of missing out or difficulty saying no, a coach reveals the underlying thought patterns that hinder effective prioritisation. Coaches also help executives discern which tasks truly demand their attention and which can be confidently delegated, fostering trust in their team's abilities and sharpening their own leadership skills.

Beyond efficiency, coaching carves out space for the high-level, impactful work that only the executive can do. It supports defining boundaries, creating protective routines, and utilising support systems to safeguard time for strategic thinking. Ultimately, a coach serves as a mirror, reflecting the executive's patterns and fostering increased self-awareness. This awareness becomes the foundation for positive and lasting shifts away from reactive firefighting and towards intentional, proactive prioritisation.

ACTIVITY

Wheel of Life

In various contexts, which include work with clients, interactions with friends and family, and even conversations with strangers, the Wheel of Life activity has been a valuable tool for me. It aids in organising and prioritising different aspects of one's life. The Wheel of Life is a fantastic and versatile coaching tool, and it works beautifully for executives and global teams seeking greater clarity on their priorities. Here's how it works and why I find it so valuable.

Understanding the Wheel of Life with Example

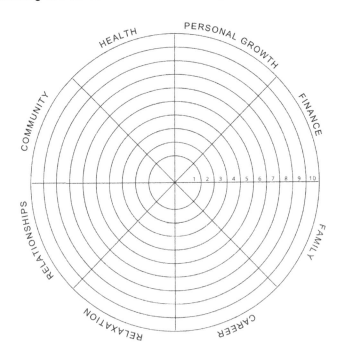

The Wheel of Life is labelled and divided into eight equal segments:

1. Health and Fitness
2. Friends and Family
3. Relationship
4. Career
5. Finances
6. Personal Growth
7. Fun and Recreation
8. Physical Environment

How to Use It

- **Reflection:** Consider your current satisfaction level in each of the eight areas.
- **Rating:** Within each segment, mark the corresponding number on the rating scale that represents your satisfaction (e.g., a 9 for Finance denotes high satisfaction; a 3 for Fun and Recreation denotes a need for improvement).
- **Connect the Dots:** Draw lines to connect your marks across the segments, creating a visual shape within the wheel.

Example

Instructions for Coaches

1. **Choose and Customise:** Pre-made wheel templates exist, or coach and client can choose categories together.
2. **Scoring and Mapping:** Explain the 0 to 10 satisfaction scale. Have them colour in their segments.
3. **Reflection:** Ask questions like:
   a. What surprises you about your wheel?
   b. Are there areas craving more attention?
   c. If you could wave a magic wand, what would change first?
   d. What actions could shift low-scoring areas higher?

4. **Goal Setting:** Wheel of Life insights provide a foundation for creating focused, achievable goals.
5. **Remember:** The Wheel of Life is a tool, not the end goal. It's the starting point for rich coaching conversations that build awareness, and it pioneers positive change.

Why It's Powerful for Executives and Global Teams

The Wheel of Life offers a rapid snapshot of an executive's or team member's current focus and energy distribution. This simple tool can highlight areas of life that might feel neglected, providing a valuable reality check. Sometimes, leaders may hold assumptions about where they dedicate their time and attention; however, the Wheel of Life often reveals a different picture. By identifying areas with low satisfaction scores, this exercise facilitates important discussions about necessary changes and helps executives and teams prioritise what matters most. This leads to effective goal-setting and a more intentional reallocation of valuable resources, such as time, energy, and finances.

Furthermore, teams can adapt the Wheel of Life tool to assess their overall satisfaction with key dynamics like collaboration, communication, and workload distribution. This facilitates open conversations about areas needing improvement and promotes greater team alignment towards shared goals. Think of each area like a spoke on a bicycle wheel—if one spoke is weak, the whole ride gets bumpy. Where are your shorter spokes? These are your areas for focused improvement.

You might find multiple areas in need of a boost. Don't get overwhelmed! The beauty of the Wheel of Life is that sometimes, by focusing on one key area, you can positively impact several others. Imagine improving your "Health and Fitness"—it might increase your energy, which in turn could enhance your career performance, social life, and overall well-being. So, give it a go, and let me know if it works for you!

In a world often defined by distance and division, coaching forges powerful connections. It bridges cultural gaps, unites diverse perspectives, and cultivates the collaboration essential for thriving in our interconnected world. The true measure of coaching success isn't found solely in achieving goals, but in the ripple effect it creates. As global leaders and teams become more empowered, resilient, and collaborative, they inspire those around them. Two questions remain: "What kind of legacy will you build?" and "How will the world be shaped by your leadership, enhanced through the transformative power of coaching?"

About the Author

Kristelle Kamini is a strategic business advisor and life coach with over 20 years of experience transforming businesses and empowering leaders. Her diverse client portfolio spans blockchain startups, technology giants, market research agencies, and the education sector. This broad exposure grants her unique insights into the challenges faced by senior executives across industries.

Kristelle's decade-long coaching experience ignites her passion for empowering individuals in optimising their careers and achieving lasting life success. She is known for developing tailor-made strategies, enhancing operational efficiency, and fostering a culture of excellence within organisations. Kristelle's coaching style fosters a safe space for self-discovery, empowering clients to make choices aligned with their authentic goals. Kristelle serves as a trusted confidant and partner for senior executives and global teams seeking to navigate complex business landscapes and achieve breakthrough results.

Kristelle believes that sustainable success starts with understanding people. Her approach uniquely blends strategic thinking with empathy and unwavering support.

Email: admin@kristelle.co.uk
Website: www.kristelle.co.uk
Instagram: @kaminikris

CHAPTER
15

Own Your Life Script

By Elena Kim
Transformational Workshop Facilitator
Santa Monica, California

*When I tell people to "write often and edit well," what I
mean is this: we are not in control of how life unfolds, but
we have agency over how we structure and interpret it.*

—ESTHER PEREL

People often turn to coaching when they are in need of external support to arrive at a desired (at least improved) outcome. This usually happens via changing something in their mindset, emotional field, or behavior. They choose a coach based on a projection that their coach of choice possesses and who embodies those desired qualities that lead to such outcome. Therefore, the more integrated we are as coaches, guides, facilitators, etc., the more effective we are in our areas of expertise.

When I embarked on my self-development journey, I was overwhelmed with the endless options of available trainings, workshops, modalities, and techniques to heal, improve, up level, and boost myself. So, whom to trust, how to choose, what to prioritize? After multiple trials and errors, I now rely on the only person that holds keys to what's right for me—me. What helped is a general understanding of human psyche development (interpreting Ken Wilber's Integral Theory and Don Beck and Chris Cowan's Spiral Dynamics based on Clare Grave's work, Andrey Stepanov's version of Spiral Dynamics via his program called "Astronauts," and others who contributed their vision and embodiment of such models).

Here's my oversimplified cheat sheet describing each developmental level of psyche evolution throughout a human life. The Spiral Dynamics Theory is called "spiral" because it increasingly becomes less linear as we go back and forth developing each level further based on conscious or unconscious choice in order of relevance to our individual life journey. In the Spiral Dynamic Theory each level is color coded:

Beige

- Main Theme: Do what you must to survive.
- Main Traits: Taking care of physical and physiological needs, instinctive-led existence, dependence on nature.
- Signs of Unintegrated Experiences: Disembodiment, numb senses, diseases, suboptimal vitality markers, low levels of energy, weak immune system, chronic pain in the body.

Purple

- Main Theme: Maintain ancestral tradition.
- Main Traits: Unconditional love and acceptance, unquestionable tribal traditions, communal existence out of safety and security, magical thinking, reliance on ancestral rituals, connection to nature, cyclical sense of time.
- Signs of Unintegrated Experiences: Superstitious thinking, over-reliance on group think and lack of personal responsibility, difficulty feeling, belonging, and asking for help, fear of trust towards people, fear of outsiders, resistance to change, lack of empathy, suppressed fantasy, tendency to over-rationalize emotions.

Red

- Main Theme: A sense of "I," being yourself, and doing what you want, no matter what.
- Main Traits: Power and autonomy, awareness and expression of intentions, claiming desires, upholding boundaries, ability to overcome fear and garner attention to self, immediate gratification, heroism.
- Signs of Unintegrated Experiences: Not knowing what you want, weak will, fear of or uncontrolled aggression, conflict avoidance, overstepping boundaries, bullying, power struggle, fear of self-expression, hiding, lack of self-confidence, egocentrism, narcissism, difficulty in complex thinking, rejection of authority, underdeveloped moral reasoning.

Blue

- Main Theme: Self-control, delayed gratification for rewards in the future, respect of social order.
- Main Traits: Order and structure, discipline, duty and responsibility, ability to set goals and work towards them, ability to be a part of a group, respecting hierarchy, adherence to social agreements and norms, choosing authority figures to rely on, initial steps in forming a sense of ethics (good/bad), ability to listen.
- Signs of Unintegrated Experiences: Overt denial and rebellion against rules or blind following of rules, guilt and shame, inability to be a part of a group or over-identifying with a group, dogmatic, rigid, uncompromising thinking, blind following of authority, inability to stick to and reach goals, problems with discipline.

Orange

- Main Theme: Achieve based on an ability to win in self-interest.
- Main Traits: Achievement and success, optimization, innovation, experimentation, reliance on rational thinking and science, extracting maximum value from resources, ability to rely on internal authority and ethics, search for absolute truth, welcoming constructive feedback, ability to create what's missing in the world.

- Signs of Unintegrated Experiences: Focus on materialism, ethical inner conflict, social inequality, fear of failure that prevents achievements, comparing with others, fear of confrontation, analysis-paralysis, inability to consider another point of view, isolation and alienation, short-term thinking.

Green

- Main Theme: Ability to manage energy for instant gratification and greater good.
- Main Traits: Movement towards multipolar view of the world, strive for peace, harmony, connection, equality, inclusion, environmental sustainability, ability to interact with shadow parts of self, search for meaning and purpose beyond personal gain, ability to observe and acknowledge difference of opinions and conscious and unconscious biases and heuristics, conscious embodiment.
- Signs of Unintegrated Experiences: Spiritual bypassing, escaping from everyday life into high-level concepts, spiritual pride, indecisiveness, inability to form an opinion, overt empathy, inability to interact with feedback and shadow parts of self, overemphasis on consensus, victimization and identity politics, disembodiment, one-sided, categorical, and divisive view of the world.

Yellow

- Main Theme: Be authentic to yourself and nature for the benefit of all.
- Main Traits: World-centric, flexible, systemic thinking, ability to digest, synthesize, and integrate complex data, concepts, and principles, self-regulation, integration of paradoxes, ability to hold the whole spectrum of polarity, comfort with uncertainty, aligned existence prioritized over material possessions, transmuting different viewpoints into win-win outcomes.
- Signs of Unintegrated Experiences: Complexity fatigue, emotional detachment, challenges with harmonizing idealism and realism, difficulties navigating power dynamics and people with predominant thinking on less-developed levels, difficulty finding peers on this level.

Turquoise

- Main Theme: Universal unity and interconnectedness.
- Main Traits: Global consciousness, integration of various beliefs into a cohesive view of the world, fluent in various languages of existence, recognition and reverence towards every kind of life, decisions are made with assessing long-term impact on society, planet, cosmos, evolutionary perspective of the Universe, and humanity's role in it.
- Signs of Unintegrated Experiences: Difficulty with crystallizing and communicating vision, inability to balance idealism and practicality, navigating spiritual experience and idealistic visions, juggling the paradox of unity and individualism, managing ethical and moral complexity, while accepting any and every point of view.

Coral

- This level is extremely rare and less studied. In general, the existential challenges on this level include managing hyper complexity, advanced technology integration, embodied transpersonal experiences, evolution of ethics and morals, and interdimensional awareness.

Through this system you can view the energy trifecta: sex, money, power—e.g., sex on the beige level is all about genital health, the ability to feel arousal, address any pain or other physiological issues around sex, keep the body free of venereal diseases, unintentional pregnancies, etc. Purple level sex adheres to adopted traditions, such as "ancestors did it this way, so will we" (e.g., no sex during menstruation or before marriage). Sex per the red level is driven by individual preference, desire to experience certain aspects of sexual interactions, specific preference of sexual partners, etc. Blue is where consent and agreement are established, so sexual encounters serve all involved, e.g., conscious sexuality practices, BDSM, role play, etc. Orange dives deeper into the hedonistic pleasure of sex. Sex on green can be transcendental and expose our shadows (Note: Shadows don't mean bad or unacceptable, but rather, they are the parts of ourselves that we were blind to until our ego is ready and willing to interact with these parts of us). Yellow, for example, offers field distortion, or "sex magic," through erotic energy to explore other versions of perceived reality. Turquoise—you can only imagine. Once again, experience of one's sexuality is not linear and can combine aspects from various developmental levels in different proportions of integration. Money and power (along with many other aspects of life) can be viewed through this model in a similar vein.

Once you identify what exactly calls for your attention, the most at this point of time, you can navigate the ocean of various offerings to choose from with more intention and ownership over what modality can help you now: improving your sleep patterns, learning how to say no, maybe treating others with dignity and respect regardless of race, gender, sexual orientation, political views, or perhaps taking a breathwork session to feel your body in a more pronounced way, etc.

A few words of caution against a tendency to bypass the "lower" levels of development: We all have an ability to find within us various markers of every described level. Incorrect self-identification, for example, of complexity fatigue from solving the world's problems when the most limiting factor is your catastrophically low levels of vitamin D or ferritin will create a greater divide between embodied integration and egoic aspiration.

Below you will find a suggested scanning practice to identify common areas for development that could hold keys to realizing your potential further. So, sit down comfortably, slowly take three deeper breaths filling with air not only your chest but also your belly, sprinkle a dash of humility over your mental meaning-making, and tune in to responses of your body as you read through the script. Read it slowly, really slowly, allowing space for your emotions to be felt. Notice what aspect your nervous system reacts to. Leave judgment and analysis for later.

Once upon a time you came into this world in a form of a human body animated by ineffable forces. You can call it "soul," "spirit," or whatever else that signifies for you something transrational, unexplainable. Your psyche was just unfolding its full potential being able to only process your key biological needs: eat, poop, and sleep, along with step-by-step exploration and discovery of the new world through your physical body. The connection with your body was direct, and there was nothing between your needs and your expression of those needs through your body. Soon it became clear that you needed other people to survive. There was zero judgment over who those people were. Usually, those around would be your parents, siblings, extended family, and friends. There was an inherent feeling of unconditional love, absolute trust, and selfless support offered to you as birthright. There was no need to earn love and affection; it was generously offered to you just because you were born. You were brought into the culture, traditions, rituals, and ways of being practiced by your tribe. You were a part of your tribe. You belonged. As you grew older, you started to develop your sense of "I" and "mine." You were given freedom and space to explore your likes and dislikes, your preferences, your sense of self, and you started feeling your individuality. Your choices were acknowledged and accounted for; your boundaries were respected. You were developing your own unique way of self-expression, and you were able to offer your voice without self-judgment, censorship, or attempt to please others. You were able to get what you wanted by asking for it, even if it involved overcoming fear. You felt centered and grounded in who you were. As you matured further, you developed an ability to empathize with others. You encountered a sense of guilt and responsibility for your actions. You became aware of your impact on others. You realized you needed to learn how to navigate the will, desires, and boundaries of others to coexist in harmony. You learned how to establish social agreements and maintain them to be in alignment with others. You became aware of societal norms, rules, and regulations that govern life on national and international levels. You had to be able to find common ground and develop communication skills to appeal to a larger group of people. You started to associate yourself with groups that share similar values, beliefs, and interests, even if those groups differed from your tribe. If you were complete with one group, you could leave it for another with grace. You learned how to be a part of society of choice.

Take another deep breath and notice what you allowed yourself to feel. This is a simplified version of a life script covering the first four levels of healthier development and could be extended to the rest of the model. It is very unlikely any of us grew up fully integrating all the described experiences without stumbles and hurt. The more we address unresolved issues now, the more we can realize our human potential and do so with more ease and joy.

Any kind of reaction to any described experience can point to a part of ourselves that requires attention, whether it's something of a novel experience (e.g., expressing our views without seeking external validation) or forgotten (listening to our body's signals on a subtle level and acting accordingly). Life's complexities make us come up with coping strategies that create solutions for dealing with some aspects yet blocking us in others. We have a chance and choice to offer ourselves integration of the key human skills to live life as mentally, emotionally, and spiritually mature adults.

How you go about integration largely depends on your worldview, level of critical thinking, beliefs, priorities, predilection, etc. Irrespective of methods, what proves to be crucial in self-development work is integrated embodied experience. Knowledge alone does not cure the issue—somatic experience is much stronger than mental awareness. With that, being properly informed with fact-based information of scientific credibility, while leaving room for methods that stood the test of time, which science has yet to prove, offers a consciously intentional, self-empowered choice over how to live your life going forward. Similarly, you can guide your clients through this exercise to identify areas that call for their zoom-in and help them with ways to address integration.

In an increasingly complex world where technology is taking more and more prerogative over our lives, the geopolitical climate is getting more and more heated, and the media is extremely polarizing, it seems to me that it's a healthy nervous system that is a sign of a well-lived life and platform for making it better. It is imperative for each of us to be rooted in our human spirit, increase our psyche's and body's capacity to navigate through the full range of human experience in a more harmonious way, and be guided by the essence of love to self, others, everything, and everyone. There are many different ways to get there, maybe you already feel in synergy with life, maybe you're just starting to pave your way—choose wisely, ask for help when needed, and enjoy your life story!

ACTIVITY

See *suggested scanning practice* within the chapter.

About the Author

Elena Kim is a UCLA Anderson School of Business MBA and former VP of business development who has selected to radically shift how she lives her life. She is currently a world-traveler, adventurer, and workshop facilitator whose goal is to allow people to live better lives through becoming more aware of their physical bodies and metal capabilities. Elena aims to allow people to engage in life with more freedom and flow.

Email: elenakim537@gmail.com

CHAPTER
16

Transformational Life Coaching: Navigating the Journey to Self-Discovery and Positive Change

By René Kok
Transformation Life Coach and Business Consultant
Cape Town, South Africa

Not all who wander are lost; sometimes, they are simply following the silent guidance of their internal compass, navigating the vast landscapes of self-discovery and purpose.

—J.R.R. TOLKIEN

Transformational life coaching is a dynamic and deeply personal journey—a voyage that requires adept navigation through the complexities of personal growth and positive change. In this exploration, we'll delve into the metaphorical concept of "The Compass of Transformational Life Coaching," a symbolic guide that represents the core principles and strategies of transformative coaching. As we unravel this analogy, we'll offer insights and guidance to fellow coaches, illuminating the path for both coaches and clients on the journey of self-discovery and positive change.

The Essence of the Compass

Imagine a compass in the hands of a transformational life coach—a tool that not only points toward cardinal directions but symbolizes the principles that guide individuals on their transformative journey. In the realm of transformational life coaching, envision the coach as the guiding compass and the client as the intrepid explorer navigating uncharted territories within themselves. This metaphorical compass, a multifaceted instrument, points the way towards unveiling potential and navigating positive change. In this chapter, we delve into the core principles and strategies of transformational life coaching, using the compass analogy to offer insights and guidance for coaches seeking to empower their clients on a journey of self-discovery and profound personal transformation.

North: Cultivating Self-Awareness

The northern point of the coaching compass represents the fundamental principle of cultivating self-awareness. Self-awareness serves as the magnetic north, providing individuals with a constant reference point as they navigate their inner landscape.

Strategy: Mindful Exploration

In the pursuit of self-awareness, coaches employ strategies centered around mindful exploration. Through mindfulness practices, self-reflection, and journaling, clients embark on a journey within, unraveling the layers of their thoughts, emotions, and beliefs. Insights for coaches include the following:

Facilitate Mindful Practices

Introducing meditation or mindfulness exercises is like offering a compass to navigate the intricacies of the mind. Guided meditation sessions can serve as a powerful tool to enhance self-awareness. Coaches can recommend mindfulness apps, breathing exercises, or guided meditations tailored to the client's preferences and comfort level.

Mindful Breathing

Incorporating simple mindful breathing techniques during coaching sessions can ground clients in the present moment. It helps them observe their thoughts without judgment, fostering a deeper connection with their inner selves.

Encourage Journaling

Journaling acts as a compass that helps clients chart their thoughts, emotions, and experiences. Coaches can encourage clients to maintain a reflective journal, prompting them to articulate their feelings, challenges, and triumphs. The act of putting thoughts into words enhances self-awareness by creating a tangible record of the client's evolving narrative.

For deeper exploration provide clients with journal prompts that encourage exploration of specific aspects of their lives. For instance, prompts like "Reflect on a recent challenge and your emotional response" or "Describe a moment of clarity in the past week" can guide clients toward deeper self-reflection.

Normalize the Journey

Coaches play a pivotal role in shaping clients' perspectives on self-awareness. By emphasizing that self-awareness is an ongoing process rather than a fixed destination, coaches empower clients to embrace the evolving nature of their inner landscape.

Celebrating Progress

Encourage clients to celebrate small victories and moments of heightened self-awareness. This not only acknowledges their efforts but also reinforces the idea that the journey itself is a significant part of the transformative process.

East: Crafting a Vision as True North

The eastern point of the compass signifies the principle of crafting a vision as true north. Just as the rising sun illuminates new possibilities, a clear vision guides individuals toward purposeful and transformative goals.

Strategy: Goal Setting and Visualization

Coaches collaborate with clients to set clear, compelling goals aligned with their values. Visualization exercises act as the compass needle, aligning clients with their desired future and fostering a deep emotional connection to their envisioned outcomes. Insights for coaches include the following:

Explore Core Values

Identifying and understanding core values is akin to setting the foundation for a stable structure. Coaches should engage clients in meaningful discussions to uncover their core values, as these values will serve as the guiding principles for goal setting.

Conduct reflective conversations that encourage clients to delve into their beliefs, passions, and what truly matters to them. These discussions lay the groundwork for setting goals that align authentically with clients' intrinsic motivators.

Utilize Visualization Techniques

Visualization acts as a compass that paints a vivid mental picture of the desired future. Coaches should guide clients through visualization exercises where they vividly imagine themselves achieving their goals. This mental blueprint enhances goal clarity and becomes a powerful motivator.

Break down the visualization into specific steps and moments. For instance, if a client aspires to advance in their career, guide them to visualize the day they achieve a significant milestone, the emotions they experience, and the impact on their life.

Emphasize Emotional Connection

Goals become more potent when connected to emotions. Coaches should encourage clients to articulate not only what they want to achieve but also why it matters deeply to them. This emotional connection serves as a magnetic force, reinforcing motivation even during challenging times.

Inquire about the emotional significance behind each goal. For instance, if a client aims to adopt a healthier lifestyle, explore the emotions linked to improved well-being, increased energy, or the ability to engage more fully in meaningful activities.

South: Embracing Change as the Compass Rose

In the southern quadrant lies the principle of embracing change as the compass rose. Change, symbolized by the varied directions of the compass rose, becomes a dynamic force propelling individuals towards growth and transformation.

Strategy: Resilience Building and Adaptability

Coaches focus on building resilience and fostering adaptability. By reframing challenges as opportunities for learning, clients develop the capacity to navigate the winds of change with grace. Insights for coaches include the following:

Strengthen Resilience

Resilience often draws from recognizing personal strengths. Coaches should guide clients in identifying their inherent strengths and capacities. Knowing their strengths becomes a reservoir from which clients draw during challenging times.

Help clients reframe their narratives around setbacks. Coaches can encourage them to view challenges not as insurmountable obstacles but as opportunities for learning and growth. This reframing fosters a resilient mindset.

Foster Adaptability

A mindset that embraces change as an inherent aspect of personal growth is the cornerstone of adaptability. Coaches play a pivotal role in fostering this shift by engaging in conversations that highlight the potential for positive outcomes in change.

Encourage clients to explore the positive aspects of change. By helping them see change as a catalyst for new opportunities, coaches empower clients to navigate transitions with curiosity and openness.

Celebrate Small Wins

Celebrating small wins is akin to marking points on the journey. Coaches should actively acknowledge and celebrate clients' achievements, no matter how modest. This positive reinforcement reinforces resilience by creating a sense of accomplishment.

Work with clients to establish realistic milestones. Breaking down larger goals into manageable steps allows for more frequent celebrations, contributing to a positive and motivating coaching experience.

West: Unveiling Potential as the Magnetic Needle

The western point of the compass represents the principle of unveiling potential, akin to the magnetic needle pointing toward untapped strengths and capacities. Coaches act as skilled navigators, guiding clients to discover and leverage their inherent potential.

Strategy: Strengths-Based Approaches and Skill Development

Coaches use strengths-based approaches to uncover and amplify client strengths. Simultaneously, they guide clients in skill development, empowering them to harness their potential fully. Insights for coaches include the following:

Conduct Strengths Assessments

Coaches can employ strengths assessment tools like the VIA Survey of Character Strengths or the StrengthsFinder assessment. These tools provide a structured way to identify and articulate clients' inherent strengths, creating a foundation for self-discovery.

Engage in meaningful conversations about the results of strengths assessments. Coaches should help clients understand how their strengths can be leveraged in various aspects of their lives, fostering a sense of empowerment.

Facilitate Skill Development

Coaches play a crucial role in guiding clients toward identifying skills relevant to their goals. Whether it's communication, leadership, or time management, coaches should help clients pinpoint areas for skill development.

Develop action plans that outline specific steps for skill acquisition and refinement. Coaches can assist clients in breaking down overarching goals into manageable tasks, ensuring a systematic and achievable approach.

Encourage Self-Exploration

Foster an environment that encourages clients to explore and understand their unique qualities. A safe and non-judgmental space allows clients to delve into aspects of themselves that may have been overlooked or underappreciated.

Encourage clients to approach self-exploration with curiosity. Coaches can provide prompts or exercises that prompt clients to reflect on their values, interests, and aspirations, creating a rich tapestry of self-awareness.

The Central Hub: Accountability and Integration

At the center of the coaching compass lies the crucial hub of accountability and integration. Here, the coach acts as the steady hand, ensuring that clients stay on course and that transformative changes become integrated into their daily lives.

Strategy: Holistic Integration and Future Mapping

Coaches engage clients in holistic conversations that go beyond specific goals, exploring the interconnectedness of various life domains. Through future mapping, clients envision how their transformative journey continues to unfold across different aspects of their lives. Insights for coaches include these:

Foster Responsibility

Coaches play a pivotal role in fostering a sense of ownership in clients. Encouraging clients to take responsibility for their journey instills a sense of empowerment and autonomy. This mindset shift transforms the coaching relationship into a collaborative partnership.

Clearly outline the roles and responsibilities of both the coach and the client. Establishing expectations helps create a framework for accountability and ensures that clients actively engage in the transformative process.

Explore Life Domains

Transformation is not confined to isolated aspects of life. Coaches should initiate discussions that explore the interconnectedness of different life domains, such as relationships, well-being, career, and personal satisfaction. This holistic approach ensures that transformative changes have a meaningful impact across various facets of the client's life.

Identify interdependencies between different life domains. For instance, a career change might influence personal relationships or overall well-being. Coaches guide clients in navigating these interconnections, ensuring a comprehensive understanding of the transformative journey.

Use Check-Ins Effectively

Regular check-ins serve as crucial milestones in the coaching journey. Coaches should establish a schedule for progress reviews, creating a structured approach to track and celebrate achievements. These check-ins allow for timely adjustments to coaching strategies based on evolving needs.

Check-ins provide an opportunity for reflective conversations. Coaches engage clients in discussions about their experiences, challenges, and breakthroughs since the last check-in. These reflective moments contribute to a deeper understanding of the transformative process.

Guiding the Journey: Insights and Guidance for Coaches

Understanding the compass analogy in transformational coaching offers profound insights and guidance for coaches seeking to empower their clients on a journey of self-discovery and positive change.

Navigating the Inner Landscape

The compass metaphor underscores the importance of guiding clients in navigating their inner landscape. Cultivating self-awareness (North) sets the stage for the transformative journey.

Setting a Purposeful Direction

Crafting a vision (East) becomes the true north, providing clients with a purposeful direction for their transformative journey.

Embracing Change as Catalyst

Embracing change (South) is not a deviation but an essential aspect of the transformative process, providing clients with the opportunity to grow and evolve.

Unveiling and Leveraging Potential

Unveiling potential (West) serves as the magnetic needle, directing clients toward their unique strengths and capacities.

Accountability and Integration

At the central hub, accountability and integration ensure that the transformative changes become ingrained in the client's daily life.

Final Thoughts: The Compass Guides, But the Journey Is Personal

As coaches, we are not just navigators but stewards of personal transformation. The compass analogy provides a rich framework for guiding clients through the intricate dance of self-discovery and positive change. While the compass points the way, the journey is deeply personal, and each client's path is unique.

In the dance between the coach as the compass and the client as the explorer, the transformative journey unfolds—an exploration that transcends boundaries and unlocks the full spectrum of human potential. As we navigate this transformative landscape, let us remember that the true north may guide, but the destination is defined by the courage and commitment of the one undertaking the journey.

ACTIVITY

Gratitude Journaling

One of the simplest yet most powerful activities a coach can use with their clients is the practice of daily gratitude journaling. This uncomplicated exercise has the potential to create a positive ripple effect in various aspects of a person's life. The purpose of gratitude journaling is to shift focus from what might be lacking or challenging in life to acknowledging and appreciating the positive aspects. It promotes a mindset of abundance and can significantly contribute to overall well-being.

Instructions

Start Small

Begin with a manageable commitment, such as journaling three things you're grateful for each day. These can be simple or profound, ranging from a beautiful sunrise to a supportive friend or a personal accomplishment.

Consistency Is Key

Encourage clients to make this a daily practice. Consistency is crucial in establishing a positive habit. Even on challenging days, finding a few things to be grateful for can be a transformative exercise.

Reflect and Elaborate

In addition to listing what they're grateful for, encourage clients to reflect on why these things bring them joy or gratitude. This deeper reflection enhances the impact of the activity.

Variety in Expression

Journaling doesn't have to be limited to written words. Clients can express their gratitude through drawings, collages, or even voice recordings if they prefer. The key is to find a method that resonates with them.

Coaching Insights

Mindset Shift

Gratitude journaling helps shift the focus from problems to possibilities. It encourages a positive mindset, which is foundational for any transformative journey.

Building Resilience

Acknowledging positive aspects, no matter how small, can build resilience. It trains the mind to look for solutions and strengths in challenging situations.

Cultivating Awareness

Clients become more aware of the positive elements in their lives. This heightened awareness can lead to increased mindfulness and an appreciation for the present moment.

Tracking Progress

Over time, reviewing past entries provides a tangible record of personal growth and positive experiences. It serves as a testament to the transformative journey.

Creating a Positive Routine

Incorporating gratitude journaling into a daily routine establishes a positive habit. Consistent engagement with this activity contributes to long-term positive change.

Despite its simplicity, daily gratitude journaling is a potent tool in the transformation coach's toolkit. It requires minimal time and effort but has the potential to create a substantial shift in perspective. By cultivating gratitude, clients lay the groundwork for a more positive and empowered approach to life, setting the stage for a transformative journey of self-discovery and growth.

About the Author

René Kok has accumulated over two decades of experience in the corporate world. For 13 years, René has dedicated efforts to a JSE-listed investment holding company. She holds a master's in business administration (MBA) and is a certified neuro-linguistic programming practitioner as well as a negative emotional therapy practitioner.

René's personal journey reads like a tapestry woven with numerous twists and turns. At its core is a transformative voyage through overcoming drug addiction—an experience that has evolved into a profound exploration of self-discovery. In the role of a Transformation Life Coach, René leverages the rich tapestry of personal experiences to guide and inspire others. René's distinctive background provides valuable insights into both personal and professional transformation, offering individuals a compass to navigate their own journeys of self-discovery. René is deeply passionate about assisting people in unlocking their potential, overcoming obstacles, and embracing positive change.

René lives in Cape Town, South Africa, with her husband and their two cats. She's an avid reader, loves spending time outdoors, loves travelling with her husband, and competes in triathlons.

Email: rene@renekokcoaching.co.za
Website: renekokcoaching.co.za
Instagram: @renekok_coaching
LinkedIn: René Kok Transformation Coaching

CHAPTER
17

Leadership Mastery: A Journey from Executive to Holistic Transformation

By Irina Kuhlmann, IAPC&M
Executive Leadership Coach, Holistic Life Coach
Bucharest, Romania

Life happens for us, not to us. It's our job to find the grace in this and every moment of our lives—that's when life is truly magnificent.

—TONY ROBBINS

I regained consciousness to the sound of a siren and realized that I was lying on the cold stone of the terrace of our house in Germany—my third home country. I will never know how many minutes I ceased to exist in the physical world. What I do know is that that moment was about to mark my life, to be a door on my path to another level, that would bring me to an upgraded version of myself—a more authentic and fulfilled one.

Life Is a Unique Journey for Each of Us

My life has been a tapestry woven with threads of diverse cultures and rich experiences. Originating in Romania, my formative years were steeped in its rich heritage before embarking on a transformative chapter in Denmark that spanned over two decades. There, I immersed myself in the essence of Danish culture while carving out a successful career in business. Founding my own company, I became a bridge between Danish and Romanian businesses, facilitating connections that fueled growth and collaboration. Subsequently, I assumed a senior executive position in a Danish company, where I embraced and embodied the Danish management and leadership style, overseeing the operations of our Romanian subsidiary with a team of 200 employees under my guidance and leadership. Life's trajectory then led me to Germany for a few years, following my husband's career. Initially, it was a time of joy and exploration, but it soon became a period marked by unforeseen challenges, including a major health setback for me.

On a cold March morning, while on the terrace of my house, I lost consciousness and fell backward, hitting the terrace tiles with the back of my head, which resulted in significant cervical issues and a concussion that would affect my health for a very long period of time. Over the following seven years, I embarked on a transformative journey to regain my physical health while simultaneously delving deeper into my inner world and embracing my personal authenticity. This profound journey ultimately led me to discover a new calling as a Holistic Life Coach.

Upon returning to Denmark, and later relocating to Romania, I encountered unexpected opportunities that paved the way for the establishment of my "Life and Business Coaching" company. Living amidst the cultural tapestries of three countries provided me with a profound understanding of the importance of attitude—towards oneself, others, and the world. Integrating Danish and German values into my life enriched me in ways beyond material wealth, fostering a sense of global citizenship and cultural understanding. In the midst of life's challenges and victories, I've unearthed the remarkable potential within each of us. This revelation fuels my commitment as a life coach—to empower individuals in discovering and utilizing their distinctive strengths, guiding them toward fulfillment and success amidst life's complexities.

My Coaching Philosophy

The core of my coaching approach reflects the following insight:

> *You can't connect the dots looking forward; you can only connect them looking backward. So you have to trust that the dots will somehow connect in your future.*
>
> —STEVE JOBS

Crafted from my life experiences, studies during illness recovery, and ongoing personal development, this quote underpins my coaching philosophy.

Drawing from my experience as a senior executive and business owner in Denmark, I've transitioned to the new role as a life coach specializing in guiding individuals within the business realm. Recognizing the vital role of holistic development in achieving peak performance and sustainable success, I prioritize working with individuals both in and behind their corporate roles. My coaching approach encompasses personal and practical dimensions, emphasizing the importance of exploring each client's inner world. True leadership mastery arises from the synergy between the individual and their role, and I've honed a holistic coaching methodology tailored for executives, business professionals, and high-performance achievers.

Mastery Leadership

Famously stated:

> *Everything rises and falls with leadership.*
>
> —JOHN MAXWELL

I firmly believe that effective leadership begins with mastering one's own personality and identity, and ultimately, inspiring and guiding others. In my approach to coaching people towards their leadership mastery and holistic transformation, I center on the following three key principles:

1. High Self-Consciousness

Encouraging leaders to attain a heightened state of self-awareness is paramount. This involves a deep understanding of their thoughts, emotions, and actions, paving the way for conscious decision-making. This fosters empathy and compassion, allowing them to understand and relate to others' experiences.

2. Authenticity

I once came across a profound quote:

> *The biggest stress of all is trying to be who you're not.*

Nothing is more true. Lack of authenticity frequently results in subpar decision-making as choices deviate from one's genuine values, overshadowed by restrictive beliefs, misunderstandings, fears, transient emotions, and external pressures. Genuine leadership, therefore, stems from authenticity—where actions, values, and beliefs harmonize with authentic intentions. Guiding leaders to unveil and embrace their authentic selves not only catalyzes personal development but also lays the groundwork for authentic connections and impactful influence.

3. Inner Alignment: Heart and Mind Coherence

Aligning the heart and mind is a powerful practice. Through coaching and intentional training, you can cultivate coherence between your emotions and intellect, resulting in more thoughtful and compassionate decision-making, behaviours, and actions. When the heart and mind are in coherence, you enjoy enhanced emotional resilience, mental acuity, and holistic well-being.

Transformation Mastery

In our constant quest for growth and achievement amidst life's challenges, we undergo profound transformations, sometimes willingly, other times propelled by unforeseen circumstances, as in my case. My own journey was profoundly altered by a life-changing accident, leading to unexpected positive transformations and alignment with my true path.

Navigating change requires clarity of purpose and defined goals. Whether mastering leadership, enhancing productivity, or transforming one's entire life, success demands a holistic commitment beyond academic knowledge—a journey marked not just by milestones, but by profound fulfillment.

Three Key Questions

When it comes to achieving what you want—a goal or a breakthrough—there are three crucial questions to ask:

1. *What* do you want?
2. *Why* do you want it?
3. *How* will you achieve it?

For a large part of my life, I devoted myself to achieving set goals, focusing on methods such as diligent study and hard work. Yet, despite immense effort, success often felt out of reach. I couldn't grasp why many times obstacles arose just before reaching my objectives. Since I've discovered the necessity of the holistic approach, I have realized success extends beyond knowledge and actions. I had overlooked the importance of mindset and inner drive, neglecting the profound impact our beliefs have on shaping our experiences.

1. Approaching the What—Goal Setting

Start by defining your goal: for today, this week, month, year, or even more.

Each of us possesses a mental framework that shapes how we interpret situations. Our mindset is shaped by beliefs, assumptions, and attitudes about ourselves and the world around us. All our behaviors, actions, and decisions are guided by beliefs accumulated over time. Wisely said:

Beliefs have the power to create and the power to destroy.

—TONY ROBBINS

Therefore, it's crucial to scrutinize our mindset and beliefs when setting our goals.

Frequently, we hold back from dreaming and believing in our ability to achieve our desires due to a limiting mindset. This lack of belief in our capability to reach our goals often results in us distancing ourselves from them without even attempting to pursue them. Visualization is a powerful tool that enables you to transcend the limitations of your mindset. It empowers you to vividly envision the specifics of your desires, identify your true aspirations, and acquire valuable insights into how to achieve them.

A Useful Exercise

Begin by imagining yourself already having achieved that goal. It's like watching a scene from a movie where you're the protagonist. What do you see, what do you hear, what do you feel? What is your state, who else is with you? Describe the entire context. What is the most important thing of all? What has helped you get there?

In conclusion, even armed with clear goals, motivation, and strategies, reaching goals can prove challenging if our mindset isn't aligned. Therefore, it's crucial to confront this aspect directly. We will delve into the realm of beliefs, exchanging disempowering notions for empowering convictions.

Reframing Limiting Beliefs to Empower Us

1. Discover and Name Your Limiting Beliefs

They often pop up in your chatter or internal dialogue about yourself and everything else. This applies to specific goals, too. It could be about your talents, your character, your relationships, your education, or anything else that triggers that little voice inside you, whispering: "You can't be what you want to be, and, therefore, you can't get what you want to get." Think of it as your inner pessimist, a miniature comedian, skilled in cracking bad jokes about your potential. It's that voice in your head that loves to repeat phrases like: "I can't," "I don't," "This is too hard for me," "I am not ...," "It's impossible." Now, direct your attention to your specific goal—the "*what*"—and recognize any inner pessimism that may surface. What messages is it conveying? How does it define aspects related to your goal?

Once identified, engage in dialogue to challenge it. What would you say to contradict its claims? Additionally ask:

- What are your beliefs regarding the achievement of this goal?
- What is the nature of your self-talk?
- When does this self-talk manifest?

2. Get to the Facts: Uncover the Truth

A fundamental aspect of limiting beliefs is their frequent lack of truth. Moreover, they wield significant influence over our emotions, rendering them challenging to displace. Nonetheless, the encouraging news is that we can diminish their hold through insightful questioning:

- What leads you to believe you're incapable?
- Why are you so convinced of your limitations?
- What barriers stand in your way?
- What evidence supports these beliefs?
- To what extent did your negative self-talk contribute to perceived underperformance?

Reflect on past experiences: How often have you confronted similar situations, and what were the outcomes? This is what happens to many people. Because they lack self-confidence, their inner critic distracts them so much that it causes them to lose power, leading to a negative state of mind. In sessions with my clients, common refrains like "I don't know" or "I can't" often surface. I encourage introspection by asking, "What if you did know?" or "What if you could?"

3. Replace Them with New Empowering Beliefs

You've reached a pivotal stage where you've identified your limiting beliefs and scrutinized their validity. Now, it's time to foster new beliefs that align with reality and propel you towards success. This step is paramount. Consider this scenario: If you catch yourself thinking, "I always mess up this sort of thing," counter your inner pessimist with a powerful affirmation such as, "Just because I haven't excelled in this before doesn't mean I won't succeed now. Keep your doubts to yourself!"

Another effective approach is to deliberately craft at least three well-founded empowering beliefs to replace your limiting ones. Allow yourself the space to deeply reflect and internalize the transformation.

Before we move forward, let's consider the following:

- Think about a time when you saw someone accomplish something extraordinary. What aspects of their success could personally inspire you in achieving your goal?
- Transform the voice and characteristics of your inner critic to reduce its influence. I, for instance, often think about a humorous cartoon character.

The Power of Our Identity to Accomplish a Goal

You cannot achieve more than what you believe you are capable of.

I was in a coaching process with Sara, a remarkable young woman who possessed extensive professional qualifications, experience, and charisma. Additionally, she was very beautiful, embodying the kind of person you imagine nobody could say no to in any situation. Despite Sara's genuine efforts and remarkable qualities, she struggled persistently in both her career and relationships. In a pivotal moment, I asked her: "Sara, how do you perceive yourself? What narrative do you construct about your own identity?"

"I am so alone. It seems like nothing I do is enough to succeed, regardless of the effort. This feeling has haunted me since childhood," she confessed.

In her response, Sara unveiled a profound narrative about herself—a narrative steeped in limiting beliefs. It was through this exploration that she discovered the multitude of constraints holding her back.

What is often overlooked in discussions about achieving goals is *your identity*—the story you tell about yourself. It plays a critical role in connecting or disconnecting you from your inner power. I've realized that in coaching, it is crucial to address the coachee with the questions: "What's your story about yourself? Who do you believe you are?" It is said that the most powerful words in the English language are "I am." Whatever you add after those two words defines you and determines your destiny. When you identify with the goal you want to achieve, you will experience extraordinary inner power.

A Powerful Exercise

Think about your most common "I am" statements. Write them down and reflect on how these statements define you. You will once again encounter limiting beliefs, which you now know how to effectively address. Identity plays an extraordinary role, tied to the next question—*why*, which we will explore further.

2. Uncover the Why Behind Your Goal

Discover your purpose and motivation.

In my coaching experience, I've noticed a common trend: Many people navigate life without truly understanding their genuine motivations. They often follow expectations or feel they have to, lacking true ownership of their actions. However, within this recognition lies a powerful insight: Understanding the "why" can illuminate the path to the "what," providing clarity and authenticity in our pursuits. I urge you: Never chase a goal without unveiling its deep-rooted purpose.

In leadership mastery, few questions are as vital as the "why." Exploring it leads to self-discovery, revealing the driving force behind our actions. Understanding our "why" empowers us to pursue our goals with authenticity and clarity, aligning our decisions with our core values and visions. This alignment taps into our inner strength and resilience—it's accessing our true power. Furthermore, the "why" acts as a steadfast compass in navigating uncertainty and adversity. When faced with challenges, reconnecting with our purpose reignites our passion, propelling us forward with determination. A crucial insight I've gained is the importance of aligning your emotions with your goals. Ensure your goals resonate with your heart.

3. The How

Crafting Your Strategies: Implementing Effective Methods for Success

Having clarified your aspirations and the driving forces behind them, you've deepened your self-awareness, moving closer to your authentic self. You've not only mastered cultivating a productive mindset but also achieved optimal motivation levels. Now, you're ready to explore personalized methods and strategies that align with you. This preparedness will propel you towards goal attainment, enabling you to fully embrace your chosen approaches without feeling burdened. Coaching questions will guide you in finding practical solutions to fulfill the "how." In the *how* phase, it's vital to focus on this crucial aspect:

Maintaining an Empowering State of Being

Your thoughts and emotions shape your state of being, influencing your behavior, which in turn, impacts your abilities. I often ask my clients: "What was your state? What thoughts crossed your mind? What emotions did you feel?"

A Brief Exercise

As a simple calibration activity, I recommend a short exercise lasting no more than two minutes. Mentally scan your entire body, from toes to the top of your head. With consistent practice, this exercise can become a natural habit, helping you stay connected to your inner power and potential, regardless of external circumstances.

And remember that the key to true joy lies in gratitude, so take a moment to give thanks for the grace you have. Feel gratitude for this beautiful life, for who you are and who you are becoming.

ACTIVITY

See *Section 1. Approaching the What—Goal Setting; Section 2. Uncover the Why Behind Your Goal;* and *Section 3. The How,* within the chapter.

About the Author

Irina Kuhlmann is an International Executive Leadership Coach, bringing a unique blend of experience as a former senior executive and business owner in Denmark, supported by 13 years of professional coaching expertise. Following a significant health challenge that interrupted her business career, Irina devoted several years to her health recovery while intensely working on her personal growth and development. Immersing herself in the study and application of neuroscience, NLP, coaching, and leadership, she underwent a profound transformation, emerging as a successful Holistic Life Coach.

Irina's coaching approach is deeply rooted in holistic and transformational principles, empowering individuals to reclaim their authenticity and unlock the potential of their minds and emotions to achieve their goals. With unwavering commitment, Irina assists business professionals, entrepreneurs, and high-performance achievers from diverse backgrounds and cultures in rediscovering their authenticity and embracing a prosperous and joyful life in an ever-changing world.

Email: coaching@irinakuhlmann.com
Website: https://www.irinakuhlmann.com/
LinkedIn: https://www.linkedin.com/in/irina-kuhlmann-574b4831/

CHAPTER

18

Scrambled Eggs

By Ashley Kuhnau
Founder, Grounded and Growing; Coach
Alexandria, Minnesota

*What's in the body is in the brain,
what's in the brain is in the body.*

—Serene Calkins, PT

Two nurses are positioned strongly, one on each side of me. The electrodes are perfectly in place. It's time to begin. The treadmill is on, and I feel like I can't keep up.

How did this happen? I am 37 years old.

Still not having the results, two weeks later I'm in the doctor's office again, bent forward in a chair with my chest heaving.

"The stress test results were all normal. Clean bill of health," he says.

"What?" was the only thought I could find.

Then he says, "Here is some medication that will calm your heart."

Without more than a few more words from the doctor, I'm on my way home.

This series of events grabbed my full attention, but it is not the beginning of the story. It wasn't until 20 years of working in physical therapy that I thought it was time to leave the field. I was burned out. Patient after patient, year after year, I heard the same complaints. So, I started looking for something else. Little did I know God was using that 20 years to prepare me for what was next.

I began schooling to work as a life coach, NLP, and brainspotting practitioner. It was during this schooling that I had the capacity to gain clarity on my physical state and how it all began. I guess we could go back all the way to childhood. My parents spent more money than they had on chiropractic adjustments for my headaches. As a teen, I developed chronic issues with my gut. In my early 20s, I had back pain that made me look like I was 80. In my 30s, as given in this chapter's opening scene, I was on a treadmill doing a stress test. In the meantime, the headaches, gut, and back pain never left and were still a daily occurrence that only intensified over the years. So, what was going on?

My body was trying to get my attention, but I didn't know *how* I was supposed to listen. I just kept beating the symptoms down with all the resources I had—chiropractor, acupuncture, massage, NSAIDS, exercise off and on.

When you work in the medical field for 20 years, you tend to have a type of blindfold on, always looking for the structural reason for pain. It's only been the last 10 or so years that this has taken a different shape throughout healthcare. This is due, in part, to the opioid epidemic, as well as the advancing science. Doctors have had to start looking outside of the box. As for me, I finally began to understand there was so much more to my own issues than structure.

> *What's in the brain is in the body, and*
> *what's in the body is in the brain.*
>
> —SERENE CALKINS, PT

Serene Calkins words are true 100% of the time, no exceptions ever! This point was driven home in one of my many hours of training for the certification process as a brainspotting practitioner. The class was called From Freeze to Thaw: Unlocking Trauma in the Body. I have a 20-year background in physical therapy. I knew the brain/body connection very well, but I didn't understand the depth of it. I guess I needed to experience that firsthand, and I had a body that was taking me on the ride of my life.

In the midst of my yearlong training for NLP and brainspotting, something odd was happening—my physical pain was going away. Headaches, back pain, control of my gut. All of it! What was the magical reason? I suppose I should have also mentioned that in the span of those 30 years, I felt the need to be perfect. I was married. I had five kids and one miscarriage. My husband was a police officer; I was running a business and serving on three committees. We had also experienced the devastating loss of my mother-in-law who'd been in my life since childhood. Then I started another business, Scrambled Eggs. It's a term I'd adapted to describe my state of mind the majority of the time. I just kept going, kept pushing. For the majority of it, there was no other choice—it was out of my control.

The challenging part of all of this is what we do to ourselves in the meantime. We shut down the signals. Our body is working for us, not against us. It's fighting to get our attention, but when it speaks, we shut it up! We take an ibuprofen, have a drink, scroll on our phone, have another snack, have a smoke, take medications, experience nerve burns, have surgeries—and the list goes on and on. In parallel to my own story, I was seeing this firsthand every day in the patients I was treating for their chronic and persistent pain.

I couldn't help but be curious about why we were all trapped in these pain-riddled bodies. The uphill battle came in "fighting" the information the medical world gives us. "It's your herniated disc. Look here, the MRI proves it!" Adriaan Louw, PT, PhD, is one of my favorite teachers when it comes to pain. He states facts around how many of us are walking around with herniated discs. Why does this affect some and not others? Why can a rodeo rider who's been beaten and bruised keep on going and smiling while someone who sits at a desk all day suffers from debilitating fibromyalgia?

*What's in the brain is in the body, and
what's in the body is in the brain.*

—SERENE CALKINS, PT

In 2020, the International Association for Pain (ISAP) revised the definition of pain. Direct from the ISAP website, it states:

For the first time since 1979, IASP introduced a revised definition of pain, the result of a two-year process that the association hopes will lead to revised ways of assessing pain. Pain is now defined as: "An unpleasant sensory and emotional experience associated with, or resembling that associated with, actual or potential tissue damage." Pain is always a personal experience that is influenced to varying degrees by biological, psychological, and social factors.

It goes on to expand this further in six key parts.

In this revised definition we have a clear picture that we now have the science to back up the state of our emotion with a physical feeling in our body. One of my favorite books to illustrate this firsthand is Bessel Van Der Kolk's *The Body Keeps the Score*. In this book, he gives countless examples and stories of what this means and looks like from a physical and psychological connection. What we know now, scientifically, is revolutionary when it comes to this connection. We are perfectly created! In understanding that very thing, we can change the picture of what we once knew of our physical pain or sensations. This is where we start.

When we begin to teach brain/body connection, we engage the inner sense that was perfectly designed in each of us. It was no accident. When we know *how* to listen, we understand our body is working *for* us, not against us. This is especially true when we understand our emotions. So, what does this look like? What does all this have to do with being a life coach? Start at the top! Let your clients know:

What's in the brain is in the body, and
what's in the body is in the brain.

—Serene Calkins, PT

I state again, direct from the ISAP website, "An unpleasant sensory and emotional experience associated with, or resembling that associated with, actual or potential tissue damage." Let me give you an example of this with our good pal, anxiety. Such a dirty word. I'm here to tell you that anxiety is needed and can be a blessing if you know how the brain and body work. It's no longer so scary. In fact, if it didn't exist, what would make you alert when you see that car coming toward you? Let's pretend you're in a crowd of people. Your body is designed to sense your environment and send a signal to your brain so that your brain can tell you what to do next. As you're bumping shoulder to shoulder into people, your heart starts beating faster, maybe you get sweaty or even short of breath. Signals, right? Signals are being sent to your brain. What's in the body just went to the brain. Now what? This is where it becomes interesting. The brain has two options. You can sense the signals and bring all of your attention to your beating heart and your shortness of breath. As you focus on these, the brain becomes hyper aware of what's happening. It is perfectly designed. Most often, if you don't have the understanding, your reaction is, "Holy smokes, I'm going to have a panic attack! I can feel it coming on! What am I going to do? Where is the nearest exit?" Now, what's in the brain is in the body ... Your body just received information that the brain is preparing for a panic attack and needs an exit. The body says, "That's our cue!" It knows, "All hands on deck, ramp it up!" And before you know it, panic sets in. Hardwired for survival, the brain and body work together.

Let's explore a different option. When you receive signals and the brain is alert to them, try saying this: "Hey, body, I hear ya. Thanks for protecting me. Let me protect you now. We don't like crowds, we know that, but we are moving, so let's stay focused on the feeling of the air, the looks on people's faces, our shuffling feet. We will get to the exit soon." What's in the brain is in the body. "Phew," says the body, "the brain has got this and knows what's going on." Suddenly, your nervous system chills out. This doesn't always mean you won't feel things like your heart pounding, but it does mean that it won't get out of hand because you understand that you're in control.

Here is another fun fact. Muscle has memory. So, had the panic taken control due to you not knowing what you know now, any similar sight, smell, sound, or touch will reactivate these symptoms for a similar response. Why? Because without the command center "at control," all the body remembers is that it has "rescued you" that one time, so why wouldn't it do it again? It is hardwired for survival. It's when we experience this time and time again that the response strengthens, which is why I chose the tools of NLP and brainspotting to address the "faulty" programming our brains develop. It's primitive and natural for the physical responses we have. We are perfectly designed. Unfortunately, we live in a world that jumps to medications and all kinds of other solutions to shut it down. This is possibly one of the biggest mistakes we can make. Don't get me wrong, we are still responsible for caring for ourselves with movement, nutrition, and sleep. Medication also certainly has its place, but if there is a plan to keep it from being a long-term solution, I think we will be better off.

Because our body will never stop fighting for us (because of its perfect design), we can't ever really shut it down. It only shuts *us* down in the end. We can take the medication, drink the drink, or have the surgery, but if we don't address the environment around us, i.e., marriage, parenting, job, etc., the signals won't stop. In fact, they only get more aggressive or they begin to recruit other parts of the body. Look at my own example of how I started with headaches, and ended up with multiple systems in overdrive when I was nearing 40. This is how we end up in a puddle of chronic and persistent pain. The body will keep pushing to get the brain's attention until we finally listen. It has the ability to push you right to a heart attack. This is why, from this point forward, when you feel pain, anxiety, or any of the things we've discussed, stop and listen. Ask yourself, "Why am I feeling that right now? What's happening around me? Was I thinking of an old girlfriend? Did I just yell at my kid and now I feel guilty? Did I get a speeding ticket?" It becomes a game of curiosity after a while, and once mastered, it's life-changing!

Some of you may be asking about your sports injury or working a hard physical job, even that car accident you were in. Tissues heal, but muscle has memory. Remember, sight, smell, sound, and touch activate the nervous system to begin communication with the brain. Real structural injuries *do* happen, but if the pain is hanging around long after tissues are healed, then the next stop is the brain. What's in the brain is in the body. If you are feeling stressed because your sports injury changed the course of your career, your body *will* hold on to that pain. You have to do the work. You have to go to the hard places and tackle the tough stuff in your environment for the signals to stop.

All of this being said, we have the scientific proof that we have the ability to retrain our brains. It's fascinating! Decades ago, we knew after someone had a stroke, we had a certain window of time in PT to retrain the brain/body function in order to maximize full potential. We now know this is far deeper. The neuroplasticity of the brain pertains to our thoughts as well. It's the precise reason why addressing those thoughts and feelings in the life I had started to change my pain.

To my clients I like to explain that thoughts are like a river. When you have a thought, it rushes down the river. The more often you have that thought, the deeper the river gets. It's a well-worn canoe trip that ends in rapids because the water just knows where to go. This oftentimes describes our negative thoughts. We have them so often, it's easy to find them and take that ride. We already know the rapids, and it ends in destruction every time. Why do we keep choosing it? Because it's easy. The next time that negative thought pops into your mind, stop. You know the river, but what about that quiet stream over there? There are cattails hiding the entrance, but I can hear the birds, and the waters look calm. Maybe I should try that path? Good thoughts. It takes work to get there, to redirect. However, in time, this path is easier to find because you take it again and again. That is the neuroplasticity of the brain and how the rewiring process begins. When we change our brains, we change our bodies. It really is incredible. This is not always easy, but being aware that *something* needs to change is the best place to start. As life coaches, we have the opportunity to educate not only ourselves but our clients as well. In a world where light has been shed on the importance of mental health, our role is essential.

Think of our job as the gym membership of the mental health world. Our job is to keep people healthy to avoid the frequent trips to the doctor's office. Assisting our clients when the signals and emotions begin—what a game-changer that will be! We have an opportunity to keep people well by giving them the tools that they need to potentially prevent serious breakdowns. It is my hope that this will lighten the load for our friends in the world of counseling. They can then attend to those who didn't receive this knowledge early on as well as to those who were created needing more complex love, attention, and education.

We also have a duty to be educators to the amazing children who are grasping the concepts of mental health. We are better trained and equipped with tools that weren't given the attention they deserved. We have the ability to take action knowing the science and our perfect design. Mental health is one thing, but an alert brain/body connection takes it to the next level!

Brain/Body Connection

Help your clients tune in to their brain/body connection with these easy steps:

1. When they identify how they feel emotionally about a person or topic, have them close their eyes and do a head-to-toe scan of their body. Ask them what they are noticing.
2. Teach awareness. In the case of negative (not ideal) body feelings, when they tune in to their body, help them understand this sensation is their "warning signal" or "awareness button" for the emotion they are feeling. This is important because as they continue to practice bodily awareness, future signals such as sour stomach (could be anxiety), back pain (could be frustration), or shaky legs (could be anger) will allow them to remember this reaction and connection. They will have awareness that their body is working for them to get their attention about something.
3. Teach "STOP." Stop and recognize what's happening. Then, teach them to thank their body for giving them the alert. Sounds weird, I know, but remember, what is in the brain is in the body. If someone is disgusted with the sensation they feel, the brain sends that emotional response to the body. If they're grateful that their body is working for them, the same is true, and the result is better nervous system regulation.
4. React. Now that they have a better understanding of what's around them and why, engaging in that process allows them to react appropriately. If they identified anger, they've taken the time to check in with all systems (which can actually happen in seconds), but it's also enough time to pause and think through what

happens next. Encourage them to let their regulation and executive function take charge instead of all emotion.

The results will be improved emotional and physical awareness as well as improved overall health and responses to those around them. This process also allows a person to understand when it's time for outside help if these signals just persist and don't go away within a reasonable amount of time.

About the Author

Ashley Kuhnau lives in Minnesota with her husband Tony and their five kids, still working in physical therapy now and then, but focusing attention on her life coaching business, Grounded and Growing. She loves teaching! One of the highlights of her job is the relief she sees when her clients are given this information for the first time. Her favorite things to tackle are helping people with "unknown" or persistent pain as well as marriage and family. Keeping our marriages and families strong by tackling our own weaknesses is key to the start of being *grounded* in our physical, mental, and spiritual well-being, allowing us to be able to *grow* as humans. She would like to invite you to learn more about brainspotting and NLP and the transformative nature these tools hold through her website as well as at brainspotting.com.

This is her first debut as an author, and she is hopeful to spread the word to as many as possible. *Change your brain! Listen to your body!*

Email: ashley@groundedandgrowing.me
Website: www.groundedandgrowing.me
Facebook: https://www.facebook.com/changeyourthoughtsandbehaviors
Instagram: https://www.instagram.com/groundedandgrowing.me/
Linkedin: https://www.linkedin.com/in/ashley-kuhnau-6a2787a3

CHAPTER
19

From Self-Sabotage to Success: Embracing Core Values for Fulfillment

By Mindy McKibbin
HR Business Partner, Certified Health & Life Coach
Des Moines, Iowa

Your core values are the deeply held beliefs
that authentically describe your soul.

—JOHN MAXWELL

As an HR professional, understanding an organization's core values is paramount in every decision you make in HR. Core values guide you on policy creation and implementation, hiring, firing, disciplinary actions, benefits, events, and employee training. Some organizations list their core values correctly, and they describe the culture of the company. However, there are organizations full of great, intelligent leaders who have yet to name their core values accurately, and their culture needs to be more precise. This is also true in an individual's life. Do even very intelligent, successful people need help understanding their core values?

Everyone has core values. When an individual knows their core values, they can make decisions that are in line with who they really are, like having the right people in their lives, where they live, what extracurricular activities they do, where they work, what their occupation is, what they eat, and much more. Sometimes, people adopt their core values from the values of society, their family, or their friends.

What could be keeping your client from discovering their core values? What could keep your client from living their core values? While there are many ways to help a client discover their core values, there is an enemy everyone has that can prevent people from discovering and living their core values: self-sabotage. How do we help clients know themselves and beat self-sabotage while also honoring the desires creating self-sabotage?

According to dictionary.com, "Self-sabotage is the act or habit of behaving in a way that interferes directly with one's own goals, well-being, relationships, etc., as by comfort eating, procrastination, or lashing out at others." Psychology Today says, "The most common self-sabotaging behaviors include procrastination, self-medication with drugs or alcohol, comfort eating, and forms of self-injury such as cutting." Berkley Well-Being Institute states, "Self-sabotage can show up as subtle patterns such as procrastination or fear of failure. But when you sabotage yourself, the behavior and thought patterns you engage in create obstacles in achieving your goals. Self-sabotage means you're getting in your own way."

While self-sabotage is rooted in a person's thoughts, did you know that a person's thoughts can create life circumstances with family, friends, and work that support their self-sabotage? The self-sabotage excuses may sound like, "I can't meet with my coach because my friends are coming over, so I must clean my house," "I had to overeat or drink too much because I was at an office party. People will be offended if I don't," "My grandma bakes the best pie; if I didn't eat it, she would think something was wrong," "My basement flooded, so I couldn't do this week's work like I agreed to with my life coach," or "My best friend needed to talk to me. She is going through so much, so I didn't follow through with my goals." There is always an excuse to be found to explain why someone doesn't do what they know and want to do. Something else is always more important than themselves

I'm sure you have heard many legitimate excuses, and you tell your client, "No problem, we can reschedule," and then you wonder if something you did or said caused them to cancel. Maybe you've had clients ghost you, and you wonder what you did. Have you had a client who has done so well you praised them for it and encouraged them, and you were so excited about their improvements, and then they ghosted you or derailed? This, my friend, is why it is essential to address self-sabotage before it happens because it will happen, and if your client feels guilty and ashamed, they may avoid you. If you can make them aware of self-sabotage, how normal it is for everyone, and that you do not have any judgment about it on any level, then your client can feel safe coming to you when they have self-sabotaged.

No one wants to spend money on a coach and start seeing extraordinary changes only to be the person who gets in the way of their goals. Then, they have to tell their coach, who has helped and praised them, that they ate an entire cake by themselves, binge-watched Netflix, and didn't get enough sleep, which caused huge problems at work. However, what if your client is doing so well and making great strides that you tell them, "I have to tell you what is most likely to happen with all these amazing changes. You may start taking steps backwards that you don't want to do." When your client takes steps backwards, they can say, "My coach told me this could happen, and they aren't going to be disappointed at all." That would be great because your client would not see you as the coach who will be angry with them, but the coach to come to.

What if you could get ahead of the self-sabotage even more? What if you not only told them that while they are experiencing this newer, better life, they will want to indulge in pleasure or be naughty, but you also helped them come up with ideas that fulfill that need without sabotaging their goals?

Change can be tricky, even good change. People have based their life decisions on their values or what they think they are, but then they start noticing that the results are not favorable to them and want better results. Those beliefs are still there; they may still believe them and expect success. I'm sure something similar has happened to you. For example, you may be the best employee and get passed up by someone who works half as much as you or doesn't know how to do their job.

As a coach, you need to recognize self-sabotage without telling your client they are self-sabotaging because this could feel judgmental to them and be unhelpful. Is your client making great strides and succeeding in everything you both are working on? Are they super excited about how they have changed? Are they referring to this as "hard work but worth it"?

Each client is different, but self-sabotage usually happens after a row of success within the first month of coaching. This is different based on how long the habits that are being transformed have been around. For example, by changing a habit that's two years old, the client may not self-sabotage until the fourth week or later; however, with a 50-year habit, self-sabotage may happen the first week. Their core values have been challenged and proven to need to be more accurate for the results they want. They may feel stupid for believing the wrong information that was kicking them in the pants. Clients are adults needing to be told they are wrong without their coach saying, "Dude, you're wrong. I don't know how you thought this would be a good choice." Every decision your client has made before meeting you they believed to be the right choice, or the best they could think of, but the results have led them down a wrong path. You can help your client transform their life in a month when they haven't been able to do it in 20 years, and this is a recipe for derailing.

How will they keep up with all these changes? Their friends and family may look at them differently, and their relationships are changing. Your client may desire to be accepted, but now there is a shift. What if now they relate to "those people," the ones they used to make fun of for being successful, skinny, or energetic? They know how their friends think about "those people," and your client doesn't want to lose relationships. This was supposed to bring success, not loss. Your client desires to be accepted.

Your client's paradigms are shifting; how they see reality and what they believe or assume about life is now different. Some people think exercise is hard work while others believe it's fun. So, the people who think it's hard work want to avoid it and dread the idea while others pay to exercise or run in the rain and snow for enjoyment. With your coaching, your client's paradigms will shift slowly, and they will see how easy life can be just by accepting a new way of thinking. They once saw climbing the corporate ladder as hard, a lifelong process, and were confused by people who reached the top quickly. Then you introduce them to another paradigm with great coaching questions and reframing perceptions. Now your client is randomly getting recognized and promoted in weeks, and life is getting easier. But wait, now what? They are having success reaching goals quickly, but the old paradigm is creeping in, and they question which way is right. Success doesn't feel normal or natural to them. The easy street is a strange feeling. Now, they may have been "good" and may desire to be rewarded and take a break from the norm, indulge in naughtiness, and do something fun, so how do you coach them in this new world they are in?

The first step in addressing self-sabotage with a client is acknowledging the desire and feelings that can cause self-sabotage and building awareness of the foe. Let your client know this will probably happen at some point soon, and it is normal. Second, ask your client to take a deep breath and relax. Ask them to describe to you any feelings and thoughts that come to their mind when they think about _____ (fill in the blank with the habit they have let go). Ask them if they would like to set a day where this behavior they are missing is OK, and plan and stick to that day. You want your client to be mindful and make this decision in their conscious mind, knowing who they are in that moment.

With your client, come up with a list of naughty activities and pleasurable activities they could do as alternatives to the habit they want to stop. Naughty ones should not be anything that would derail their goal and might include relatively innocent ideas such as pranking a loved one, pretending to be someone else when talking with a stranger, or going commando. Pleasurable activities could be taking a long bath, painting, dancing, or having sex in an unusual place. Whatever your client comes up with for ideas should not cause them harm or bother their ethical beliefs.

It's imperative that you remain supportive and encouraging. Two steps forward and one backwards will still get them to their goal. They need to know that you have not rejected them, and you are not disappointed in them. Your client is in a vulnerable position to have to admit they didn't follow through or messed up. However, they also need you to hold them accountable; this is why you are the coach.

Each week, you will help your client set goals. These goals should support them in their life and the direction they want to go in. If they want a goal that you have observed would be damaging to their progress, be sure to ask them clarifying questions and bring this to a place of mindfulness. Remember, some of their decisions have only been the best solution they could come up with on their own. Equip your client with the right tools to complete their goals, develop the belief that this will be easy for them, and have enough pleasurable and naughty things to do so that they can honor those feelings without bringing about guilt or shame. If your client feels guilt or shame, this can affect your relationship, or end it, and stop all progress. Success is inevitable if you proceed. Even if your client tells you that they told off their boss when what they were working on was a raise, don't judge that as bad. Show them you are curious. Ask curiosity questions. "Isn't it interesting that ...? How did that make you feel? What outcome did you want?"

The first time I had a client self-sabotage, I felt like I was banging my head up against a brick wall. I wasn't prepared for it. The homework was simple, so simple I thought a two-year-old could accomplish it, I could praise my client, and we would develop a great relationship. Instead, my client was happy that she even returned to our session. She knew she needed accountability, and that's why she had me as her coach. I dialed back her homework to an even smaller and more manageable task, understanding this may have been easy in my eyes, but it was not, in her opinion.

Unfortunately, I could not celebrate a win during that session, for my ego was damaged. I was shocked and questioned if I should continue to meet with her or even if I should be a coach. However, I pulled myself together after the session, saw her choices through her eyes, and realized I was there to coach her. Neither of us was there to boost my ego. At our next meeting, she had made progress, less than she could have made, but it was progress. I wholeheartedly celebrated with her the victory she had and let her know she was enough.

Everything was going great for a few weeks when another self-sabotage moment came. This time, she questioned whether she should be spending money on herself for coaching. She was reaching her goals but felt selfish for spending their family finances. She was feeling distant from her spouse. However, by me asking a series of curious questions, such as what would be a better way to spend your money, will that get you where you want to be, would your daughter or your husband be worth this, are you worth it? She came to the conclusion that she was worth the coaching, and we came up with new fun activities she and her spouse could do together to build their closeness in a different and healthier way that would meet their needs and not sabotage her goals.

Self-sabotage will happen; bring this to your client's awareness and practice mindful techniques, so they are aware of their options, choices, and what decisions they want to make consciously. Give your client support and accountability and be their biggest cheerleader while also asking them about their homework to hold them accountable. Make sure their goals are in line with their values. Empower your client with positive talk and encouragement, building their confidence and not agreeing with guilt or shame. Be shocked that they feel you could think any shame or guilt about them. You are holding the vision that your client wants for themselves. Ask curiosity questions without judging them. Help your clients develop their naughty and pleasure lists. Your client's desire to be accepted, rewarded, and have aligned priorities that aren't selfish are natural desires that will need to be fulfilled by healthy options.

As a human resources professional, I consider what the employee experiences from the moment they apply to the time they leave the company. As a coach, you need to decide what you want your clients' experiences to be from the moment they see your website to the time they end services. Give your clients an amazing coaching experience that will transform their life.

ACTIVITY

1. Make your client aware of self-sabotage. It's normal and every-one will self-sabotage. Your client has feelings and desires that are normal
2. Self-sabotage is fulfilling a need your client has so come up with a plan together how that need gets filled without causing self-sabotage to their goals and life.
3. Have your client relax and describe their thoughts and feelings about letting go of certain habits in order to create habits that will give them the results they want. Is there a day the client wants to indulge in this habit?
4. With your client come up with a list of naughty activities and plea-surable activities they could do as an alternative to the habit they want to stop.
5. Each week set goals with your client.
6. Equip your client with the right tools to complete their goals, and help them develop the belief that this is going to be easy.
7. Celebrate every win big or small.

About the Author

Mindy McKibbin is a certified HR leader. She is also the founder and cer-tified coach with MD Master Your Health and Life Coaching LLC, which reflects her profound dedication to the holistic well-being of individuals and is an illustration of her compassionate, transformative leadership and dedica-tion to excellence as well as an enduring commitment to the empowerment of those around her. She guides her clients toward a holistic transformation where people can grow, and positive change flourishes.

Amidst her exceptional professional achievements, her role is a nurturing and dedicated mom to three accomplished adult children, McKenzie, Keisia, and Kolton, and four adorable grandchildren, Nicholas, Noah, Amelia, and Annaliese. Mindy has demonstrated leadership in various organizations, dedicating time and expertise to numerous nonprofit initiatives. With a strong commitment to community service, Mindy has also served as a public speaker at various events, sharing insights and inspiring audiences across different organizations.

Having established herself as a leader and public speaker in various organizations, Mindy has profoundly impacted the lives of many through her coaching. In the following quote clients share their personal stories of transformation and growth under her guidance "Thank you from the bottom of my heart for all you have done to give me my life back over these past 12 weeks. I am truly a new woman who's ready to go after what I want in life, something I haven't felt in years. I didn't realize what a dark place I was in. Thank you for bringing me back out into the light."

"Before coaching with Mindy, I struggled with using my voice to claim the life I want. I've always been a people pleaser & shoved a lot of emotions & desires down thinking it was selfish of me to put my needs & health first. Then she taught me that I have to take care of myself first to be my best for others & that I have a right to my thoughts & feelings & to pursue the life I want & passions of my heart."

Mindy's collection of accomplishments is a testimony to the transformative power of resilience, empathy, wisdom and visionary leadership. It leaves a lasting legacy that continues to shape and elevate the lives of those she touches, guiding individuals toward recognizing their intrinsic potential and fostering a mindset of personal growth and self-discovery.

Email: mindy@mdmastercoach.com
Website: http://www.mdmasteryourhealthandlife.org/
Instagram: MD Master Your Health and Life (@vitalitywithmindy) | Instagram profile
LinkedIn: https://www.linkedin.com/company/md-master-your-health-and-life-coaching

CHAPTER
20

Voice of Wisdom

By Tanya Newbould, ACC, ICF
Life Transformations Strategist
Beverly Hills, California

*Between stimulus and response, there is a space. In
that space is our power to choose our response. In
our response lies our growth and our freedom.*

—Viktor E. Frankl

If you are reading this, you are a coach. That means you have been called to do something great in your life—greater than yourself, your beliefs, your doubts, your worries, and your outcomes. Being a coach means you are divinely called and given the opportunity to serve. Whether it be an individual, company, organization, or corporation, it is a calling that God put you on this mud ball called Earth to do. You were born to do something great with your life and being a coach is just that.

What is coaching? The International Coaching Federation (ICF) defines coaching as partnering with clients in a thought-provoking and creative process that inspires them to maximize their personal and professional potential. Dr. Maria Nemeth, founder of the Academy for Coaching Excellence (ACE) program, defines coaching as a process consisting of clarifying your intentions, designing goals, and taking authentic action within a safe, supportive relationship.

Coaching is not psychotherapy, nor should it be used as a substitute for counseling or legal, financial, or medical services. Coaching is a calling, for both the coach and the client, group, organization, or corporation. It is a privilege, an honor, and should be held with great reverence.

Before you begin coaching, whether it's with an individual on Zoom or walking on a stage to a corporation of 500 or 10,000 people, how do you prepare or clear yourself? Are you coming in Mach 6 with your hair on fire, distracted from a stressful day or the moment before? Did someone say something to you that knocked your self-confidence? Did you just have an argument with a loved one? Or, even worse, do you doubt yourself and allow that to creep into your psyche like a thief in the night? If any of this occurs, it doesn't mean there's anything wrong with you; it simply means you're a human being.

Even if none of this is occurring, it is of the utmost importance that you take the time to clear yourself. There are many ways to do this. I personally have a strong faith in God, so I like to pray for my clients, myself, and for God to give me the wisdom and words that He wants me to say, what *they* need to hear, so I become a vessel for change. It's not about me *telling* or *giving* advice. Why? Because each person already has their own answers. We are simply here to hold space, like holding a mirror up until they can see their own magnificent reflection.

Dr. Maria Nemeth of ACE developed the Green Lens and I Am Willing techniques. I'm going to go over these principles as a guideline for any coaching practice that you have, so let's begin. She looked at admired leaders and asked: "What were they seeing that has led them to act in such an empowering way?" There are five key conclusions:

1. This person is a hero, whole and complete.

"Whole and complete" means we lack nothing. The idea of *a* hero we take from mythologist Joseph Campbell. He wrote that we are drawn to heroic myths because we see ourselves in them. We all go through a "hero's journey" as we undertake new pursuits. We depart from the familiar; we enter unknown territory where we encounter fears and mysteries; we are initiated into new skills; and finally, we gain new abilities to contribute to others.

2. This person has goals and dreams and a desire to make a difference.

We take this from Mother Teresa, who saw each person's life as having tremendous worth and value. One of the intentions of her mission in Calcutta was for the poorest of the poor to experience, if only once before they passed away, that their life makes a difference.

3. This person has their own answers.

By this we mean, they have a wellspring of wisdom. We take this from all great teachers, who see their role as drawing out the innate wisdom and intelligence of their students.

4. This person is contributing to me right now.

We take this from Nelson Mandela, whose power came not from inspiring others but by being inspired by others. In fact, while he was imprisoned, his jailers had to change out his guards every several months because he would befriend them!

5. This person deserves to be treated with dignity and respect.

We take this from the Dalai Lama, for whom every person is the Buddha, worthy of compassion, respect, and reverence.

What do these five conclusions mean to you as a coach? Are they automatic? Do you think of your client from this lens when spending time with them? Like yoga, this is a practice. Not only can and should we utilize these five conclusions in coaching, it will also change your entire life when you look at each individual or group this way.

As a coach, we get to support clients in seeking their passion, power, and purpose. Too many times coaches want to "coach" and impart their own opinion or wisdom onto the client. It comes from a good place, but it is far more rewarding for the client when they work through their own situations and empower themselves with their own answers.

As an Academy for Coaching Excellence Licensed Academy Trainer, it is our responsibility to be ethical, have integrity, and most importantly, listen. Being present to what is, and by allowing spaces and silence and not feeling like that void must be filled, allows the client to look, see, and tell the truth. From there, as coaches, we give them the space to create small, sweet steps (action). No matter how much reflection, discovery, and conversation takes place, if it's not followed by action, there will not be the results a client needs to create a life that they love.

There are several simple tools and activities that can be done with a client to quickly create impact in their lives. One of the most powerful tools a client can learn is to recognize the power of the words used and how it affects their life. These are three of my favorite phrases I learned and implement from ACE:

1. Anytime you say the phrases "I have to," "I need to," "I should," or "I could," try replacing those words with: "I choose to."

Language is important. We can trick ourselves depending on the words we use. When we "have to" do something, we give that task a lot of negative weight; when in reality, many of the "have to do," "need to do," "could and should" can wait. "Choose to" gives the brain a sense of freedom of choice and helps a person prioritize what truly matters.

2. When words are spoken like "It's just who I am, I can't change," or there's negative self-talk like "I'm stupid, I can't, I always …," try replacing those statements with: "Up until now."

In other words, "Every time I try, I can't do it" is replaced with "Up until now when I've tried, I haven't been able to do it." Read this last part out loud and notice how your body and brain react to the shift in language. You will notice an ease, and instead of a solid statement of fact, there is possibility present. "Up until now" suggests that a change or new development is expected or happening at the present moment, which allows the brain to grasp possibility instead of a statement being spoken as a fact that isn't accurate and more like a taskmaster.

3. The third one I love the most is this: Instead of saying phrases like, "I am," try replacing those with "I am willing" or "Therefore, I am willing."

Here is a great example: If I were to ask someone with a modicum income to say, "I am financially successful and wealthy," what do you think their sweet brain would say to them? It's going to say, "No you're not!" Now try saying, "I am willing to be financially successful and wealthy." What do you notice? The brain relaxes, and there is an ease that takes place. The brain is open to possibility. There may even be a sense of excitement present.

What Is "Being Willing"?

"Being willing" is our capacity to say yes to whatever is before us on our life's journey, no matter what we are thinking or feeling. We may not want to do something, we may not think we can, we may not know how to do it—and we can nevertheless be willing—whether it's going to the dentist, taking out the garbage, writing a book, or experiencing the pain of childbirth.

Being willing comes from who we are in our hearts and souls, and transcends our doubts, worries, and skepticism. It is undimmed by time and is a capacity that is always available to us. It defines who we are and gives us strength. When we see that we are willing, we tap into the core of our being.

Say yes to all that will be, and you're taking a step every bit as courageous as those knights who entered the dark forest in search of the Holy Grail. Think about it, you put one foot in front of you, you don't know what your path will look like, but you are going ahead anyway. No more standing at the outskirts, waiting for the trail to show up, you have begun. Even if those customary limiting inner thoughts are yelling at you to stop, you're on your way. By simply being willing, you automatically energize yourself to take action. This is true no matter how long you've put that action on hold. You get in touch with the power that resides in your hero's heart. When you do this with your clients, it gives them an opportunity to see for themselves the difference and how the brain reacts based on the language used.

What Is "Voice of Wisdom"?

The last coaching piece I want to touch on is using your voice of wisdom. Some people call it their higher power, their intuition, or their inner knowing. How do we know when we are listening to it? There are several ways:

- It's gentle, kind, and has reasoning.
- Your body relaxes, your heart opens, and your breathing slows.
- It makes sense and is clear.
- Some humor is present.
- It is always empowering.
- There is a sense that all is well.

Choose to operate from this space and listen intently for your voice of wisdom. Not only will you be a profound coach for others, but your life will also become magical too. We are all human beings on our own hero's journey, and my prayer is that some of the wisdom from this chapter will help all of us to create a better world. In our growth and freedom lies our own voice of wisdom.

ACTIVITY

See section on the three phases learned and implemented from ACE within the chapter.

About the Author

With 20+ years in the entertainment industry as an actor, Tanya Newbould chose to leave that behind to follow her passion, being a Life Transformation Strategist, Executive Coach, Entrepreneur, and Jewelry Designer. With five businesses to her name, Tanya stays active coaching others to grow and see their true magnificence, so that they will transform their world and the world around them with power, passion and purpose.

Tanya is an ACC Coach with her International Coaches Federation (ICF) and is a Licensed Academy Trainer (LAT) for the Academy for Coaching Excellence (ACE Coaching). She is a passionate advocate for Postpartum Depression, so she attained her Certification and Advanced Certification from Postpartum Support International (PSI) in Perinatal Mood & Anxiety Disorders (PMAD's). After suffering and surviving her own PPD trauma, Tanya had the forethought, Co-Created and Co-Produced "When the Bough Breaks—A Documentary about Postpartum Depression" Executive Produced and narrated by Brooke Shields, viewed in over sixty countries and six languages. Tanya co-authored the book *Absolute Vision* and is wrapping up her memoir of her PPD journey.

Tanya won the 2019 Flaunt It Award for her work in Postpartum Depression from 'Don't Hide It Flaunt It' (DHIFI), and she chose to not only survive but thrive from her experience and help others know they are not alone. Look for Tanya's memoir about her journey through postpartum depression.

As an Executive Coach and Consultant, Tanya transforms the workspace as the missing link in mindset which translates on every level in business.

Websites:
https://www.tanyanewbould.com/
https://delpozzojewelry.luxury
https://www.whentheboughbreaksfilm.com
https//www.sozoheart.org

Instagram:
https://www.instagram.com/tanyanewbould/
https://www.instagram.com/delpozzojewelry/
https://www.instagram.com/sozoheart
https://www.instagram.com/whentheboughbreaksfilm

Facebook:
https://www.facebook.com/tanyanewbould
https://www.facebook.com/whentheboughbreaksdoc/

LinkedIn:
Tanya (Newbould) Del Pozzo
https://www.linkedin.com/company/del-pozzo-designs/
https://www.linkedin.com/in/tanya-newbould-b57930232/

CHAPTER

21

Unveiling Your True Self:
The Five Pillars of Transformation

By Joyce de Nooijer
Founder, JoycedeNooijer Coaching
Spijkenisse, South Holland, Netherlands

The privilege of a lifetime is to become who you truly are.

—CARL GUSTAV JUNG

h, the rollercoaster of life for today's young adults and young professionals—grappling with self-doubt, choice overload, and the ever-persistent critical voice that seems to have taken up residence in their heads! It's like trying to navigate a maze blindfolded while juggling flaming torches. As a Transformation Life Coach, what surprised me is that each and every one of my coachees was looking for something to hold on to. This also indicated that they were not at all connected to their authentic self, so they did not only feel lost, they were actually really lost in this world. I saw an opportunity here to offer these young adults' insights into their inner world, so they could get reconnected again with their true values.

Over the past few years of setting up my own practice, I have come up with something I like to call my "Five Pillars of Transformation." These are not ancient secrets whispered by wise mountain gurus, but rather, practical tools to help these amazing young individuals discover their true selves. It's like a GPS for the soul. It guides them through the twists and turns of self-discovery with a touch of flair and maybe a little fairy dust. Let me take you through my five pillars and unravel the mystery of identity.

1. Self-Awareness: Unveiling the Epic Saga of Authenticity

In my coaching universe, we embark on a cosmic quest where each coachee takes center stage—they are the shining star of our grand show. Picture it as a captivating adventure, an exploration into the very essence of who they are. We kick off with the basics, venturing beyond the surface into the depths of their values, beliefs, and the mysterious corners of their thoughts. This isn't a mere surface-level exploration; it's a deep-sea dive into the uncharted territories of self-awareness. As a life coach, I guide them through the process of shedding layers—stripping away the opinions, the noise from social media, the expectations of family and friends, and the influence of society at large. It's about untangling from the external web and connecting with their authentic true selves. Together, we navigate through the maze of influences, peeling back the layers until we reach the core.

This is where the magic happens. We're not just scratching the surface; we're diving deep into the very essence of their being. The exploration becomes the ultimate kickstart, propelling them on a transformative journey of continuous growth and self-discovery. It's like opening a treasure chest filled with hidden gems, where each revelation unveils a new chapter in their extraordinary story. As a life coach, my role is akin to that of a seasoned navigator, guiding them through this uncharted terrain. The process is about more than just self-awareness; it's a reconnection with their true values and beliefs. It's a cosmic journey that untangles them from external influences, allowing their authentic selves to shine. This pillar lays the groundwork for the coachee to understand and appreciate their unique narrative, setting the stage for the profound transformations that lie ahead. So, fellow life coaches, prepare to embark on this epic saga of authenticity with your coachees as they uncover the hidden treasures within themselves.

2. Self-Acceptance: Hugging It Out, Even in the Less Brilliant Moments

Having embarked on the cosmic quest of self-awareness, our brave coachees now stand at the threshold of a transformative era—the age of self-acceptance. This isn't just about acknowledging their existence; it's a profound journey into embracing every facet of who they are. Imagine it as the dawn of a new era where self-love becomes the guiding star illuminating the road to happiness. As we navigate through the maze of self-discovery, we delve into the realm of what they truly like and love about themselves. It's not just about recognizing talents; it's about shining a spotlight on the unique qualities that make them extraordinary. In this phase, we discard the cloak of self-doubt and welcome the warmth of self-acceptance, bidding farewell to the inner critic that has lingered for too long.

Together, we explore the vast landscape of their inner world, uncovering passions, interests, and the very essence of what they genuinely adore. It's like stepping into a vibrant garden of self-appreciation, where every bloom represents a newfound love for themselves. This pillar is the catalyst for a ripple effect—as they start accepting themselves, love begins to bloom, unlocking the door to the road of their happiness where resilience arises.

As a life coach, I see my role is that of a compassionate guide, navigating them through the terrain of self-acceptance. I encourage them to not only acknowledge but embrace their uniqueness. The setbacks and challenges that once felt like stumbling blocks are now viewed as unexpected plot twists in the beautiful story of their lives.

3. Clear Goals: Plotting the Adventure of a Lifetime

Every adventure needs a roadmap. If self-acceptance is the canvas, then goals are the vibrant brushstrokes that paint the masterpiece of their lives. These aren't just any goals; they are the beating heart of our journey—challenging, yet undeniably realistic. In this phase, the coachee becomes the visionary, the mastermind behind the script of their epic life movie. We collaboratively plot these goals, each one a compass guiding them through the uncharted territories beyond their comfort zone. It's like being both the protagonist and the director of their life's blockbuster, creating a narrative that not only captivates audiences but also leaves the architect of this narrative—themselves—in awe.

As a life coach, my role is to act as their co-pilot, guiding them through the process of goal-setting with wisdom and enthusiasm. We navigate through the possibilities, ensuring that each goal is not just a checkbox but a stepping stone towards their personal summit. This pillar lays the foundation for a journey that is purposeful, intentional, and aligned with their newfound self-acceptance.

4. Conscious Choices: A Personal Cheerleader with a Wise Wink

Building upon the foundation of clear goals, our coachees now enter the enchanting realm of conscious choices—a space where I, as their devoted coach, step into the role of a personal cheerleader with a sprinkle of wisdom. It's not just about making choices; it's about cultivating a skill that harmonizes seamlessly with their goals and values. Imagine this phase as the continuation of our cosmic adventure, where together, we choreograph a dance of decisions. Each move is intentional, a step towards the spectacular performance of their dreams. In this vibrant, energetic routine, every decision resonates with purpose, propelling them forward in the direction of their aspirations.

As their personal cheerleader, I encourage them to embrace the notion that not making choices is akin to standing still. It's the "what-if" scenario that often holds them back. We unravel the magic in the art of making conscious choices, where the fear of the unknown transforms into an exciting anticipation of what lies ahead. A timeless wisdom echoes through our journey:

> *If you do what you always did, you*
> *get what you always got.*
>
> —HENRY FORD

I actually always use this quote, and it gives almost all my coachees the insight that that is indeed what they have been doing lately, and it did not get them anywhere.

Together, we break the cycle of stagnant choices, opening doors to new possibilities. I guide them in understanding that making a choice, regardless of the outcome, is a stepping stone in a direction, far more powerful than remaining immobilized in uncertainty. In this pillar, the coachee learns that conscious choices aren't just decisions; they are milestones in their journey. Every choice, even if it diverges from the expected path, offers valuable insights and opens the door to new opportunities. It's a dance where they lead and the choices follow, creating a rhythm that propels them towards the destiny they envision.

5. Taking Action: From Dreams to Reality, One Step at a Time

At the fifth pillar, we now stand at the threshold of the grand finale—the era of taking action. Picture it as the exhilarating climax, where coachees transform their dreams into reality, step by exhilarating step. It's not just about envisioning; it's about rolling up sleeves and diving headfirst into the script they've meticulously crafted. Building upon the foundation of conscious choices, my role as a coach takes center stage in ensuring that the coachee's dreams don't merely remain in the realm of imagination. Through regular check-ins and a healthy dose of accountability, I become the anchor, ensuring they don't get lost in a sitcom marathon of indecision. The journey becomes a steady, purposeful march forward, even when unexpected plot twists arise.

Imagine this phase as the construction of a sturdy bridge—a bridge that spans the gap between what they desire and what they do. We transition from being dreamers to becoming architects of our destiny, constructing a pathway that bridges the gap between aspirations and achievements. It's not just about hoping for a blockbuster; it's about scripting, directing, and starring in one's own chart-topping story. In this pillar, coachees learn that action is the catalyst that propels dreams from the abstract into the tangible. Every step taken is a building block, each check-in a reassurance that they are on the right path. It's about transforming the energy of ambition into the fuel that powers their journey.

So, fellow life coaches, prepare for this grand finale as you inspire your coachees to orchestrate stories destined for the blockbuster charts. The narrative isn't just about turning dreams into reality; it's a saga of resilience, triumph, and the unyielding spirit to transform aspirations into tangible achievements. This is their movie, their magnum opus, and the action has just begun. Lights, camera, action—let the blockbuster destiny unfold, and may the applause be a testament to the transformative journey they've undertaken.

Conclusion: Illuminating Transformation

As we draw the curtain on this cosmic odyssey of self-discovery, guided by the five pillars, we find ourselves at the nexus of transformation where dreams transition into tangible reality. These pillars, like sturdy columns, have not only provided a solid foundation but also sculpted the space for profound self-discovery.

In this coaching journey, each pillar is not just a stepping stone but a portal to a deeper understanding of oneself. Through tailored exercises and coaching techniques, we navigate the unique landscapes of individual experiences, seamlessly intertwining them with the universal themes encapsulated in these pillars. (1) Self-awareness becomes the compass, guiding coachees through the labyrinth of values and beliefs, untangling them from external influences, and reconnecting them with their authentic selves. (2) Self-acceptance is the warm embrace, inviting them to appreciate the symphony of their strengths and uniqueness, transforming setbacks into unexpected plot twists in the grand narrative of their lives. (3) Clear goals act as beacons, illuminating the path to self-discovery, crafting a roadmap that not only challenges but also aligns seamlessly with their deepest aspirations. (4) Conscious choices become the dance of decisions, each step resonating with purpose, propelling them forward and breaking free from the inertia of indecision. (5) Taking action is the grand finale, the moment when dreams cease to be ephemeral and materialize into the tangible substance of achievements. Regular check-ins and accountability serve as the wings that ensure their flight continues, even when faced with unexpected plot twists.

At the culmination of this transformative journey, the coachee emerges, equipped with tools, bathed in illuminating insights, and adorned with a positive self-image. Clear goals act as lighthouses, guiding them towards their redesigned, happier life. As a coach, witnessing this metamorphosis is an indescribable satisfaction. It's not merely observing a change; it's being a part of the tapestry of transformation. The coachee, once a seeker, now stands as the architect of their destiny. The once-muted dreams now resonate with life, and the once-diminished self-esteem shines with newfound radiance.

In the end, as a coach, there's a profound joy in knowing that the impact of this journey ripples far beyond the coaching sessions. It's the satisfaction of having played a role in unraveling the cocoon, allowing the coachee to spread their wings and soar into the expanse of their potential, ready to script the next chapter of their blockbuster life.

ACTIVITY

Unveiling Your Inner World Compass

Objective: To dive deep into the depths of values, beliefs, and inner thoughts.

As a life coach, one of the first and crucial steps in guiding your coachees towards self-awareness is to embark on a journey of uncovering their values, beliefs, and the hidden corners of their thoughts. This activity, Unveiling Your Inner World Compass, serves as a powerful tool to initiate this exploration.

1. Values Exploration (15 minutes)

Begin by presenting a list of common values, ranging from integrity and freedom to creativity and compassion. You can find comprehensive lists online or curate your own based on the coaching context. Ask your coachee to select the top five values that most resonate with them. Encourage them to reflect on instances in their lives where these values played a significant role.

2. Belief Identification (20 minutes)

Move on to beliefs by presenting a set of open-ended questions designed to uncover core beliefs. Examples include: "What do you believe about success?" or "What beliefs about yourself may be holding you back?" Encourage your coachee to journal their responses without overthinking. This exercise is about capturing raw, unfiltered thoughts.

3. Journey into the Mind's Maze (15 minutes)

To explore the mysterious corners of their thoughts, introduce a mind mapping exercise. Ask your coachee to draw a circle in the center of a page and write their name inside it. From this central point, have them draw lines outward, connecting to various aspects of their lives—relationships, work, passions, fears, etc. Encourage them to jot down thoughts, memories, or emotions associated with each aspect.

4. Reflection and Connection (10 minutes)

After completing the activity, guide your coachee in reflecting on the patterns and connections they observe. What values consistently appear in their stories? Are there recurring beliefs that influence their thoughts? Discuss how these revelations contribute to their self-awareness and what insights they can draw from this exploration.

5. Next Steps (5 minutes)

Conclude the activity by brainstorming actionable steps. What changes or adjustments can they make to align their choices more closely with their values? How can newfound awareness of beliefs guide them in making conscious choices? (They can use this as a building block for pillar number four.)

This activity serves as a compass, pointing clients in the direction of self-discovery. It unveils the intricate tapestry of their values, beliefs, and thoughts, providing a solid foundation for the transformative journey that lies ahead.

About the Author

Joyce de Nooijer, a seasoned manager of office operations and Transformation Life Coach, guides young individuals through life's journeys with a unique perspective. Fascinated by the intricacies of the human mind, her passion stems from a personal journey of self-discovery, navigating a challenging path without a GPS. This profound understanding drives her commitment to supporting the next generation.

Completing coaching training five years ago, Joyce specializes in unraveling the unconscious mind through her "Five Pillars of Transformation." Inspired by the wisdom of Carl Gustav Jung, she cherishes his quote, "The privilege of a lifetime is to become who you truly are." Guided by this principle, Joyce empowers young individuals to navigate their inner world, fostering resilience and strength in their transformative journeys. Her mission is clear: You don't have to do it alone. As a steadfast guide, Joyce helps others discover the privilege of becoming their authentic selves.

Email: info@joycedenooijer.nl
Website: www.joycedenooijer.nl
Instagram: @joyce.transformationcoach

CHAPTER

22

Mindset Mastery: Navigating Stress when Building Your Practice

By Jennifer Richardson
Founder, Rediscover Happiness; Stress Management Coach
Newmarket, Ontario, Canada

*Take care of yourself then you can
take care of your neighbor.*

—Tony Robbins

S tarting a coaching practice was exciting and rewarding; however, it came with a lot of challenges. A lot of my self-doubts and worries turned into stress, which affected my mental and physical health. Before I transitioned to full-time coaching, I balanced a full-time schedule from my marketing company while building a part-time coaching practice. It was exhausting, and I was eager to open my coaching doors. I knew that developing coaching skills and gaining clients took time and patience, but that soon became an after-thought once my limiting mindset took over, and it led to many mistakes and stressful days.

In the beginning, I faced time pressures, financial worries, high expectations, and fears that I overanalyzed everything and eventually shifted my focus. The anxiety was growing, and it prevented me from being my best. I later realized I had to change my mindset and balance the transition with a thoughtful approach to ensure a more rewarding journey.

Asking myself, "Remember why you started," helped transform my limiting mindsets to empowering ones. Limiting beliefs can hinder your ability to offer optimal client support and prevent you from reaching your full potential. Naturally, we start to question when something doesn't happen right away or easily. But good things take time, and right now, it's about balancing patience with awareness and using stress management strategies to reframe your mindset.

So, when you're ready to open your doors, avoid overthinking or rushing at the start. Practice patience and mindfulness to manage your stress, set realistic expectations, and seek support from mentors or peers. Let's take a closer look at why a limiting mindset often stops coaches from reaching extraordinary success.

High Expectations

Limiting Mindset

When you're learning to be a coach or starting your practice, don't set overly high expectations on yourself and others. First, nobody said you need a fancy website right away and have to know everything about your field or business from the start. Just as we say to our clients, as long as you have a willingness and are open to learning, know that it takes time to grow, and you can learn things bit by bit.

Second, let's talk about the support you may expect when building your practice. I'm fortunate to have a wonderful husband who has supported me from the start though I came to realize later that not everyone may have the same backing. While I had his support and some from friends and family, not everyone agreed with the life I envisioned for myself. Your life is yours to live, and no one should make you feel guilty for living it your way.

As people offer you support in ways they can understand, some will be cheerleaders while others will quietly believe in you. There will also be those who don't care and can be a negative influence. It took some time for me to realize that everyone has their limits when being supportive. However, before figuring that out, it added unnecessary stress and distractions to my already growing list of problems and self-doubts. I had to check my expectations and tell myself to never question my dreams or allow others to make my life complacent.

Empowering Mindset

Embrace a mindset of continuous learning, recognizing that as information evolves, we evolve. By staying curious and open to new ideas, experiences, and perspectives, you enrich your understanding of the world and yourself. Be confident in your decisions and set realistic expectations for yourself and with certain people in your life. Remember, not everyone will be on the same page as you, so be sure to understand their limits. Avoid the stress of self-sabotage and focus your efforts on calming the mind while checking your expectations.

Imposter Syndrome and Imitation

Limiting Mindset

In the beginning, you might feel like you're not enough and start comparing yourself to others who may be further along in their journey. I'm here to remind you that learning is part of the process and doesn't require perfection from the start. I understand that we feel pressure to know everything and be perfect in the eyes of our client, but this mindset can make reaching your goals seem impossible, adding unnecessary stress and self-doubt. Feeling like a fraud or that one doesn't deserve success, due to self-limiting beliefs, also creates a constant internal struggle where you doubt your accomplishments and abilities, and instead of growing and learning, you end up contributing more to your stress and anxiety.

While imposter syndrome and imitation share some similarities, they are different ideas. Imposter syndrome means you have the fear of being exposed as a fraud, even when you're doing well. It's doubting your abilities and feeling you don't deserve your achievements. On the other hand, imitation is about copying or replicating the behaviour, actions, or ideas of others.

Be mindful when you're planning your practice and you're deep into research mode. It's easy to get caught up on trendy social media posts, sleek websites, top-selling e-courses, and professional videos. While you might feel drawn to these successful examples, copying them can lead you further away from your original focus. It may seem like the easier, faster route, but it actually diminishes your authenticity and unique selling point. More importantly, you start to blend in with everyone else, and clients and other coaches can see right through that.

Empowering Mindset

Overcoming these limiting mindsets is crucial for growth and learning. Start by acknowledging your achievements and expertise. Reflect back to the moment you decided to become a life coach and what your story looked like. Then, focus on your unique strengths and what sets you apart. Embrace your individuality and use it as your selling point. You can still research successful professionals, just be sure to write out your goals and branding before you cruise the internet. Fuel the empowering mindset by keeping a record of positive feedback from clients or colleagues to remind yourself of your capabilities. You don't have to get it right from the very start; just remember why you started and make that your focus moving forward.

Difficulty in Setting Boundaries

Limiting Mindset

Setting boundaries can be tough, as this stress leads to burnout because we're all trying to balance our work and personal life, struggling to say no, and not prioritizing our mental and physical health. A common problem is people-pleasing, where you prioritize other people's needs over your own. People-pleasers tend to say yes to everything, even if it's too much, just to avoid upsetting someone. The stress comes from the fear of disappointing others or being afraid of what people might think, and while you want to make everyone happy, it can leave you feeling overwhelmed. There needs to be a balance between helping others and taking care of yourself without always saying yes to everything. It's about setting healthy limits to reduce stress and promote overall well-being.

Neglecting to set boundaries can become challenging to manage workload, prioritize essential tasks, and maintain a healthy work-life balance, ultimately leading to over-commitment and burnout. As a life coach, it can also affect the quality of support you provide to your clients, potentially hindering their progress and overall experience. Setting clear and healthy boundaries is so important for maintaining the well-being of both you and your client, thus creating a more effective coaching relationship.

Empowering Mindset

I want you to identify and understand your personal limits—recognizing what you are comfortable with and what causes stress. This self-discovery provides insight into your priorities, values, and the activities that contribute positively or negatively to your stress levels. Next, explore what specifically triggers stress when it comes to setting boundaries (for example: exploring past experiences, fears, or societal pressures). By uncovering the root cause, you can develop a deeper awareness of where the stress stems from and work towards addressing that.

The final step involves developing practical strategies you can manage and that create healthy boundaries. This may include how to communicate to others what your limits are, time management techniques to prioritize self-care, and building an empowering mindset that values personal well-being. That shift in mindset can help you create a balanced and less stressful life, where you can thrive personally and professionally.

Shift in Focus

Limiting Mindset

When you start your practice, be mindful of where your attention goes. If you've faced challenges to get started, maybe even made some financial sacrifices, the urgency to make money quickly might shift your focus from your original mission. For example, you might get overly focused on social media metrics, like followers and likes, forgetting that building authenticity online takes time. Stress shows up when you expect quick results and overlook the gradual process of turning viewers into clients.

As you kickstart your practice, the temptation to quickly earn money through affiliate marketing or sponsorships may arise. It's okay to want more income, but relying too heavily on these sources instead of your coaching practice can bring short-lived success accompanied by stress and guilt. This approach limits your possibilities and may redirect your goals unexpectedly. Having a mindset focused on quick profits might give you a bad reputation and work against you, leading to a loss of followers on social media, fewer visitors to your website, and negative reviews. Building any kind of business takes time, just like building relationships and trust, so make sure to do regular check-ins with yourself to ensure you don't veer off mission.

Empowering Mindset

Take a moment to reflect on why you started the practice in the first place and what your core values are. Write them down and keep them visible. When you notice your focus shifting towards quick gains or external pressures, refer back to your mission to realign your priorities. It might take more time, energy, and resources, but building something you're proud of, something valuable to others, speaks volumes in the long run.

Complacency and Procrastination

Limiting Mindset

It's important to admit when we've been afraid of failing or when we didn't put in enough effort and settled for less. Waiting for the perfect moment or more knowledge can stop us from taking action. Avoiding important tasks or tough situations because of fear or discomfort can slow down our progress and success. This delay creates stress and makes it harder to achieve our goals. For example, during my first full year of stable income, I got so comfortable in my day-to-day work that I turned down opportunities and slowed down on my continuous learning. This limiting mindset of complacency, procrastination, and inaction created barriers to learning and growth, blocking my self-promotion and success and easily fueling my self-doubts.

When you think that you don't have much to offer or worry about what others might think, this can make it stressful to promote yourself as a coach.

This hesitation can make it tough for you to get clients and grow your practice. If you keep fearing that you won't succeed, it may lead to procrastination or missed deadlines and opportunities.

Empowering Mindset

Embrace a growth mindset, knowing that you'll continue to learn and grow as you progress. Start by identifying what's creating situations of fear and discomfort. Challenge negative beliefs by replacing them with positive affirmations, practicing self-compassion, and cultivating mindfulness. It's a gradual process, so patience and persistence are key. Regularly review and adjust your goals to keep momentum and ensure your growth. I find it best to seek an accountability partner or mentor to provide support and encouragement along the way and help you stay focused on your objectives.

Perfectionism

Limiting Mindset

Starting a coaching practice, building a website or course, writing a book, or creating videos won't ever be perfect or happen at the exact right time. Not feeling "ready" and waiting for the perfect moment can hold you back from taking action. Thinking, "I'm not experienced enough," and feeling like you lack the necessary skills to be a successful coach adds to self-doubt and undermines your confidence. "I don't have enough credentials" shifts you to believe that a lack of specific certifications diminishes your ability to succeed.

Constantly focusing on your shortcomings not only increases stress, but it actually makes decision-making and productivity harder. Striving for perfection to an unrealistic degree can stop any progress you've made, as it often leads to procrastination, fear of failure, and self-criticism. I often felt overwhelmed when I worried about my limitations. I had this constant pursuit of perfection, tweaking and reworking everything, that it left me stressed and drained. I was stuck in a cycle of waiting for the perfect moment to launch something or seeking more information before deciding on an opportunity. Perfectionism delayed me from taking action, consumed so much of my time and energy, and impaired my decision-making ability.

Empowering Mindset

Accept that perfection is unattainable and that mistakes are part of the learning process. Prioritize your progress and improvement over flawlessness. Start by setting realistic goals and deadlines, breaking them down into smaller, more manageable ones. By focusing on smaller, achievable goals, you can make progress, build momentum, and reduce stress and anxiety. Don't forget to celebrate your accomplishments along the way, reinforcing a positive mindset and motivating yourself to tackle the next step. Move forward confidently and embrace the journey. There's always time to tweak your work later. You just have to get it out there!

Limitations and Fears

Limiting Mindset

Worrying about being rejected or judged can stop you from promoting yourself and your coaching services. This fear, rooted in limiting thoughts, can make it tough to get clients and grow your practice. It's important to know not everyone will connect with your approach, but those who do will benefit greatly from your guidance. When fear or your limitations take control of your mindset, you start to avoid change and then stay in your comfort zone.

Thinking that failure is bound to happen, or success is impossible due to your limitations, can be paralyzing. It can stop you from taking risks or trying new things. I experienced this during my start, and I was physically and mentally exhausted. I stayed in my comfort zone, stuck to my routine, and avoided any new projects. Later I recognized that my fears stemmed from a lack of confidence and worrying about what others think, so I worked hard to move past this limiting mindset and only accepted happy thoughts and opportunities that supported the life and business I wanted to create. It's crucial to realize that failure is not always going to happen, and you can succeed if you work hard and are open to learning and changing. These are self-limiting beliefs, and it's time to think differently and more proactively.

Empowering Mindset

To overcome limitations, I advise my clients to practice more in areas where they feel restricted. I believe that competence comes from learning and practicing, leading to improved confidence. Keep yourself in check by scheduling time for journaling and reflection or create a vision board that reflects the person you want to become, the type of practice you desire, and the goals you aim to achieve. Develop affirmations based on these ideas and repeat them daily. When negative thoughts start creeping in, take time to reflect or journal. Tony Robbins often emphasizes that changing your thoughts can influence your mood and actions.

———

Navigating stress and overcoming a limiting mindset when building a coaching practice is an integral part of the journey toward success. When you recognize the impact of these stressors, only then can you transform these challenges into opportunities for growth. By understanding why you started coaching, you can transform your thoughts and break free from self-doubt.

Just think of the positive impact you can make on others and use that as your driving force. During the start of your journey, I cannot emphasize enough the importance of managing stress, fostering resilience, and maintaining a positive approach to everything. By mastering an empowering mindset, you can also achieve a fulfilling and successful coaching practice.

I can go on all day about stress management strategies and business practices, but it all comes down to strengthening your mind and keeping your focus. If there's one thing to take away from this chapter, let it be a reminder of the passion that led you to coaching, helping you not just become a coach, but an extraordinary force for positive change. Remember why you started.

Mindful Release

This stress management technique combines mindfulness, visualization, and physical relaxation to help aspiring life coaches release stress related to self-limiting beliefs and foster a positive mindset. These steps are to be performed in sequence, so you may identify the negative thought, visualize its release, and then focus on positive affirmations.

Identification of Stress and Limiting Belief

Begin by acknowledging the specific stressors and self-limiting beliefs causing anxiety in your coaching practice journey.

Mindful Breathing

Find a quiet space and sit comfortably. Close your eyes and take slow, deep breaths. Inhale positive energy and exhale stress, visualizing the release of tension.

Visualization of Stress

As you continue breathing, visualize the stress taking a tangible form. It could be a dark cloud, heavy weight, or any image that represents your stress.

Mindful Release

With each exhale, imagine releasing this stressor from your body. Visualize it dissipating or floating away, leaving you feeling lighter and more at ease.

Affirmations and Reframing

Introduce positive affirmations related to the self-limiting belief. Challenge the negative thoughts by reframing them into positive, empowering statements. For example, if the belief is "I'm not good enough," affirmations could include "I am a skilled and impactful life coach," or "I am confident in my ability to help others succeed."

Grounding

Now bring your awareness to the present moment. Feel the support of the ground beneath you. You can even touch an object nearby to anchor yourself to the present.

Progressive Muscle Relaxation (PMR)

(Your eyes should still be closed.) Starting from your toes, tense and then relax each muscle group progressively moving up to your head. This physical relaxation enhances the mental release.

Nature Imagery

Visualize a serene natural setting—perhaps a calming beach or a peaceful forest. Picture yourself in this space, away from stress.

Guided Imagery for Success

Lastly, create a mental image of yourself successfully navigating challenges in your coaching practice. Imagine positive interactions with clients and the joy of accomplishment.

Closing Mindfully

Slowly open your eyes and take a moment to appreciate the sense of calm and empowerment.

About the Author

Jennifer Richardson is a certified life coach practitioner, proud mother, and an advertising honours graduate with over two decades of experience in professional and personal development, business, and marketing. She started her coaching journey as a volunteer mentor, devoting more than a decade helping young women and aspiring entrepreneurs. Jennifer later obtained certification as a life coach and started practicing part-time until officially transitioning to full-time coaching in 2018.

Having weathered numerous life challenges, Jennifer's experiences have shaped her into the person she is today. She dedicates herself to the service of helping others and shares innovative strategies wherever possible. Jennifer has redefined her practice, specializing in stress management, the promotion of happiness, and the rediscovery of one's best self. Her passion is her family and helping others navigate stress, rejuvenate their careers, and uncover a newfound sense of happiness.

Download Jennifer's other free activity, Mindful Beginnings, at: RediscoverHappiness.com/mindful-beginnings-activity

Email: contact@rediscoverhappiness.com
Website: RediscoverHappiness.com
LinkedIn: @jennifer-richardson-rediscover-happiness
Instagram: @rediscoverhappiness_
YouTube: @rediscoverhappiness
Facebook: @rediscoverhappiness

CHAPTER
23

Flip Your S.C.R.I.P.T©:
From Fiction to Reality

By Nick C.I. Schaart, MBCI
Founder of S.C.R.I.P.T.©, Resilience Expert, Neurocoach
Haarlem, North Holland, The Netherlands

If you can dream it, you can do it.

—WALT DISNEY

Internal Restaurant–Café of Your Choice

*Y*ou are drinking coffee at a table next to a window, gazing, and minding your own business. Music is playing and people are talking and laughing out loud. It is your favorite place to be to relax on your free Saturday mornings. Suddenly a famous Hollywood producer walks right up to you.

PRODUCER X

Good morning, so nice to see you! I'm producer X. Tom Cruise, Steven Spielberg, and I noticed you from across the street. I am working with them on a new Hollywood film, and I think you are the perfect person to play a role in this film. If you like the script and you agree to participate in the film, I am willing to pay you five million dollars.

YOU

Uh ...

———

Chances are you will be a little excited, maybe a little shocked, or maybe even a little scared, right? What I would like is for you to play with me for a moment. See where this comes together. Let's assume that after several weeks of testing and conversations / discussions, you agree to take on this challenge and that you will do your very best to play this role. You sign the agreement, he hands you the script, and now you have agreed to this role.

What do you do first? If you really want to master the role and make sure that people believe you when you act and filming has started, then I imagine you first practice by reading the script and acting (playing) the role you imagine in your head. You do this over and over again, for as long as you need until you actually feel comfortable playing it. And I imagine with practice, in your mind and through your behavior, you begin to integrate the role from the script, and you start to become the role because you have become more and more familiar with the role as time goes on, right? What if this would happen in your life? What would you believe, feel, and do? Is this not realistic, more like fiction?

Flip Your S.C.R.I.P.T.©

*A lot of people will tell you that you can't do it,
that you don't have what it takes, but if it is in
your heart and you feel it, there is nothing that*

will stop you. It is like the sun–you can't block it: it
will shine regardless, if that is what you want.

—Tom Cruise

It is really possible with the right script for you. Therefore, I've created S.C.R.I.P.T.© It is the basis of realizing your profound want, your need. It is not like the law of attraction, which states that if you say a lot of affirmations, etc., then the universe will provide. And on your terms. No, sometimes hard work and endurance are needed. Also—acceptance, when the result doesn't or didn't go exactly at the pace or in the shape as you want or wanted it to be. However, with the right focus, mindset, and trust in the process, it will happen. It will bring you happiness, wealth, health, relationships, and so on. Fake it until you make it, with the right S.C.R.I.P.T.©

Take on the Leading Role

What does S.C.R.I.P.T.© stand for? It is a method to clarify in detail what you desperately want. Why do I say "desperately"? There must be a great sense of urgency, a big need. So much so that you will go the extra mile to get the results you envision. Feeling it in all your veins and already feeling the emotions when you will succeed. With the slightest doubt, the path will be cloudy, and the results will be less impactful. You, yourself, a coach, or an accountability partner must keep you accountable if you won't or don't take the action steps you need to take. However simple or small the steps might be. Every detail counts. This system will give you direction. It will pull you to your goal instead of pushing. It will make it sustainable and repetitive; a way of living.

Your S.C.R.I.P.T.© in the Spotlight

It is urgently time to transform aspects of your life. Go for what you dream of. Get rid of the negative stuff and keep focusing on the positive outcome. Individuals, as well as coaches, can use S.C.R.I.P.T.© Coaches can use it as a tool for an intake and for a structure to do multiple sessions. In that case, it takes a minimum of six hours, one session of one hour for each character in the word S.C.R.I.PT.©

In this section I will cover the intake option. It will take a maximum of one hour to create a script. The client does the work, and you will guide them through it with helpful NLP techniques. It will give them an idea of which direction they have to go in order to transform and get the results they envision. The main goal of this intake for you, the coach, is showing them, the client, that you are the person to come to in order to enable them to overcome their obstacles and achieve their goals, or at least help in finding a way to do so. Keep asking questions and exploring their world model. What's going on within them? What do they really want?

Most essential is that you put the whole S.C.R.I.PT.© in their circle of influence. The client is the director. The client has to play the starring role and has to act. If they don't have an answer to a profound question, then you can ask: "What if you would know it? What would be the answer?" It is a cognitive thing. It takes the pressure off things. People are sometimes doubtful and don't dare to say their answer immediately. By asking this question, the doubt diminishes, and they say: "Then the answer would be …" Nine out of ten times this will work.

The Six Steps of S.C.R.I.PT.©

1. Scenario—Defining the Goal

Find out what the client really wants. You can do that in so many ways. My way is doing a visualization, a NLP technique. For example, the Dickens process. It is important that people can "dream" freely with no limitations. Ask what they see, hear, feel, and when applicable, smell or taste. Make it as vivid and positive as possible. In doing so, the client experiences emotions. It stimulates the production of dopamine, endorphins, and serotonin, which are happy hormones that will lift them up and make them want to achieve their goal even more. It will be a great anchor to hold on to. Especially if the client wants to quit during the process of "playing" the chosen role.

Ask at least every time: "What do you want, and what will be your role?" If the client isn't into visualizing, you can use the analogy of a favorite book or piece of music. People need to feel, see, and find out what they yearn for. That's key in this phase. Explore the need and the role. The role is necessary to know for establishing context. When you look at the Disney strategy, a NLP technique, then this is the part where Walt and his team start to dream. In order to do that, create a safe environment for your client first, so they can go—

To infinity and beyond!

—Buzz Lightyear

When the client knows the goal, they create an inspiring storyboard. Together with you, as coach, they determine what is the best way to record it—as a vision board, a drawing, a written text, a video, or an audio, etc. It has to be visible and/or tangible. Eventually the actor in the S.C.R.I.P.T.© must be held accountable for the "acting."

2. Continuity—Defining the Obstacles and Options to Stay Resilient

Find out what your client is really afraid of. Will they be left alone if they will be the star in their movie? What will be the "costs"? Breakups, bankruptcy, illness, or loneliness? What is keeping them from achieving their goals? What is their trigger? Again, it is essential that the coach puts the obstacle(s) within the control of the client, so they cannot blame their parents, significant other, or the weather. The actor must think of their own lines, exercising their influence.

You often see people are holding themselves back. "No time," they say. In this case, they don't take responsibility for their actions. By changing their time management, they can create more time for themselves or loved ones. Take control. The show must go on! Questions to ask are:

- What keeps you from achieving your goal?
- What is essential to hold on to in this scenario?

People have standards and values, like freedom, safety, harmony, or logic. It is important to take these into account. If people can't act congruently with those, the script is doomed to fail. It is a fact that people want to be consistent with their self-image. For example, when I see myself as rich, I am rich, and then I will do everything in my power to hold on to that identity. So, buying clothes to look rich is one of those actions.

If you dare, depending on the safety setting you already managed to create for your client, you can ask in what way they are stopping themselves from achieving their goal or doing certain things. Maybe you discover a pattern which you, as a coach, will be able to break, so they can turn their fiction into reality anyway. In this stage you need to find out what is crucial to hold on to: relationships, income, health, etc., and what are the resources, e.g., people, a network, materials, or a skillset, required to make the dream come true. Your inquiry:

What are the dependencies and what are the resources required to obtain your goal?

Maybe not all resources are available in the time of need. However, the assumption is that we, as individuals, have all the resources within us. As coach, it is your job to let the client come up with more options to achieve their goal. What can be done to make it possible anyway? Having one option is like a machine, two options is like a dilemma, and three or more options is freedom of choice. That's real resiliency.

3. Result—Defining the Outcome: Make It Smartie and Vibrant

Let the client, with your assistance as coach, make their goal:

- Specific
- Measurable
- Achievable
- Relevant
- Timely
- Inspiring
- Engaging

Add as much data as needed. How much do you want to earn? What kind of skills do you need to learn, and in what amount of time, that helps you to achieve your goal? Is an education really relevant or are you procrastinating? Ask as many questions as you can think of to make it entirely SMARTIE for your client. The result must have an inspiring, pulling effect. Make it vibrant, so the client can persevere, conquer, and go all the way. Also, the engaging aspect is important. What are the pros and cons? Are they in line with the values of the client? When that's the case, the client will stay eager to do the work.

4. Impact—Defining Who or What Will Benefit

In this step, you help your clients to map out what impact their S.C.R.I.P.T.©
will have on whom or what. First of all, on your client. Let them make a drawing of five circles, like a ripple effect. Put the client in the center of the circle
and determine with them who will experience a positive effect as well. For
example: the partner in the second circle around the center, kids and parents
in the third circle, friends in the fourth, and colleagues in the fifth. It can also
be done with money, health, skills/intelligence, career, and things like a place
to live. This phase is to show in which areas the impact is going to be.

5. Plan—Defining the Small Simple Steps

This is the most relevant phase for you as a coach. In this phase, you can
show your added value by helping your clients to plan the process to overcome the obstacles, to determine how to hold them accountable when they
threaten to relapse, and to help them eventually to achieve their goal in the
role and with the result they have put down in their S.C.R.I.P.T.© Break it
down into small, simple steps for them.

I talked earlier about "the intake option." In this part, you can show
what you will do in order to help your client, which tools you will use, and
how many sessions you will need. Always giving the client the control. They
are the director, and you will be the assistant. Your client needs to see in what
time and what steps they can transform and turn their dream/goal into reality.
Otherwise, the client will go elsewhere.

To make that happen, "write" the plan:

- Positive
- Sensorially perceptible: see, hear, or/and feel
- Within the control of the client
- In an appropriate context, e.g., work or private life
- Engaging

You can do it coach!

6. Try Out—Time to Play!

End the S.C.R.I.P.T.© with your client playing their role in the "as-if" frame. It can be done by visualization or by taking one or more small steps. These steps make it easier for your client to achieve the goal. Taking steps creates movement.

By visualizing, the client will be able to imagine how it will be when they achieve the goal. The client looks back on the journey towards the goal. You can assist with that. This way of working has the following advantages:

- It makes it more realistic for them to play the role.
- They are able to associate with the setting in which they already achieved their goal.
- They feel, hear, and/or see the result and impact. They will feel differently, and it can give them new insights. For example, changed beliefs, seeing new people, and having created and persevered in their habits.

You can close the session by proposing several sessions to your client to be or seeing them the next session. Make sure to celebrate when you both made progress and created successes. Good luck client and coach! And they lived happily ever after.

ACTIVITY

S.C.R.I.P.T.© In a Nutshell

Scenario—Wants and Needs

1. Create a safe environment for the client.
2. Do a visualization, so the client can "dream" without limitations.
3. Ask the questions: "What do you want? In what role?" (for context).
4. Record the outcome in the most appropriate way (vision board, drawing, etc.).

Continuity—Values and Resilience

1. Define the relevant values of the client.
2. Define their obstacles and independencies: What keeps you from achieving your goal and what is essential (can't do without values) to hold on to in this scenario?
3. Define the resources they need: What are the dependencies and what are the resources required to obtain your goal?
4. Prerequisite: We have all the resources in us.
5. Let the client come up with options to get and stay resilient during the process of achieving their precious goal.

Result—*SMARTIE and Vibrant*

1. Use the SMARTIE analogy to make it tangible for the client.
2. Make it possible to see and record the progress.
3. Be able to hold them accountable.

4. Don't forget the "inspiring" aspect for the pulling effect. Make it vibrant!
5. Always take the "engaging" aspect into account.

Impact—Circle of Influence

1. Determine the impact the client wants to make.
2. Draw five circles like a ripple effect and put the client's name in the center.
3. Explore with the client the people or areas in which the scenario has an impact on.

Plan—One Small Step for Man, But a Giant Leap for Mankind!

1. Break down the steps the client has to take.
2. Make them as small as possible, so the client will experience progress quickly.
3. Make it at least positive and sensory-perceptible.

Try Out—You Can Dream It. If So, You Can Do It!

1. Create a setting where the client can take the first step or visualize the goal as if the goal is already achieved by acting in their new identity.
2. Let the client reflect on their insights.
3. Celebrate them on the work done.

You and your clients will soon turn your fiction into reality with S.C.R.I.P.T.©

About the Author

Nick Schaart is a resilience expert, and his purpose is to enlighten people by helping them to lift their burden and set them into the light of becoming—more—themselves. He transformed his life several times in some extreme ways.

He is a highly individualistic, neurodivergent man and believes in the resiliency of people. He thinks out of the box and sees hardly any limitations. He helps like-minded people to create an enlightened life.

The impact of S.C.R.I.P.T.© is positive, huge, and sustainable. This multilayered method has become Nick's way of living and hopes that coaches will put it in their Life Coaching's toolbox.

Nick is an influence psychologist and studies the way people choose. He is a NLP practitioner, neuro/systemic coach, and is writing a book on enlightenment. *Unleash the Power Within* by Tony Robbins was his game changer in life where his biggest transformation started and his S.C.R.I.P.T.© came successfully to light.

Email: welcome2scipt@gmail.com
Website (in Dutch): www.nickschaart.nl
Learn more about S.C.R.I.P.T.© on www.flipscript.nl
LinkedIn: https://nl.linkedin.com/in/nickschaart

CHAPTER
24

Believe

By Mary Beth Schrudder
Founder, Day One Life Coaching, Spiritual Coach
Cincinnati, Ohio

You'll see it when you believe it.

—Dr. Wayne Dyer

Your true nature is limitless. You will likely question this fact repeatedly at the beginning of your life coaching career, but I promise you that if you focus on keeping yourself in alignment with your purpose, then you will inevitably attract your dream clients. When your main intention is to be in service to others and you can focus on appreciating your life and your work, the money will naturally follow. You will become a money magnet. You will put yourself in a state of flow. Applying the advice in this chapter will quickly catapult both you *and your clients* into next-level success!

So, how can you do this? For me, spiritual transformation was the key to my success. I used to have horrible habits that affected my body, mind, and spirit. I drank alcohol every day, had a lot of negative thinking, and did not realize my self-worth or potential. My recovery was spiritual. I did not attend

AA or do anything traditional. I knew that if I was able to recover from alcohol abuse (and all the negative things that come along with it) using spiritual methods, then I could also help others do the same. This became my passion.

Maintaining a high vibration and positive mindset by deliberately using law of attraction techniques will put you in alignment to attract the right clients and reach all your career goals. Once you understand and implement these manifestation skills, your personal reality will shift, and the ideal clients will find you. Hustling is not the best approach; it is all about alignment. Align your energy and then take inspired action.

What is the law of attraction? The basic premise is that everything is energy, and we attract people and experiences into our lives based on what we focus on, expect, feel, think, and believe. We attract exactly what we believe we are worth. We even attract what we judge! Essentially, we attract anything that has an energetic spark whether it is in a high or low frequency. The law of attraction does not make mistakes. It is a universal law that exists whether we believe in it or not. This is why it is extremely important to at least learn the basic concepts because it is life-changing information. It is not a religion; it is more like quantum physics. We now have the technology to prove the theories outside of personal experience. If you want to take a deep dive into the scientific views on the law of attraction, I highly recommend researching the work of Dr. Joe Dispenza and Gregg Braden. They do an amazing job marrying science and spirituality. I will stick to the basic premises for this chapter.

The easiest way to describe the law of attraction is to think of it like tuning into a radio station. It is impossible to hear what is playing on an FM station when you are tuned in to an AM station. We are like magnets constantly sending, receiving, and attracting on an energetic level. In essence, unless you are going out of your way to deliberately change your thoughts and feelings, you might be tuned in to a frequency that is blocking your dream clients and success. In other words, unless we are energetically in alignment with our desires, we are inadvertently attracting the absence of our desires.

Once you learn how to line up your energy with your desires, manifesting them will feel effortless. Can you make things happen by taking physical action only? Sure, taking action steps will eventually get you there, but it will feel forced and much more difficult. Applying law of attraction principles is like taking a quantum leap as opposed to baby steps. The key is in changing your point of attraction, which consists of (1) all of your programming and beliefs you have acquired since birth, (2) your momentum on a specific topic, and (3) your current vibration, i.e., how you feel right now about a certain subject.

Much of this reprogramming happens through self-awareness and repetition. We have brainwashed ourselves with limiting beliefs and negative thoughts, and much of this programming occurred during our childhood. The work is in becoming aware of our subconscious personal blocks, catching ourselves, and reprogramming our minds to believe the opposite. The limiting beliefs are never true. According to Abraham-Hicks, a belief is only a thought you keep thinking, and guess who oversees these thoughts—you do! You are not your thoughts, but you can master them once you make a conscious decision to be the witness of your thoughts. Your thoughts do not control you unless you allow them to take over. It is always your decision what thoughts you choose to focus on, so it is important to pay attention to what you are thinking.

Most of us are running on autopilot and think the same thoughts and have the same feelings as we had the day before. Then we wonder why our lives never change. According to writer and lecturer Bruce Lipton, subconscious programs are in control of 95% of our lives. He also states that 70% or more of the downloaded behaviors we acquired before the age of 7 are programs of limitation, disempowerment, and self-sabotage. This is why it is extremely important to bring this subconscious programming to the conscious mind where we can change it.

The simple law of attraction manifestation formula is Ask + Believe = Receive. Guess which step everyone gets stuck on? That's right, *believe*! We can only create within our personal belief system, so this is why we see varied results with people when they first attempt to apply law of attraction teachings. We must learn to change our own limiting beliefs if we ever hope to help our clients change theirs. Your clients will argue for their limitations. Try not to give up too easily on a client because some of my most difficult clients have turned into my biggest success stories.

My favorite technique to help my clients change their subconscious programming is called "afformations." It is different than "affirmations," which are defined as positive statements. Afformations are in the form of a question instead of a statement. The purpose is to help shift the subconscious mind in the areas we do not quite *believe* yet. Our thoughts and feelings must be in alignment if we expect to manifest something into our physical reality. This is why afformations work. Instead of trying to convince yourself of something you do not believe yet with a positive affirmation such as, "I am abundant in all areas of my life" (when you clearly are not abundant yet), *ask* instead, "How did I become so abundant in all areas of my life?" Your subconscious mind will immediately look for ways to line you up with abundance! It is a wonderful tool to help both you and your clients break the negative thinking cycle and believe in yourselves again. We must recondition our subconscious to believe and know our worth, and until we line up our feelings with our words, these afformations will help bridge the gap for you and your clients until the new belief is established.

Why does this technique work so well to crush negative programming and fear-based beliefs? Our subconscious mind has no sense of humor. It does not distinguish between the past, present, and future. In fact, our subconscious mind does not even discern between our reality and our imagination! This question method will switch your subconscious mind into action mode and start searching for solutions. According to science, we are not stuck with our conditioned thoughts from childhood. We can reprogram our brains, and the term for this is "neuroplasticity." It is defined as the ability of neural networks in the brain to change. We can rewire our brains even if we have had the same programming since we were 5 years old. Your subconscious mind will believe whatever you tell it, so it is time to start focusing on the future you want to create and get rid of those fear-based lies you keep telling yourself.

Some believe that the reticular activating system (RAS) is the only way we manifest. The reticular activating system is a bundle of nerves that sits in your brainstem, and its job is to regulate behavior, consciousness, and motivation. We have all experienced the phenomenon where we decided we wanted to purchase a certain car, for example. Let's say it was a white Toyota Supra. Suddenly, we begin to see white Toyota Supras *everywhere* when we never saw them before making this decision. The reticular activating system plays a role in these occurrences; however, the energetic law of attraction is also attracting these experiences to you. They work in unison to deliver synchronicities, serendipities, and spiritual rendezvous right to you. This is following the path of least resistance.

Allowing the universe to conspire and introduce you to the right people at the perfect time is going to take your coaching business to the next level. When your energy is in alignment, you will feel inspired to act, and it will feel exciting, not like an action you are forcing simply because it is your job. My point is to take advantage of the way your reticular activating system works so beautifully with the law of attraction and be sure to follow that inspiration that comes to you. Pay attention to the signs the universe is sending you and listen to your inner guidance. We always get signs, but most people stay way too distracted with their devices and work, so they forget to pay attention to the guidance.

How do we hear our inner guidance when we are so distracted? The answer is remaining present as often as possible throughout the day. I like to start my morning out with 15 minutes of silence or a guided meditation when my mind feels too busy. Breathwork is another powerful tool to get you grounded, back into your body, and in the state of consciousness that will allow you to "hear" your inner being, leading you on the path of least resistance toward your career and personal goals. If you only have a moment, put your hand over your heart and simply take a few deep breaths. Do this several times throughout the day to line up your energy. I also set my phone alarm for times throughout the day as a reminder to just be in the present moment.

Keep your focus on the future you wish to create. When you start worrying and doubting yourself, try to catch yourself and return to the future vision you wish to create. Visualize yourself successful, busy, giving speeches, and having a huge waiting list of clients. Your imagination is powerful. This is powerful advice, not only for you but also for your coaching clients! Like the Dr. Wayne Dyer quote at the beginning of the chapter states, "You'll see it when you believe it." Change your beliefs, and you will change your life. Never forget that you create your personal reality, so be sure to make it a magical one.

Morning and Evening Routine Prompts

Morning Meditation Prompts

Today I am so excited because _____.
My focus for today is _____.
Three small goals I will accomplish today are _____.
One big goal I will accomplish today is _____.

Evening Meditation Prompts

Goals I accomplished today are _____.
Things I did today that made a positive impact are _____.
Today I learned that _____.
Three things I am thankful for this evening are _____.

About the Author

Mary Beth Schrudder is a Spiritual and Transformational Life Coach. She is founder of Day One Life Coaching, author of *Addiction Recovery with the Law of Attraction,* and the host of the *Spiritual Transformation Podcast with Mary Beth.*

Mary Beth will help you heal addictions and transform relationships, including your relationship with yourself. Her approach is holistic, and her areas of expertise include relationships, marriage, divorce, mindset, happiness, freedom from addictions, optimal fitness, life purpose, and career. As a professional life coach with years of experience, Mary Beth's life-changing coaching will help you step outside of your comfort zone, and together, you will create extraordinary results using innovative techniques.

You may email Mary Beth to schedule a complimentary discovery call at: marybeth@dayonelifecoaching.com

Mary Beth's social media links may be found here:

LinkTree: https://linktr.ee/DayOneLifeCoaching

CHAPTER
25

What Takes You from Pressure to Stress? How Do You Rebalance?

By Alex Webb
Founder, TLRdynamics LTD; Co-founder Resilient Women Leaders
Surrey, England, United Kingdom

*The truth is that stress doesn't come from the boss,
your kids, your spouse, traffic jams, health challenges or other circumstances. It comes from
your thoughts about these circumstances.*

—ANDREW BERNSTEIN

What takes you from pressure to stress? Do you know? Within this chapter we introduce you to our Uncertainty Spectrum from Resilient Leaders Elements (RLE™), a spectrum, which, depending on your levels of resilience and ability to cope, highlights how we cope with pressure and stress, at any point upon it. By building this awareness as to where you are right now, you can start to focus on what you can do to support yourself in bringing yourself back to a state where you can perform at your best. To note: Pressure is motivating and stretching; it makes us want to jump out of bed in the morning. Stress is debilitating and makes us want to hide under the duvet. First, let's introduce you to the two important axes.

Axis 1: What Is the Uncertainty Spectrum?

Coined by RLE™, this spectrum highlights a few things:

1. Where do we do our best work? Is it at—
   a. Equilibrium: We know what is happening each day and nothing much changes.
   b. Change: Things can change on a daily basis, and we have to show flexibility to ensure we stay on track.
   c. Crisis: The pace has picked up, and we're having to make decisions faster and get things done more quickly. We're still in control.
   d. Chaos: We have lost control with things not happening in an organised fashion.
2. As leaders, we are constantly moving up and down this spectrum, depending on our own performance, the behaviours of others, and our environment.

Whilst some of us will do some great work in Crisis, and even Chaos, there is a question of how sustainable that is over extended periods of time. Coping strategies help us to move down the spectrum after periods of heightened uncertainty. Consider what helps you rebalance. Are you looking after yourself, so you can continue performing at your best rather than hitting burnout?

Axis 2: Resilient Leadership—What Do We Mean?

We know that a resilient leader has the capacity to cope when navigating uncertainty, change, or even crisis. The greater their resilience, the greater their ability to make better decisions for themselves, their team, and the organisation. The definition of a resilient leader is as follows:

A resilient leader knows where they are strong and their areas of development, they know what takes them from pressure to stress and how to rebalance. A resilient leader has confidence in who they are and what they do so they create, build, and take opportunities, bouncing back, knowing they will find a way through uncertainty, change, and even crisis. (RLE™ 2024)

To increase our levels of resilience, we need to build awareness of where we are on this spectrum at any given time. This understanding helps to devise ways of managing events that we are not used to, or not expecting, and discover ways to help us cope and thrive. This awareness will naturally give us an increased ability to cope.

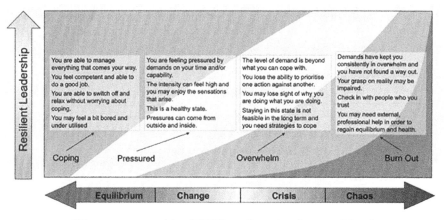

Diagram created by RLE™ co-founder, Jeremy Mead.

When looking at the above diagram, where are you currently? Are you coping? Feeling pressured? In overwhelm? Or feeling burnt out/unwell? We want you to be able to stay in Coping and Pressured and help you find ways of moving from Overwhelm to Pressured.

What Takes You from Pressure to Stress?

Everyone leads in some capacity and being able to lead anywhere on this spectrum is important. Some level of pressure is good; it helps us perform at our best. The more we are aware of our behaviours, the earlier we can notice when we need to rebalance. Developing your understanding and awareness here will help you grow "resilience" muscle. You will have more capacity to cope when events become more challenging. The following exercises are a great way to start building this awareness:

Exercise I: Who Am I at My Best?

When you can visualise who you are at your best, it brings a clearer picture to the person you want to be or want to go back to being.

Step 1: On a piece of paper, list out everything that describes you at your best.

- What are you doing?
- Who are you with?
- What is your environment?
- Are you in a specific place?
- How are you behaving?
- How are other people around you behaving?
- What is your mood?

Step 2: Underneath this list, draw two columns and title the first column "What Helps Me Be at My Best" and the second column "What Hinders Me Being at My Best." In each of these two columns, list all the things that help you be at your best or hinder you from being at your best. For example,

- The amount of sleep you have
- The food you eat
- The exercise you do, including physical and meditative
- The type of work you're involved with
- The mood of those around you (radiators or drainers)
- The behaviours of those around you

- Writing a list
- Feeling in control versus overwhelmed through procrastination
- The type of environment in which you thrive
- The time you spend on your phone

Step 3: Reflection Notes

Look at each list separately and rank each statement, number one having the most impact on you. By completing this exercise, it reminds you of the person you want to be—the high-performing you. It also highlights the things you can do to support yourself when you start moving up the Uncertainty Spectrum. Even if you just focus on the top three "What Helps Me" behaviours, this will provide coping strategies to keep you performing at your best. Remind yourself of your top "What Hinders Me" list and make every effort to remove those from your day.

So, what do you need to do more of or less of to keep yourself performing at your best? Note: Once completed, print this out, so you are reminded of your "Helps" and "Hinders." You could even share it with your team/family, so they can support you in being the best version of you too.

Exercise 2: Your Triggers

This exercise aims to give you greater awareness of those things that contribute to you moving you up the Uncertainty Spectrum. With this awareness of your triggers comes the ability to do something about it.

Step 1: Identify Your Triggers

1. What is it? Is it getting stuck in traffic or a certain meeting or situation?
2. Who is it? Seventy-six percent of stress at work is due to people.
3. Where is it? Is it in a certain environment? Work? Home?
4. When is it? When you're running late or you're up against a deadline?

Answering these questions is increasing your awareness of yourself and how you react to things, other people, and the environment.

Step 2: **Manage the Impact**

Knowing your triggers means you can do something about it. For each of your answers in Step 1, imagine a different response. What could be a calmer approach? How could better communication support you? Are your assumptions getting in your way? What happens if you lead with empathy over opinion? Is your ego stopping you from being more open? You get the picture.

Step 3: **Reflection**

What one thing are you going to change? What different response are you going to commit to? What impact will that have? Visualise the scenario and how the levels of stress reduce due to your new response.

Exercise 3: Asking for Support

We are often hardwired to think that asking for help shows weakness. It shows that we're not good at our job. This is a myth. Think back to Exercise 1. Our aim is to keep to the left on the Uncertainty Spectrum. This allows us to work more effectively as we are more energised and at our best. Question: What does it feel like when someone asks you for support, for your advice, or for your help? It feels good, doesn't it? So why deny that gift to other people?

Step 1: **What Support Do You Need from Others?**

From your reflections in Exercise 1 and Exercise 2, you now have greater awareness of who you want to be and what is stopping you from getting there. Who do you need to get involved to help you make progress? Is it your spouse? A family member? A colleague? A boss? Maybe you have something to ask each one of them. Do you need someone just to listen without judgement? Ask them. Do you need someone to bring you a cup of coffee/juice when you're struggling? Ask them. Do you need someone to say thank you more often or show appreciation because you need it? Ask them. Do you need someone to get you away from your desk, so you have time for your mind to settle or rest? Ask them.

Whatever you need from someone to help you be at your best and to help change your trigger response, ask them. The more you are clear on what you need, the easier it will be to ask for the right support. In an increasingly complex world, we can't do this alone, and as the African proverb says, "If you want to go fast, go alone. If you want to go far, go together." As a leader, whether you're leading yourself, your family, your team, or your organisation, the more you open up and ask for support, the more others will do the same, creating a more open and trusting environment.

Conclusions

Knowing what takes you from pressure to stress brings greater clarity. You now have the tools to be able to visualise yourself performing at your best, knowing what helps you and what gets in your way. With this more developed clarity comes focus, and with focus, comes energy. This energy helps us start to make changes and increases confidence that we can find a way through anything that comes our way, wherever we are on the Uncertainty Spectrum. Focusing on what helps us be at our best gives us permission to prioritise ourselves in this moment.

You have identified your triggers and understand some simple changes you can make, accepting them as triggers and potentially choosing a different response. You've also considered who you're going to go to for support, giving them the gift of knowing they are valued and helping to create a more open and trusting environment in which you can thrive.

> *The first step toward change is awareness.*
> *The second step is acceptance.*
>
> —NATHANIEL BRANDEN

All of the above exercises have come from our ReNew You programme—a five-week course designed to support people with a need to refocus, rebalance, and re-energise when they have lost a bit of confidence in who they are and what they do! It has been developed based on the Japanese concept of *ikigai*—your reason for being—your direction or purpose in life. As part of our five-week programme, you will get the opportunity to explore your beliefs and values, who you are at your best, and how the roles and relationships that surround you can energise as well as de-energise you. To bring even more to your clients, join us for this complete programme experience at www.tlrdynamics. com/courses or https://resilientwomenleaders.com/renew-you/

ACTIVITY

See *Exercise 1*, *Exercise 2*, and *Exercise 3* within the chapter.

You can find more information and activities using the RLE™ by reading Chapter 4 –Building confidence and self-worth — written by Skye Deane co-founder of RWL.

About the Author

Alex Webb is a business and leadership behaviour coach working with individuals and teams to optimise their performance and build organisational health through self-awareness, leadership, and resilience development.

Starting her career in education and teaching, Alex has had a mixed career within events, sports TV and media, entrepreneurship, and technology. With her roles as an Events Director and Programme Director, Alex has created, designed, and facilitated workshops, events, and programmes for an array of ages, including clients such as TfL, Innovate UK, UK Trade and Investment, Prince's Trust, Nectar, Sky, Vodafone, Coca-Cola, Umbro, Lego, AXA, and GSK.

Following a change in priorities, after having a family, Alex worked alongside one of the Dragons from Dragons Den, learning entrepreneurship and the basics of building and growing a business. Using these skills and her experience in the events, sports, and business worlds, Alex runs TLRdynamics Ltd, focusing on developing leadership skills and high performance, motivating and inspiring leaders to be confident in both what they do and who they are, wherever they are on their career journey.

With a passion for supporting women leaders, knowing the impact of imposter syndrome and lack of confidence following her time out to have her family, Alex, alongside her business partner Skye Deane, created Resilient

Women Leaders in 2020. This was an opportunity to focus on developing the capabilities of women leaders, so they can lead through uncertainty, overcoming the seven commonly shared barriers that keep women from reaching their full potential. (Research RLE™ Women as Resilient Leaders (WaRL) March 2020 and 2023).

Alex has worked across many industries including pharmaceutical, technology, TV & media, education, telecommunications, charity, and FMCG. Her knowledge of working with B2B and B2C gives Alex great experience to guide clients with their development needs.

Alex's qualifications include accreditation in C-Me™ Colour Profiling, Resilient Leadership Elements, and The Six Types of Working Genius. She is a facilitator in Positive Intelligence and Lego Serious Play, a qualified teacher, and possesses over 25 years of experience in business, events, and facilitation. Alex is an international sports coach, tutor, assessor, and gold medalist, as well as author of the FSXP "How To ..." series on enabling employability for school leaders and graduates available on Kindle, Amazon, and Audible.

Emails:
alex@tlrdynamics.com
hello@resilientwomeleaders.com

Websites: tlrdynamics.com
resilientwomenleaders.com
flyingstartxp.com
Facebook: facebook.com/TLRdynamics/
facebook.com/FlyingStartXP
Instagram: @tlrdynamics
@flyingstartxp_2016
Twitter: @tlrdynamics
@flyingstartxp
Linkedin: https://www.linkedin.com/in/alex-webb-nee-spring/

CHAPTER

26

The Self-Compassionate Way to Stop Second-Guessing

By Sabrina Vogler, CPC, CEC, CGSS
Life and Executive Coach, Grief Specialist
Asheville, North Carolina

Safety is not the absence of threat; it is the presence of connection.

—Dr. Gabor Maté

If you were to ask me which client concern stands out head and shoulders above the rest when coaching, I'd have to say self-compassion because there's nothing that will stand in your client's way more than *your client.* So then, how do you help stop this form of self-sabotage?

I'm here to walk you through the ins and outs of second-guessing, overthinking, perseverating, ruminating, and all the other fancy phrases that reduce your clients to begging for an exit ramp out of their overactive minds. Spoiler alert: The secret to helping your clients stop second-guessing is the *opposite* of what you might think. Keep reading to find out why!

What You'll Walk Away Knowing:

- A simple way to understand *why* second-guessing happens in the first place
- A four-step tool for calming the stressed-out body, clearing the mental cobwebs, healing the heart's wounds, and invigorating the beleaguered spirit

Are you ready? Great. Let's dive in!

What Is Second-Guessing Anyway?

Take me out to the ballgame ... Do you know that familiar jingle? This phrase emerged in the late 1930s to describe hecklers criticizing and judging the umpire's decisions from the baseball bleachers. Thus, the term "second-guessing" was born.

Why Do We Do It?

Rule #1 for humans will always be the same: safety at all costs. If there's even a remote chance that your client's decisions or actions could invite criticism or judgment, your client's brain will kick into high gear fast. Because, let's face it, the body, mind, heart, and spirit are all impacted by the threat of discomfort. The brain's way of minimizing this danger and creating safety is to revert to storytelling. The story attempts to make sense of a stressful situation by retelling it in a way that identifies who and what is to blame.

You'll notice the story spun by your clients is judgmental and negatively biased. This is because somewhere along the way humans learned that it's safer to assume the worst and adopt a negative outlook—just in case a saber-toothed tiger is nearby. Those who believed the worst escaped with their lives far more often than the open-minded and optimistic ones. In addition, self-criticism is a surefire proactive way to prevent looking foolish. If you berate yourself before anyone else can, you can modify your behavior before the critical external world rejects you. The idea is that remonstrating yourself for past mistakes allegedly prevents them from repeating in the future.

So, now that you understand the judgmental nature of your client's inner narrative, let's talk more about its function. This mini-novella is supposed to put you out of your misery by forcing some clear conclusion that eliminates all "threats" of ambiguity. Regardless of accuracy, this second-guessing story is told and retold on an endless loop. Each time the story repeats, the brain's reward center releases dopamine into the blood supply. Oddly enough, the story that makes you miserable produces an addictive reward, which then demands its retelling.

So, how do you help your clients defeat the threat and retire the second-guessing? Dr. Gabor Maté's quote offers that you create safety by connecting supportively with your clients. And that's not all. Teaching self-compassion to your clients helps them connect with themselves in a whole new way. Here's a tool that enables you to do exactly that.

The Four-Stepper Tool

Preface

Interrupting the emotionally hijacked state of second-guessing first requires that you set the stage with a statement of intent. It begins with some version of this three-part script based on Mindful Self-Compassion co-founder, Dr. Kristin Neff's *Self-Compassion Break:*

1. *This is a moment of second-guessing myself.*
2. *Second-guessing is a natural part of being human.*
3. *I'm choosing at this moment to pause and support myself.*

You can encourage your client to make these phrases their own, which is one of the most crucial self-compassion skills. Now that you've helped your client start with this script, it's time to activate step one of the Four-Stepper Tool.

Step One: Home Base

This step addresses your client's nervous system. As the body eavesdrops on second-guessing, it kicks into the stress response and cues up the self-critical story. That's why it's so essential to begin by calming the body. Besides, changing thinking patterns and shifting emotions is much more challenging without first feeling calm and comforted. The easiest way to help your client cue up a grounded state is by following the home base steps:

- Take three full, nourishing, deep breaths while lengthening the exhales. Breathing this way calms the alarmed body.
- Direct the exhale down the body through the feet into the ground while sinking into the solid surface of the chair and ground below.
- Place a hand or two on the heart while focusing on the weight and warmth of the hand. This practice activates the primal human circuity shared by all mammals. It releases a cascade of neurochemicals like oxytocin and naturally occurring opioids into the bloodstream, lowers cortisol levels, and creates a sensation of peaceful connection.
- Assess and address physical needs: hunger, thirst, fatigue, and body aches. Caring for these needs results in clear thinking and enhanced coping.

Step Two: Erase

Step two focuses on the story that your client wishes they could delete. It's intended to help your client reframe their situation through a fresh, clear perspective. You begin by suggesting that your client imagine they are kind observers of their stories, as if they were playing on a stage. From this balcony view, your client takes a step back from the intensity of the plotline. The balcony perspective invites your client's inner knowing and intuitive wisdom. It creates a way to view themselves through the lens of a supportive and understanding friend. Step two is the following journaling practice:

- Jotting down from the perspective of a kind observer on the balcony: "What second-guessing story do I wish I could erase?"
- Writing down whatever answers arise off the top of your head:

  "This part of me feels …"

  - o Why "this part of me"? Because it's easy to feel like emotions are all one way. And chances are, there's more than one emotion in play.

o   When your client is stressed out and stuck, helping them identify words that describe their specific emotions creates clarity. It redirects the blood flow in the brain from the lower limbic regions (emotionally intense) to the upper brain neocortex (self-composed). The overwhelm can now dissipate at a quicker rate.

"This part of me thinks …"

o   Describing thoughts builds space between the "on-stage self" who is thinking and the "supportive observer" on the balcony. This distance invites flexible open-mindedness instead of rigid self-criticism.

o   When journaling thoughts, the practice is freely writing without concern for grammar or spelling. There are no wrong answers here!

"This part of me believes …"

o   It's easy to believe everything you think when stressed out from second-guessing. This prompt helps your client describe what feels *true* now, even if it seems irrational. You reflect these beliefs back to them without a trace of judgment. You might remind your client that believing everything you think is normal. It's part of the human journey!

"This part of me needs …"

o   One of the central tenets of self-compassion is that unmet needs drive all forms of resistance. This aversion shows up as unwanted feelings or thoughts that cause unrest in the body. Examples of needs are *to be seen, heard, understood, validated, respected, loved, or believed.*

"This part of me notices these body sensations …"

- o   This step invites interoception, a fancy way of describing the ability to notice how your body feels. The more body awareness your client has, the easier it will be for them to calm and care for their stress.

"This part of me wishes I could change …"

- o   Your client might feel their wishes are too far-fetched or unrealistic. Your non-judgmental support as their life coach helps them discern the root of their second-guessing.

Step Three: Supportive Space

It's time to reveal the surprising secret of why ending overthinking is the *opposite* of what you'd expect. The truth is that trying to stop anything just makes it worse. As Carl Jung taught, "What you resist persists." Once your clients tell themselves to stop thinking, the word "stop" cues up the nervous system's response to a high-level threat. The addictive story loop gets reactivated to secure rule #1: safety at all costs.

Dr. Gabor Maté's quote reminds us, "Safety isn't the absence of threat, but the presence of connection." You're guiding a client to find safety in their connection with you as their coach. At the same time, they're learning how to create that safe connection between their kind observer in the balcony and their on-stage self.

And so, the real secret to stopping overthinking is not stopping at all. Instead, it's compassionate connection. Once your client understands their unmet needs from the perspective of a kind observer on the balcony, self-compassion allows your client to talk to themselves in a way that meets that need.

- •   Direct the breath toward the parts of the body that are holding tension.
- •   Place a hand on the heart to activate the caregiving response shared by all mammals.

- Compose an "ally statement" based on the identified unmet need. This statement conveys what your client would say to a good friend in the same situation (or what that friend would say to them). It offers understanding and acceptance without judgment or giving advice.
  - o For instance, if the unmet need is to be seen or heard, your client might say to themselves, "I see you" or "I hear you."
  - o They might remember that feeling this way is part of the human experience.
  - o They might say to themselves, "This is a lot to take. I'm here for you."
  - o Other possibilities might include: "Of course, it makes sense you'd feel this way. I hear you. I understand what makes this so hard for you. I'm here to support you, no matter what, etc."
- If creating an "ally statement" seems challenging, you might encourage your client to practice being present with their feelings without trying to fix them.
- Your client may wish to visualize a supportive figure. Some often-used examples are Mother Teresa, Mr. Rogers, or perhaps a beloved grandmother. They might recall a favorite tree from childhood or a relaxing location like warm sand on a beach.

It's important to mention that the practice of talking to yourself in the same way you'd address a friend will likely feel awkward at first. You can reassure your client that these words don't have to land perfectly. In fact, talking to yourself in a self-compassionate way sometimes causes you to feel worse, which self-compassion refers to as "backdraft." The way around this is encouraging them to respond supportively to their irritation or frustration. As their life coach, you'll want to remind your client to return to the home base step and reground themselves anytime the process of self-understanding triggers feelings of overwhelm.

Step Four: Replace

This final component of *the* Four-Stepper Tool builds upon the three previous ones. As the second-guessing narrative is unpacked, your client is encouraged to write a new ending from the perspective of a kind observer on the balcony:

- What are the most challenging parts of this story?
- What lessons have I learned that will help my future self?
- What can't I change about this story?
    - Am I ready to radically accept what I can't change? If not, can I care for the parts of me that need my kind attention?
- What can I change about this story?
    - Am I ready to take radical responsibility for an action step? If so, what's the first small step I could take?
- This intersection between radically accepting what you can't change and taking radical responsibility for what you can draws upon Reinhold Niebuhr's well-known Serenity Prayer. Here's a diagram to conceptualize that sweet spot:

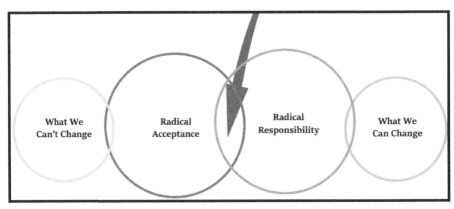

2024 Copyright Heart in the Moment Mindfulness Coaching, LLC.
Please do not reproduce without written permission.

- The new ending to the story invites self-forgiveness of the past self and alignment with the desired future self.
- The good news is that time doesn't restrict self-compassion. That means it's never too early or late to support any aspect of the self with an unmet need.

To sum it all up, you've now walked your client through a framework that interrupts their overwhelm, calms their stress, grants crystal clarity on what's bothering them the most, identifies their unmet needs, and teaches them to comfort their difficult emotions from the perspective of a kind friend. You've empowered them to stop second-guessing themselves and create a brand-new ending to their story. And now that you've helped them get out of their own way, there's no limit to the life you can help them create

The Four-Stepper Tool

Step 1: Home Base

Shift your nervous system from a state of survival into calm connection.

- Take three full, nourishing, deep breaths while lengthening the exhales.
- Send the exhale down the body through the feet into the ground.
- Place a hand or two on the heart.
- Assess and address physical needs: hunger, thirst, fatigue, body aches.

Step 2: Erase

Jot down from the perspective of a kind observer on the balcony:

- What second-guessing story do I wish I could erase?
- This part of me feels …
- This part of me thinks …
- This part of me notices these body sensations …
- This part of me needs …
- This part of me believes …
- This part of me wishes I could change …

Step 3: Supportive Space

- Direct your breath toward the parts of your body that are holding tension.
- Place a hand on your heart.
- Compose an "ally statement" based on your identified unmet need.
    - This reflects what you'd say to a friend in the same situation as you.
    - These words communicate acceptance without judgment or giving advice.
    - For instance, if the unmet need is "being seen" or "being heard," you might say to yourself, "I see you" or "I hear you."
    - Other possibilities: "Of course, it's understandable you'd feel this way. I hear you. I understand what makes this so hard for you. I'm here to support you no matter what, etc."
- If this feels too challenging, practice being present without trying to fix it.

STEP 4: Replace

Compose a new ending to this story from the perspective of a kind observer.

- What are the hardest parts of this story?
- What lessons have I learned that will help my future self?
- What can't I change about this story?
    - Am I ready to radically accept what I can't change? If not, can I care for the parts of me that need my kind attention?
- What can I change about this story?
    - Am I ready to take radical responsibility for an action step? If so, what's the first small step you could take?

2024 Copyright Heart in the Moment Mindfulness Coaching, LLC. Please do not reproduce or distribute without written permission.

About the Author

The first in her industry to introduce self-compassion to one-on-one coaching, Sabrina Vogler trained under program founders at UC San Diego Center for Mindfulness. She is a certified professional coach, executive coach, grief counselor, and globally recognized expert in Mindful Self-Compassion. Her career began in the 1990s as a licensed master social worker in acute medical and hospice settings. Inspired by work with the dying, Sabrina vowed to discover her *No Regrets Life* and help others do the same. Heralded as a "game-changer" and "magical," Sabrina supports diverse clientele, from C-suite executives to soccer moms. She offers empirically studied mind-body practices with a unique blend of neuroscience-based badassery. In addition to coaching, Sabrina is an author, keynote speaker, thought leader, and mama to twin sons.

Email: Sabrina@HeartintheMoment.com
Website: HeartintheMoment.com

CHAPTER
27

Bridging Ancient Wisdom and Modern Science in Life Coaching

By Po Wu, MD
Holistic Wellness and Performance Coach, Neurologist
Vancouver, British Columbia, Canada

The wisdom of the five elements lies in their balance. Nurture each element within yourself and find harmony in their dance.

—CHINESE PROVERB

I n founding and leading an integrative medical practice in New York that fused neurology, sleep medicine, medical acupuncture, and traditional Chinese medicine (TCM), my aim was to harmonize the holistic perspective of TCM with the analytical approach of allopathic medicine. This endeavor transcends conventional symptom-focused treatments and uncovers the root causes of health challenges to achieve overall wellness and balance.

This journey revealed connections between my integrative medical practice and life coaching principles. In particular, the combination of TCM's five elements—wood, fire, earth, metal, and water—with conventional medicine proved potent for treating patients and offered insights into the interconnectedness of physical health, emotional balance, and personal development. TCM's framework, deeply rooted in ancient Chinese philosophy, serves as a powerful tool, going beyond mere representation of natural forces to understanding and enhancing well-being on multiple levels. This chapter merges the ancient wisdom of the five elements with modern neuroscience insights to enhance life coaching. My journey from a traditional medical practice to embracing TCM has been transformative and prompted me to look beyond immediate medical symptoms to the stories and potentials hidden within perceived imbalances.

The Five Elements and Their Dynamics in Life Coaching

Within us, wood, fire, earth, metal, and water each uniquely contribute to our makeup. Typically, one element predominates, shaping our strengths and challenges and playing a crucial role in our personal development. However, some individuals may find two elements equally influential. These elements reflect their diverse impacts on our lives and underscore the importance of harmonizing our dominant element(s) for holistic well-being.

Understanding the five elements involves comprehending the yin and yang principle within each, symbolizing the balance of opposite but complementary forces. Achieving equilibrium between the yin (passive, receptive) and yang (active, expansive) aspects is crucial for harnessing each element's strengths. Additionally, the elements are interconnected and exert influence on one another, maintaining balance within us. As illustrated in Figure 1, the sheng (generating) and ke (controlling) cycles depict this balance: The sheng cycle shows how the elements support the growth of the next, promoting regeneration, while the ke cycle describes how the elements ensure balance by moderating another element to maintain harmony.

Figure 1.

THE FIVE ELEMENTS

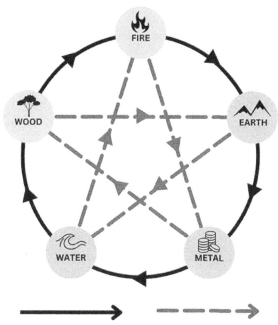

SHENG (GENERATING) CYCLE   KE (CONTROLLING) CYCLE

Example (Fire)
Fire is generated and nurtured by Wood.
Fire is controlled and moderated by Water.
Fire helps generate and nurture Earth.
Fire helps control and moderate Metal.

Coach's Tip

Use the provided questionnaire to identify your client's primary (or dominant) element(s), including their generating and controlling elements according to the sheng and ke cycles. With these insights, develop personalized strategies that leverage your client's elemental strengths and address imbalances. The illustration of the sheng and ke cycles, summary table, and reflection questions are helpful tools for effectively incorporating the five elements framework into your coaching practice. The upcoming sections will delve into each element's emotional and health implications, their correlations with neuroscience, and their application in coaching.

Wood: The Element of Growth and Adaptability

The best time to plant a tree was 20 years ago.
The second best time is now.

—CHINESE PROVERB

In TCM, wood signifies new life, growth, and renewal—mirroring the emergence of spring. Wood's qualities are rooted in the principles of emotional regulation, which entails maintaining composure and flexibility in the face of life's challenges, and adaptability, ensuring smooth transitions through changes. It also embodies strategic and visionary qualities, akin to a sapling striving towards sunlight. Individuals with a dominant wood element radiate with intrinsic motivation, purpose, and the capacity to conceive and execute plans.

Balanced wood manifests as a harmonious blend of flexibility (yin) and determination (yang). Yet, imbalances can stir stress, anger, and frustration, manifesting physically as tension headaches, migraines, muscle stiffness, menstrual irregularities, or digestive discomfort. These physical signs are wood's cry for equilibrium, often accompanied by emotional manifestations like irritability or hasty decisions.

As the proverb goes, "The bamboo that bends is stronger than the oak that resists," highlighting the strength found in adaptability and resilience. Nourishing wood involves immersing oneself in nature, participating in outdoor sports, and practicing yoga or tai chi to enhance physical and mental adaptability. Engaging in creative endeavors, such as art, writing, or entrepreneurial projects, also channels wood's growth potential into productive outlets.

Neuroscience offers a compelling analogy to wood through neuroplasticity, highlighting the brain's remarkable capacity to evolve and adapt its neural connections throughout life. This concept is similar to exercising muscles; mental and physical activities strengthen neural pathways, improving cognitive and emotional health. Imbalances in neural networks, akin to elemental disharmony in TCM, may manifest as mental health challenges. Life coaches can employ cognitive behavioral strategies, mindfulness, and continuous learning to promote neurogenesis and enhance cognitive function. Physical exercise and prioritizing quality sleep further support neuroplasticity, underpinning the balanced attributes of wood. Incorporating sheng and ke cycle principles provides a strategic approach to leveraging wood's dynamics. Water's nurturing influence of intuition and adaptability supports wood's growth while metal's disciplined and organized energy helps moderate wood's expansiveness.

My journey, shaped by the challenges of a first-generation immigrant family, violence, cultural assimilation, and my father's tragic suicide, sowed in me seeds of anger and pain. These feelings propelled me forward but also precipitated stress and health complications. By embracing forgiveness and release, I tapped into wood's capacity for renewal, which guided me towards a path of integrative medicine and wellness coaching. It drove me to nurture resilience and adaptability in others, reflecting wood's essence. My past experiences became the foundation for my holistic well-being and personal development work, allowing me to channel my energy constructively and to embody wood's vitality.

Fire: The Element of Passion and Energy

Thousands of candles can be lit from a single candle,
and the life of the candle will not be shortened.
Happiness never decreases by being shared.

—BUDDHA

In TCM, fire epitomizes summer, embodying warmth and the vibrancy of life. It is closely associated with the heart, recognized not only for its crucial role in our physical well-being but also as the seat of joy, passion, and connection. When harmonious, fire blends warmth and connectivity (yin) with vitality and passion (yang). However, imbalances may lead to restlessness, diminished vitality, or emotional disturbances such as anxiety or detachment. These can be accompanied by physical symptoms like cardiovascular issues, sleep disturbances, and skin inflammation. To nourish fire, engaging in group celebrations, dancing, or pursuing creative hobbies can reignite inner joy and connection. Practices and exercises promoting heart health and mindfulness cultivate a luminous and balanced fire, ensuring both emotional and physical health.

Neuroscience sheds light on fire by examining the brain's emotional regulation networks. These networks enable us to experience joy, maintain emotional balance, navigate social interactions, and build fulfilling relationships. This mirrors the warmth and vitality of a well-tended flame. A balanced fire element in TCM parallels the harmonious functioning of these networks, highlighting the interplay between our emotional health and overall well-being.

Employing principles from the sheng and ke cycles offers strategic ways to balance fire. Wood's growth and visionary qualities nurture fire's expansion while water's introspection and adaptability temper excessive fire, ensuring equilibrium. My journey, marked by a profound personal transfor mation, ignited a passion within me that reshaped my holistic practice and coaching philosophy. It underscored the power of sharing one's inner light and fostering an environment of connection. This path not only led to my own emotional and spiritual balance but also inspired me to guide others in discovering and nurturing their inner fire.

Earth: The Element of Stability and Nourishment

The more you know yourself, the more you know others.

—Lao Tzu

In TCM, earth represents the nourishing essence of late summer, embodying stability, support, and sustenance. Earth's qualities foster empathy, practicality, and a deep-rooted sense of belonging, essential for our well-being and for grounding us in our lives and relationships. Earth in balance radiates stable comfort (yin) and dependable practicality (yang). Imbalance may present as digestive issues, fatigue, muscle weakness, and edema, coupled with emotional states like excessive worry or overthinking that impair adaptability. Nourishing earth calls for grounding activities: connecting with nature, practicing mindful eating, maintaining consistent routines, and being involved in a community. Cultivating gratitude through journaling or meditation enhances a sense of inner fullness and contentment, harmonizing with Earth's nurturing spirit.

Neuroscientifically, earth's stabilizing influence mirrors the default mode network (DMN), active in introspection and identity. Just as earth provides a foundation for growth and connection, the DMN integrates our past and present, continually shaping our narrative. Disruptions in the DMN echo Earth's imbalance, leading to psychological distress. Mindfulness, social engagement, and fostering self-compassion recalibrate the DMN, affirming a balanced, grounded state akin to a well-nourished earth.

Within the sheng and ke cycles, earth's grounded nature is fueled by fire's warmth and connection and balanced by wood's growth and shaping influence. This balance illustrates the importance of harmonizing self-care with adaptability and empathy. Overcoming personal challenges has deepened my empathy and self-awareness, which are foundational to my approach in holistic coaching. Inspired by earth's principles of stability and care, I've navigated my healing journey and have committed to assisting others. Embracing earth's essence enables coaches to offer nurturing guidance, enhancing a sense of belonging and shared humanity, underscoring that understanding oneself is crucial to effectively help others.

Metal: The Element of Clarity and Organization

Letting go gives us freedom, and freedom
is the only condition for happiness.

—THICH NHAT HANH

As autumn unveils its clarity and coolness, the metal element in TCM stands as a symbol of structure, precision, and refinement. Metal encompasses the vital processes of taking in new experiences and releasing what no longer serves us, representing the essential cycle of renewal and letting go. It challenges us to establish our values and boundaries, steering us towards organizational mastery and self-reflection. Imbalance in metal can manifest in a range of physical symptoms, such as respiratory issues including allergies, skin conditions, and digestive disturbances. Emotionally, it might express as difficulty in letting go or coping with change, excessive rigidity in thoughts and behaviors, or a lingering inability to move past old wounds. Unresolved grief is particularly associated with metal imbalance, calling for a reconnection to metal's cleansing and refining energies to process and release these deep-seated emotions.

To nourish metal, practices that instill mindfulness and foster an orderly environment are essential. Engaging in martial arts or qigong enhances physical discipline and focus while deep breathing exercises and meditation support lung health and emotional serenity. Decluttering physical spaces acts as a metaphor for internal cleansing, facilitating a clearer, more organized mental state. Writing, especially reflective journaling or intention setting, can process emotions and solidify personal goals, echoing metal's essence of definition and determination.

Neuroscientifically, metal correlates with the brain's executive function networks, primarily located in the prefrontal cortex and interconnected regions. These areas are responsible for organizing thoughts and actions, making clear-minded decisions, and controlling impulses. Strengthening these cognitive abilities through focused tasks, problem-solving exercises, and strategic planning embodies metal's discipline, aiding in adeptly navigating life's complexities.

Within the sheng and ke cycles, metal is nurtured by earth's stability and self-awareness and moderated by fire's dynamism. Earth's support helps metal solidify core values and structure, whereas fire prevents metal's precision from turning into rigidity. This balance allows for adaptability and discernment in facing life's challenges.

In my journey, the metal element's qualities—structure, clarity, and the art of embracing change—have been crucial to my evolution. Venturing into entrepreneurship and exploring avenues beyond traditional medicine have required metal's discipline and openness to letting go of past certainties. This process has uncovered a sense of freedom and joy in continuous self-improvement and transformation. Influenced by metal, my coaching approach has evolved to guiding others in finding their clarity and encouraging them to embark on meaningful life transitions.

Water: The Element of Adaptability and Depth

Empty your mind, be formless. Shapeless, like water.
If you put water into a cup, it becomes the cup. You
put water into a bottle and it becomes the bottle ...
Water can flow or it can crash. Be water, my friend.

—BRUCE LEE

Water in TCM symbolizes winter, and the essence of adaptability, depth, and introspection. Water is crucial for sustaining our foundational energies and resilience, enabling us to navigate and adapt to life's changes. A balanced water element is characterized by profound wisdom and introspection (yin), combined with the capacity to adapt and overcome adversity (yang). Yet, imbalances may manifest physically as issues with fluid regulation, lower back discomfort, chronic fatigue, and knee issues. Emotionally, a water imbalance may present as feelings of fear, anxiety, or an inability to effectively manage stress, alongside a diminished sense of will or drive.

To nourish the water element, engaging in water-based activities, like swimming, aligns with its essence. Introspective practices, such as meditation and journaling, foster deep reflection and emotional insight. Exploring new ideas fuels water's pursuit of wisdom. Mindfulness strengthens emotional resilience, leading to a more adaptable and resourceful approach to overcoming life's obstacles.

The neuroscience of water corresponds to the limbic system's role in emotion and stress management, emphasizing adaptability and introspection. This system, encompassing the amygdala and hippocampus, manages emotional responses and memory consolidation, reflecting water's qualities in TCM. Its flexibility in processing emotional stimuli echoes water's adaptability and resilience. Importantly, quality sleep bolsters this adaptability, aiding emotional processing and memory during rest, akin to water's restorative capacity.

In the cyclic interactions of sheng and ke, metal's refining and organized influence nurtures water's wisdom, promoting clarity and introspection while earth's grounding and self-aware force provides necessary boundaries, preventing water's expansiveness from becoming aimless and lacking direction. Navigating life's adversities, I tapped into water's adaptability and depth, embracing the flow of change. Embracing the perspective that "life happens for us, not to us" shifted my narrative from victimhood to empowerment. This mindset of seeking deeper understanding and embracing change resonates with the enduring spirit of water. By embodying this fluidity and resilience, we, as coaches, can inspire others to explore their own depths, cultivate resilience, and navigate life's shifts with grace, echoing the ethos of being like water—formless, adaptable, and powerful.

Figure 2. Summary Table

Element	Exemplar Attributes	Strengths (In Balance)	Challenges (Out of Balance)	Physical Traits When Stressed	Balance Strategies
Wood	Visionary Leader	Flexibility, Renewal (Yin); Assertiveness, Determination (Yang)	Anger, Over-dominance, Aggression (Excess); Indecisiveness, Submissiveness (Deficiency)	Muscle & Tendon Stiffness, Headaches; Menstrual Issues, Digestive Discomfort	Outdoor Activities, Mind-Body Practices (e.g., Yoga, Tai Chi), Creative Pursuits
Fire	Inspirational Motivator	Warmth, Connection (Yin); Energy, Passion (Yang)	Anxiety, Restlessness, Impulsiveness (Excess); Emotional Coldness, Disconnection (Deficiency)	Heart Issues, Insomnia, Digestive Challenges, Skin Inflammation	Social Enjoyment, Creative Expression, Mindfulness, Heart-Healthy Exercise
Earth	Empathetic Caregiver	Nurturing, Support (Yin); Practicality, Stability (Yang)	Worry, Over-protectiveness, Smothering (Excess); Lack of Empathy, Neglect of Self-Care, Overthinking (Deficiency)	Digestive Issues, Weight Fluctuations, Muscular Weakness, Edema	Grounding Routines, Mindful Nourishment, Community Engagement, Gratitude Practices
Metal	Discerning Analyst	Reflection, Precision (Yin); Organization, Discipline (Yang)	Unresolved Grief, Rigid Thinking, Resistance to Change (Excess); Disorganization, Emotional Detachment, Letting-Go Challenges (Deficiency)	Respiratory Concerns (e.g., allergies, asthma), Skin Conditions, Lung and Large Intestine Imbalances	Mindfulness Practices, Martial Arts/ Qigong, Structured Routine, Breathing Exercises, Decluttering

			Fear, Overwhelm, Paranoia (Excess); Lack of Will, Emotional Disconnection, Apathy, Insecurity, (Deficiency)	Kidney and Urinary Concerns; Fatigue, Reproductive Issues, Low Back Discomfort, Knee Pain	Resilience-Building, Mindfulness Practices, Learning, Aquatic Exercises
Water	Intuitive Philosopher	Insight, Contemplation (Yin); Resourcefulness, Adaptability (Yang)			

Conclusion

This chapter explored the five elements of TCM—wood, fire, earth, metal, and water—integrating their wisdom with neuroscience to boost life coaching. It calls on coaches to utilize the unique strengths and address the challenges of each element, leading clients to balance and fulfillment. Reflect on the elemental dynamics within yourself and your clients, being mindful of the yin and yang balance and the sheng and ke cycles' effects on well-being. Use this insight to develop strategies for continual growth and adaptability, promoting a holistic approach that benefits both coaches and clients. Let the elemental harmony inspire your development and that of those you guide. Embrace these timeless concepts in your practice and enjoy their transformative potential.

ACTIVITY

Five Elements Self-Assessment Questionnaire

Directions: For each question, rank how relevant each statement is to you from 1 to 5, where 1 is "Least like me" and 5 is "Most like me." At the end, add up your scores for A through E to identify your dominant and secondary elements.

1. In decision-making, I: ___A. Strategize and look at the big picture. ___B. Trust instincts and consider the impact on others. ___C. Weigh the practical implications and seek stability. ___D. Aim for efficiency and clear outcomes. ___E. Deliberate deeply and consider the philosophical angle.	**5. When things don't go as planned, I:** ___A. Forge a new path or find an alternative. ___B. Look for the silver lining and stay optimistic. ___C. Seek comfort in my community and shared experiences. ___D. Re-evaluate and adjust my strategy meticulously. ___E. Reflect on the lessons learned and plan for the future.
2. The quality I most value in myself is my: ___A. Determination and drive. ___B. Enthusiasm and expressiveness. ___C. Reliability and thoughtfulness. ___D. Precision and dependability. ___E. Insightfulness and introspection.	**6. I recharge by:** ___A. Engaging in physical or outdoor activities. ___B. Being around friends and lively environments. ___C. Participating in community or family events. ___D. Planning my next steps and organizing my thoughts. ___E. Spending time alone or in contemplation.

3. I feel energized when I am:	7. I express creativity by:
___A. Starting new projects and pioneering.	___A. Innovating and experimenting with new ideas.
___B. Interacting with people and inspiring them.	___B. Engaging in artistic or dramatic expression.
___C. Helping others and creating harmony.	___C. Cultivating growth and harmony in my surroundings.
___D. Organizing my space and setting goals.	___D. Designing systems and structures for efficiency.
___E. Learning new things and exploring ideas.	___E. Pondering complex concepts and theories.
4. I am most fulfilled when I am:	**8. In social settings, I am more likely to:**
___A. Overcoming challenges and leading.	___A. Direct conversations and activities.
___B. Engaging with others and sharing experiences.	___B. Be the center of attention with my warmth and charisma.
___C. Providing support and advice to friends and family.	___C. Ensure everyone feels included and cared for.
___D. Achieving a goal or completing a task efficiently.	___D. Observe and analyze the dynamics before engaging.
___E. Deepening my understanding of a subject or myself.	___E. Engage in meaningful one-on-one discussions.

Total Scores:	**Dominant Element(s):** _____
A (Wood) _____	**Secondary Elements:**
B (Fire) _____	_____
C (Earth) _____	_____
D (Metal) _____	_____
E (Water) _____	_____

Follow-Up Questions (Refer to Figures 1 and 2 If Needed):

1. Examine the interactions between your primary and secondary elements. How do they complement each other, and what areas of imbalance can you identify that need more attention for greater harmony?
2. Reflect on the positive impacts of your dominant and secondary elements in your life. Can you identify specific instances where your generating element has supported your dominant element?
3. Consider instances where your controlling element has tempered the excesses of your dominant element. How has this moderation manifested in your behaviors or decisions?
4. Think about the elemental dynamics with those close to you. How do your elements interact with theirs, and what steps could you take to enhance mutual understanding and support in these relationships?

About the Author

Dr. Po Wu holds board certifications in neurology and sleep medicine from the American Board of Psychiatry and Neurology and in medical acupuncture from the American Board of Medical Acupuncture. As a holistic wellness and performance coach, he employs a multidisciplinary approach, empowering individuals to find balance, enhance their relationships through his expertise in the Gottman method, and reach their full potential. Achieving financial independence through business and real estate investment, Dr. Wu combines diverse expertise with a passion for life. He cherishes being a husband and father of two while living in beautiful British Columbia.

Dr. Wu is an avid endurance athlete, having completed numerous marathons and ultramarathons, including Boston Marathon finishes, and enjoys triathlons. His adventurous spirit extends to skiing, scuba diving, hiking, and runs with his Rhodesian Ridgeback. A children's book author, he also delights in playing the ukulele with his children, weaving creativity into family moments.

Dr. Wu is also the co-host of The Rich Life Podcast—Wealth, Health, & Happiness.

Email: connect@drpowu.com
Website: www.drpowu.com
Social media, podcast, and online assessment quiz: www.beacons.ai/drpowu

DID YOU ENJOY THIS BOOK?

If you enjoyed reading this book, you can help by suggesting it to someone else you think might like it, and **please leave a positive review** wherever you purchased it. This does a lot in helping others find the book. We thank you in advance for taking a few moments to do this.

THANK YOU

You might also like other Thin Leaf Press titles:

The Life Coach's Tool Kit, Vol 1
The Life Coach's Tool Kit, Vol 2
The Successful Mind: Tools to Living a Purposeful, Productive, and Happy Life
The Successful Body: Using Fitness, Nutrition, and Mindset to Live Better
The Successful Spirit: Top Performers Share Secrets to a Winning Mindset
Winning Mindset: Elite Strategies for Peak Performance
Winner's Mindset: Peak Performance Strategies for Success
Peak Performance: Mindset Tools for Sales
Peak Performance: Mindset Tools for Leaders
Peak Performance: Mindset Tools for Business
Peak Performance: Mindset Tools for Entrepreneurs
Peak Performance: Mindset Tools for Athletes
Ordinary to Extraordinary
Explore.

Made in the USA
Monee, IL
30 August 2024

64672791R00174